ONE LAST SHOT

Brian Gartland
with Mark McCadden

www.**HERO**BOOKS.digital

HEROBOOKS

PUBLISHED BY HERO BOOKS
1 WOODVILLE GREEN
LUCAN
CO. DUBLIN
IRELAND

Hero Books is an imprint of Umbrella Publishing

First Published 2022

ISBN 9781910827215

Cover design and formatting: jessica@viitaladesign.com
Ebook formatting: www.ebooklaunch.com
Photographs: Sportsfile, Ciaran Culligan and the Gartland family collection

DEDICATION

To my late father Bernard, my mother Carmel and my
brother Neil, who gave me the drive and passion to chase
my dreams. Thank you for your love and support

To my wife Bronagh for all her love, support and laughs

To my children Bobbie and Jesse, who have brought
unimaginable joy to my life in such a short space of time

This book is for them

CONTENTS

ACKNOWLEDGEMENTS

FIRSTLY, I'D LIKE to thank Liam Hayes and Hero books for the opportunity to tell my story so far, and Mark McCadden for decoding and transcribing my ramblings in such a fine manner. Their patience, co-operation and hard work is sincerely appreciated.

I've been blessed with the people I've come across in life so far. So many people have supported, encouraged and helped me to get to where I am now. Without all of you, I would not be living out my boyhood dream of being a professional footballer, playing in beautiful stadiums all over Europe, experiencing cup final days in the Aviva, and league-winning clinchers like 'Oriel 2014'.

Thank you to former Ballyroan BNS principal Gerry O'Brien and all the influential and sport-loving teachers who made growing up such a ball. Also, a big thank you to Coláiste Éanna, and to Mary Pat Prendergast and Alan Moody, and the teachers and coaches who infused sport into my life in such a positive and fun manner.

Thank you to all the coaches, teammates and parents at my local football club Knocklyon United FC, GAA club Ballyboden St Enda's, basketball club Delta Notre Dame, Leicester Celtic and Verona FC. A special thanks to Alan McGovern and John Curran. Alan took me under his wing at a young age and thought me so much in football, while John saw something in me and set me on my LOI journey.

Thank you to all my friends down through all the years. The great memories of games in Ashton, Elkwood, Ballyroan, Templeroan, Coláiste Éanna, Cherryfield and so many other 'fields of dreams' live long in my head. The highlight culminating in the Knocklyon Galactico era, getting to play with some of the finest footballers who could have played at any level in the world had they wished… so they tell me!

And more thanks…

To Dr James Foley and the staff at St Vincent's University Hospital for their expertise and care. To Bronagh Byrne for all your help since we first met over 10 years ago.

To all the staff, management, teammates, volunteers and fans at Bray Wanderers, Shelbourne FC, Monaghan United and Portadown FC. Good or not so good, the experiences stood to me and I moved forward better equipped for what was next in life.

To the whole footballing community on this island. Rivals on the pitch but, for most, we have a mutual respect off it and I've had great encounters and laughs with fans of all clubs.

A special thank you to Dundalk FC and the town

And to Andy Connolly and Paul Brown for starting something incredible that I was so fortunate to be part of, and Martin Connolly for his help along the way. To all the volunteers and staff at the club for their tireless work.

I'm eternally grateful to the incredible fans that I got to share so many spine-tingling moments with over the past 10 seasons. Whether it's in person or on social media – positivity always has an uplifting effect on a player. I wish we could have had you with us at the Emirates and the Aviva when we played during lockdowns in recent years. The support has been incredible and hugely appreciated.

Moving to Dundalk was made all the easier with how welcoming everyone in the town and Pearse Park were, and none more so than my in-laws, the O'Briens in Pearse Park (Pat, Margaret, John, 'Wee' Pat and their families). I arrived into their house with them excitedly expecting a 'Brogan or Connolly' to walk in… after Bronagh said she had met a 'footballer from Dublin'. Even after the disappointment, I was made feel right at home from the very start.

Football is beautiful. And it can also be a tough industry at times. I've been blessed with the teammates I've had everywhere, especially at Dundalk FC over the last 10 seasons. I've been surrounded by great players and great people.

Stephen Kenny! Thank you for bringing me to be part of your Dundalk adventure. For the demands you placed on me and for then creating an environment where I could pursue my dreams. You helped me develop in so many ways and bred confidence into us all that took away any limits or ceilings. I am eternally grateful.

My devotion to the game has meant football coming before everything else. Not being there for others sometimes, and missing the 'big days' in their lives. Regardless, these friends and family have always been there and never held my absence against me. Despite going on the 'missing list' so often, you were still there if I ever needed you, and that is something I value and appreciate so much.

With family also on the other side of the country or abroad, it has meant limited time with them. I want to thank you all for your support. Most notably my brother Neil and his family – his wife Hannah and daughters Lola and Bronte. Neil, you have been a great friend and were always there for me since the day I was born.

My late father Bernard, whom I wish so much could have seen even just one trophy win.

My wife Bronagh and our children Bobbie and Jesse. Bronagh still sacrifices so much for me to continue to chase my dreams and devote myself to football. Thank you for your patience, understanding, love and support. Success is all the sweeter when shared with you. The arrival of our children brought a greater meaning to the joy of life. I owe so much to you and I definitely wouldn't be still going without you.

Finally, I want to thank my mother Carmel. A woman who has led by example my whole life. When faced with adversity and hardship, you stand tall, up-skilled and work like a trojan to get where you need. More admirably, you do this while always putting others first and living life to the full.

My role model and best friend.

Brian Gartland
March 2022

♦ ♦ ♦ ♦ ♦

MY CONTRIBUTION TO this book would not have been possible without the loving support of my wife Tara, and daughters Aoibhinn and Caoimhe. I'm not sure how they have remained so patient with me, but their acceptance of my poor timekeeping and dreadful adherence to deadlines has been equalled only by the good people at Hero Books.

When this process began, I was given encouragement by my former sports editor Eoin Brannigan. It was his crazy decision almost 20 years ago to hire me that set me on this course. It took him a while to realise the error of his ways, but once he did he hightailed it north to the *Belfast Telegraph*, where he now works as editor-in-chief.

Years before I joined the *Irish Daily Star*, it was with the help of my parents Joe and Evelyn that I enrolled in a journalism course at Griffith College Dublin, where I made friends for life and gained a fine education.

The *Irish Daily Star's* current sports editor Brian Flanagan is another whose support has been invaluable. Brian's son has also benefited from Brian Gartland's basketball coaching expertise.

There are countless colleagues and friends that I'd like to thank for their support and friendship, including my brother David and his family.

Finally, and most importantly, my eternal gratitude to Brian Gartland. His honesty and no-holes-barred approach to our chats made this, my first effort at writing a book, far easier than it might have been. I have learned so much about Brian over the past 18 months and respect him for much more now than just his tireless endeavours and talents as a footballer.

He is as driven off the pitch, as he is on it. Brian will make a huge success of his life outside of football.

To anyone I have forgotten to mention, apologies and thank you.

Mark McCadden
March 2022

♦ ♦ ♦ ♦ ♦

FOREWORD

IN MANY WAYS, it was a dramatic change for me. Within two years I'd gone from walking out as manager of Dunfermline against a Gordan Strachan-led Celtic in front of 50,000 passionate fans in the Scottish Cup final at Hampden Park, to managing back in the League of Ireland First Division.

I was back where I started. Derry City, like Shelbourne and Cork City, had entered administration and were automatically relegated. It was a period of reflection and introspection for me, as just a few seasons earlier all three clubs had been challenging for the Premier Division title.

It may be too simplistic to suggest that Derry, as a city, felt marginalised and was considered isolationist. However, I was intrigued by the Basque model at Athletic Bilbao and to a degree Real Sociedad, and while it was considered dramatic I imposed a guideline that every player must be from the City of Derry, its environs, or have come through the youth structures.

Only four players remained as we rebuilt from the ground up, with a group of young players coming through. Daniel Lafferty would go on to be Northern Ireland left-back and James McClean would have a really successful career on the left wing for the Republic of Ireland.

There were the McEleney brothers Shane and Patrick – the most gifted 17-year-old I coached – and, of course, an incredible human being in Mark Farren, who walked into my office one day to tell me he had a brain tumour. Mark had an operation and came back from his treatment to score the goal to win the First Division, only to later tragically relapse. Ultimately the illness would take his life.

Monaghan United were a dark horse in the title race that year under the shrewd guidance of Mick Cooke. Experienced players like Big Alan Byrne, Philly Hughes, an emerging Shane Grimes and Gabriel Sava formed a really well organised team.

A more recent phenomenon – and expanded upon by Chris Wilder at Sheffield United – is the overlapping centre-back in a three-man defence. Several years earlier in Bayer Leverkusen's Champions League challenge, Lúcio, the brilliant Brazilian defender, was overlapping from centre-back in a conventional back four, breaking forward, appearing everywhere at will. He was unorthodox, yet thrilling to watch.

At the Brandywell, during the game between Derry City and Monaghan, this physically imposing centre-back by the name of Brian Gartland was joining in attacks and appearing all over the pitch.

I turned to my assistant Declan Devine and said, 'This guy thinks he is bloody Lúcio!'

Brian scored his trademark headed goal that day and was instrumental in driving Monaghan all the way to the promotion play-off that season.

While rebuilding Dundalk in 2013 we had a largely inexperienced group of young players with talent and a point to prove, together with Stephen O'Donnell and Mark Rossiter. Young Andy Boyle had signed and he would later go on to play for Ireland.

Initially, his defensive partner was Mark Rossiter, whose versatility meant he could also play right- or left-back. But we didn't have a really dominant aerial presence and we needed another centre-back for the season ahead.

Whilst I had not seen much of Brian playing for Portadown, reports were he had been playing right-back for a period. I was aware that he had finished up there and was available on a free transfer.

I spoke to him regarding signing for Dundalk before our trip to play Derry City in the Brandywell, but he needed more time to consider, having had an offer from Shelbourne who were, of course, Dublin-based and had better overall facilities than we had. It was never straightforward. All we could offer was our ambition.

The daily commute would not be easy, but Dundalk as a club had tradition, even if success had skipped a generation. We knew if we were successful it would inevitably draw a passionate response from the town.

On the journey home from the Brandywell, word filtered through from the staff that some players had reservations whether Brian would improve the team. From what I had seen of him at Monaghan United, he had exactly the characteristics that we needed as a team to improve – and his subsequent contribution has been outstanding and has exceeded everyone's expectations.

Brian has a keen interest in sports science and is highly intelligent. His broad shoulders and imposing frame could be misleading as his percentage of body fat was absolutely minimal. His diet and level of professionalism were extremely high.

He was 26 when he signed for Dundalk, and he went on to become one of the most decorated defenders in the history of the game in Ireland. His is an incredible story, a story of fortitude, of real desire and leadership.

To understand the value of clean-sheets, yet to score 50 career goals as a centre-half is significant. His 245 appearances for Dundalk and 37 goals helped change the club's history, as they contributed to two Europa League group stage qualifications, one Champions League play-off, five Premier Division title wins, three FAI Cups and three League Cups.

To be truthful, personally I don't measure success solely on a trophy count. It is also about the effects success has on every town or city, the joy it brings, how it elevates the mood, self-esteem and pride of all of its supporters and inhabitants of the region.

Sean Gannon, Richie Towell, Patrick Hoban, Daryl Horgan, Patrick McEleney and Michael Duffy would have been some of the favourite players of all of the young Dundalk supporters. But if the question – *Who is your favourite player?* – was asked of some of the more experienced fans, they would have identified with Brian Gartland and Chris Shields; players who consistently put their bodies on the line throughout every game.

Brian has a ferocity, yet is intelligent and streetwise in defending. It is often asked, *How do you define leadership?* Dundalk has been blessed with some great leaders, such as Stephen O'Donnell.

Incredibly for a centre-half, Brian scored the winning goal in two games to clinch league titles – the epic game against Cork City in 2014, and against Bohemians in 2016. And it was his brilliant header in the Champions League qualifier against Rosenborg in Trondheim that gave us the lead in that tie.

To score goals when the stakes are highest illustrates his strength of character.

His desire to improve and his willingness to set high standards around him have contributed to the culture of achievement in this period. That's leadership.

His central defensive partners – initially Andy Boyle and Mark Rossiter, then Paddy Barrett and Nicholas Vemmulund, and later Sean Hoare and Daniel Cleary – have always benefited from Brian's experience. There is no doubt they all improved as players playing alongside him.

Brian can be very proud of his contribution to Dundalk FC, representing the jersey with real pride. He has been an important leader in a significant period in the history of the Lilywhites.

Stephen Kenny
March 2022

♦ ♦ ♦ ♦ ♦

PROLOGUE

IT WAS TWENTY past ten on February 27, 2014 when the phone rang. Dad's partner's voice trembled. 'He's gone Brian… he just took his last breath. You should get to the hospice as quick as you can.'

Mam and Bronagh were with me in the living room.

I jumped off the couch and raced out the front door. I barely got the words out… 'He's after passing away'… before slamming the door behind me. It was only afterwards that I thought about mam, leaving her behind like that. She had been married to dad for 30 years and I'd left without her. Worse still, I'd left her with Bronagh, someone she hardly knew. I'd only been seeing Bronagh for a few months.

But I was in my own world.

I jumped in the car and sped to Our Lady's Hospice in Harold's Cross, breaking a few red lights on the 15-minute drive. The road was quiet and I floored it. So much so that I nearly flipped the car as I turned into the hospice car park.

What an eejit… the reckless driving, leaving mam behind with Bronagh, leaving poor Bronagh behind with mam! But all I could think about – if I was even *thinking* at all – was seeing dad one more time.

I HAD SPENT most of that day with dad.

I needed a break. So, when Bronagh said she was coming down to see me, I told her to go to mam's house in Knocklyon. Our relationship was getting serious at the time, but not bring-her-to-see-my-dying-dad-in-the-hospice serious. By the time I got back to mam's house, Bronagh was already there. She'd come all the way from Dundalk. I said I would go home and meet Bronagh for an hour or two, and get back to the hospice for 10pm. When I *was* home, I felt I'd only been there for a short time… so I pushed it back to 10.30pm. I'd go then… but at 10.20pm the phone rang.

I needed the break. I *needed* to get away for a bit. I'd practically been living in dad's room for several weeks at that stage. So I didn't feel too bad about leaving him. And it's not as if he was alone. His partner Caragh was with him.

People ask whether it haunts me, not being there when he passed away, but my honest answer is … no, it doesn't. He was unresponsive at that stage. *What difference would I have made?* I certainly don't think anyone should torture themselves over something like that.

I was with dad throughout the whole process, from diagnosis to his last day. We were in the middle of pre-season with Dundalk, ahead of my first full campaign with the club. I was sleeping every night on an inflatable mattress in dad's hospice room at the end.

We talked about lots of stuff as he was lying there, but even as death approached there were topics he simply would not discuss. He wasn't a *feelings* man.

If I'm haunted by anything, it's that.

Dad died on his 62nd birthday, still a young man.

PART **ONE**

Awakenings

When we moved to Knocklyon, nothing could keep me from hitting the front green daily for any sort of game with a football – here I am sporting my new Republic of Ireland strip. We were one happy family in the beginning (top). Mam and dad and my brother Neil (left) celebrate my Confirmation Day.

TOP: The Knocklyon United team that travelled west and played Westport United (the pitch was at the back of my grandad's house) included me (left on the back row) and my friends Colm O'Neill (next to me), Graham Coffey (front left) and Eoin Ryan (front right). Here I am proudly receiving the club Player of the Year award.

MIDDLE: Gaelic football and hurling were also a huge part of my young life, and what a thrill I had (left) getting to wear a Kilkenny kit before the 1998 All-Ireland final between the Cats and Offaly. But I also fancied myself as a footballer – belting the ball (right) for Ballyronan Boys School in a final in Croke Park and celebrating with Eoin Casey afterwards.

BOTTOM: We queued for hours to meet Roy Keane at his book launch in easons on O'Connell Street, but just before the photo was taken, I unzipped my coat to reveal my devotion to Man United's arch enemy Liverpool.

• CHAPTER 1 •

I WAS 15 years old when mam and dad separated.

Bernard Gartland was a drinker. He had problems with depression. For years they argued. No abuse, just shouting. Not that mam was much of a shouter herself. It took a lot to get her worked up.

For years they just lived together.

No relationship, no marriage to speak of, just anger.

Ultimately my older brother Neil and I sat mam down and said she needed to get a separation. She told us how she had been waiting for us to grow up before taking that step. For mam, it was always about helping others first. Neil and I figured mam had been suffering for years. I remember sitting on the stairs as a child, roaring crying as they shouted at each other.

It wasn't constant fighting, although the memories still remain vivid.

They had lived together for years but wouldn't talk to each other. They shared a house, but there was no relationship to speak of. After their separation, the relationship my brother and I had with dad improved ten-fold. I really wish it had happened sooner.

DAD WAS A damp proofer when I was young. He would work all over the country, Monday to Friday. Then he became a hackney driver. He was out of work for a while before he got a taxi plate later in life.

We lived in Dublin, in Tallaght for the first few years of my life, before moving to Knocklyon. The roads were only half-done and the bus didn't go all the way to our house. Mam was working, effectively paying the mortgage.

Neil saw more of the rows than me. He would also have his own arguments with dad. Neil might come in after a night out, dad would have had drink on him and they'd row. I was more oblivious to the drinking when I younger. I might find an empty vodka bottle down the back of the couch. Or, if I went to the shed to get my football I'd see empty bottles thrown down the side.

On one occasion I came in from an evening out with friends. I was 15 at the time. Dad had been drinking and we got into a row. I can't remember what it was about, but things got heated and I ended up pushing him onto the couch. I felt so guilty afterwards, but when I think back he probably deserved worse for what we were going through at the time.

My brother and I had regular arguments with him.

But we had no idea what was behind the drinking.

Dad wasn't one to open up. He never spoke to us about his feelings.

MY GRANDAD ON dad's side was one of the founders of Westport United, along with Pat Duffy's dad. Pat has long been one of the good guys in the FAI, a lovely man with a great sense of humour. Whenever I read any negative headlines about the FAI, it's people like Pat that I feel for. He has put his heart and soul into football. He is such a familiar face at grounds up and down the country, always quick to offer a handshake and share a joke.

My granddad and Pat's dad were the two main men behind Westport United at a time when the GAA banned its members from having anything to do with football. My dad loved the 11-a-side game, but that love came at a pretty hefty cost. He often got a beating in school from the Christian Brothers, because he was into football. The physical scars healed pretty quickly, but he struggled to cope with the mental scars. Especially as he wasn't someone who'd open up about it.

There's a lot about dad that I'll never know, stuff that he took with him to the grave. Being battered in school every day, being made feel like an outsider because he wanted to play football; he carried that burden alone. He was conditioned not to talk about it.

Even on his deathbed, when I was sleeping next to him on a blow-up mattress, he didn't open up. Neil and I were both completely on mam's side whenever they'd row. But at the time we didn't realise that dad was suffering from depression, that he was being tormented by the memories of his childhood. All we saw was the drink, the anger and the havoc they caused.

It was all-consuming at that stage.

Day one of my Junior Cert, I wanted dad to be there when I got home, but he was down the pub. When Ireland played Germany in the 2002 World Cup, I had an exam that morning; English Paper Two, if I remember correctly. So I watched the start of the game before heading into the exam hall. I remember hearing noises from outside. *Was that a cheer? Did Ireland score?*

That morning loads of my classmates were cramming in a last bit of study. But my pals and I, we thought… *Who gives a f**k about the exam, Ireland are playing at the World Cup.* I was football-mad. It was all that mattered to me. I was a Liverpool supporter and was fairly fanatical about it when I was younger. The older I got, I still followed them and enjoyed seeing them winning. But it wasn't life or death anymore.

By the Junior Cert, it was all about Ireland. I was – and still am – as big a Boys in Green fan as you will ever meet. It's my country, my team. For years I had a season ticket in the singing section behind the goal. The only reason I stopped going to as many games was because things got so full-on with Dundalk. I still get to as many matches as I can, including the odd away trip.

To say the Germany game was a bit of a distraction would be an understatement. I recorded the game on an old VHS tape and the plan was to go home and watch it with dad. I finished the exam and raced home on my bike, but he wasn't there. He was at the pub. Dad wasn't working at the time. He could have been there for me. So, I watched the second-half of the game on my own, after bursting into tears. I was gutted.

For as long as the 2002 World Cup clashed with my exams, I was coming home and watching games when I should have been getting some last-minute study in. I did well enough results-wise, but I could have done better. But it was all about sport for me and football was my number one priority. If only I could have shared more of it with dad. Like the good times we did have, because we did have good times too. He took me to the Goat Sportsbar for the Cameroon game. It was a 6am kick-off, but a mate of dad's got us in the back door. I still have such vivid memories of the joy and celebration when Matt Holland equalised.

With dad, it was only much later that I understood the role depression played in his life.

AS DAD WAS dying, I tried really hard to get him to talk about his life, about the things that made him the man and the dad that he was. *But what chance had I when he wouldn't even face up to the fact that he was dying?* Eventually, I mustered the strength to ask him whether he wanted a funeral or a cremation?

Dad wanted to be cremated. It wasn't long after that conversation that the hospice staff had to up his medication. Dad started to drift in and out of consciousness. It was clear that he was nearing the end. One day, I was sitting beside his bed and a Leinster rugby game was on the television in his room. Someone was kicking a penalty and dad was in such a state that he thought it was me on the telly.

He had followed my career, but it was only after he died that I found out how proud he was of me. I met someone in a pub, about a year after dad passed away, who asked me if my dad was a taxi driver. I replied, 'Yeah', and he said that he was in a taxi once with dad, and that he didn't shut up about me for the entire journey. I've since heard the same story from a few different people.

Dad didn't go to many games. I don't think he was in Oriel Park once in the few months that I was playing there before he died. He didn't get to see me win anything. There were a couple of runners-up finishes – the league up north, and in the EA Sports Cup with Monaghan against a really strong Sligo Rovers side. He actually made it to the Showgrounds for that one.

It was kind of sad to hear from strangers that he was proud of me, because it wasn't something he ever told me. I knew he kept in touch with literally everything that was said or written about me. He read the forums, the newspapers and Twitter. But he wouldn't say a whole lot. Occasionally, when we'd talk about my career, he'd give a little chuckle, accompanied by a misty eye. On reflection, that might have been his tell.

One thing I always appreciated about him was that he wasn't one of those dads that would shout and roar at their kids from the sideline. He'd never say, 'You should do this or that'… he'd always leave the big decisions to me.

There were times when I could have done with the advice. I could have done with him being a friend or a confidant. Especially when it came to a big disciplinary issue early in my career with Bray, which I'll get to later. Or even during contract negotiations with clubs – something I was never very good at.

I was always on my own when it came to talking money with people who were far more skilled than me. I learned over time that it would have been a lot easier discussing terms with someone by my side. I'd definitely be a lot richer by now! A lot of my teammates – current and former – would have had their dads with them for contract talks. I'd love to have had that relationship with my dad, but it wasn't to be. At the same time, I had to learn quickly on my own, and experience in those situations helped make me the man I am.

I will always regret the fact that he never saw me win anything. He was so proud of me despite the fact that my career was bang average while he was alive. Imagine if he was alive now to *see* me win five titles with Dundalk. *And to see me lifting the Premier Division trophy in 2019 as captain? The 2016 European run?*

My grandad was a huge football man and dad loved the game too. One of my most treasured possessions is a medal – but it's not one that I won myself. Grandad won a Connacht title decades ago. He passed it onto dad and, before he died, dad gave it to me. I think that was his way of telling me how proud he was.

MY MAM CARMEL is from Galway and dad was from Westport in Mayo. Mam is a very forgiving and gentle person. But dad held their separation against her. He wouldn't talk to her, even in those final days.

He came to my brother's wedding but refused to talk to her even there. Dad literally had just a few bob in his suit pocket and that was it. He had inherited his parents' house, yet mam had to pay him half the value of our house after the separation – even after she had paid most of the mortgage. He was fighting his addiction during this period of his life, so I now understand too that it wasn't easy for him.

That summed up my mam; she never contested the terms of the separation. She re-mortgaged half the value of the house so that dad would be looked after, yet even on his deathbed he couldn't put the grudge aside. It was hard to imagine that they were kids once, that they were in love. But they were. That it ended in this way was so disappointing.

I told him that mam wanted to say goodbye, but he refused to see her. That broke my heart. However, I had to give mam one last opportunity to say goodbye. One day, when dad was at the stage where he didn't really recognise anyone, I rang mam and told her to come down. I couldn't let her live the rest of her life knowing that she didn't get the chance to say goodbye. I wanted her to have some form of peace.

I kept this from dad's partner Caragh. She was adamant that mam shouldn't see him. I'll be honest, I don't blame her. Dad had spun his side of the story so much that he painted mam in a really bad light. So, naturally dad's partner was going to be on his side. The job of organising the funeral fell entirely on my lap and I told her, 'If mam isn't there, I won't be there!'

The funeral took place at Mount Jerome in Harold's Cross. On top of the grief, I remember feeling a great deal of anxiety over how dad's partner would react to mam being there. When we arrived, Caragh came over and gave mam a hug. I can't describe the relief I felt. Even telling the story now, I can feel my shoulders tense up.

I HAVE SO much admiration for mam. She worked in Littlewoods. It was while working in Manchester that she met dad. When Littlewoods – it was then called Family Album – opened up on O'Connell Street in Dublin, she was able to move back home, where she was promoted from the call-centre in Manchester to supervisor. She worked her way up the ladder, all the way to director, before retiring in 2019 after 44 years of service. She worked from the bottom right up. It's from mam that I get a lot of my traits. I like to think I'm hard-working, just like her.

When we were really young, she had just seven weeks' maternity leave and then had to send Neil and myself in with our neighbours, Helen and Terry Carthy, while she worked. Helen was like a second mother to us. They were all Shamrock Rovers fans in that house. Little did they know that they were minding someone who one day would be going toe-to-toe with their beloved Hoops.

Mam would leave work at seven in the morning and come back at seven in the evening, when it was pitch black. The bus would drop her off beside Aherne's pub, almost a mile-long walk from the house.

The older we got, the more our admiration for mam grew. She worked her way up the ladder in a male-dominated world and had to put up with plenty of shit along the way. But she persevered and became a director of a massive company. I have learned a hell of a lot from what she has gone through.

On one side, mam is sensible, serious and incredibly hard-working. But there's another side to her. She says I have this little Del Boy streak about me. I know where that comes from. We call mam 'Crafty Carmel', because she is always bargaining, always wheeling and dealing. And she loves an adventure.

In the past 10 years she has been all over the world. On one trip she spent time in Argentina, Brazil and Uruguay. She has been on tours to China, India and New Zealand, where she sky-dived from 15,000 feet, and where she rented a car for three weeks and drove the length of the country. She has taken a train ride through the Rockies, cruised through Alaskan glaciers and has had many more trips to the U.S. There's barely a country in Europe that she hasn't visited. As for further afield… Thailand, Vietnam, Cambodia… the list goes on. She would usually go with a friend or with a group.

MAM ALWAYS SAYS she needs to look after her money, that she always thinks about what she is leaving behind for Neil and myself. But every time she hums and haws over another trip, we tell her we're grand, not to worry about it, to spend her money on herself. You never know when you won't be around to enjoy it anymore.

Mam wouldn't be one for extravagance, but what she has done – travelling, seeing the world, and doing so at her age when most others would be slowing down (and she has a better social life than me!) – is a real inspiration. She believes in living life!

Now that she has retired, she has started to work in a voluntary capacity with SAGE – a charity that supporters vulnerable people, the elderly and healthcare patients. She's nearly busier now than when she was working. There'd be days when she would have several meetings back-to-back. Mam loves helping the elderly, helping them with their finances, advising them in disputes with their families. She is a bundle of energy.

Mam is also a big sports fan. She has been to a few of my games in Oriel Park, Dalymount Park and Tallaght. I have often seen her sitting with my wife in the middle of the Jodi Stand. I'd have a good rapport with the Bohs fans. I seem to get a decent amount of abuse from them, and I'd be sure to have a bit of craic back.

Whenever my mam attends a game at Dalymount, she'd ask me afterwards, 'Did you hear the things they were saying about you?'

Mam went to Tolka Park for a bit but stayed away after a while. A lot of the language was quite vulgar. For some it's a bit of craic, but for others it might come across as aggressive. Maybe that made her take a little step back from attending matches. That and the nerves.

When she's into a sport or a team, she's all-in.

Especially when it comes to Galway or whoever I'm with. Mam gets so worked up. She made it to the title decider in 2014, against Cork City on the final day of the season. At one stage during the second-half she was such a bag of nerves that she had to leave the ground. She spent the last five minutes or so pacing up and down Carrickmacross Road.

We were 2-0 up. I had just scored our second, after Stephen O'Donnell's opener shortly after half-time, and she had to leave. At that stage, what were the odds that Cork would come back? If the roles were reversed, I would have been in the stand laughing and cheering, yet she was more nervous than ever.

Thankfully, she was back in the ground for the final whistle. I ran straight over to her and gave her a big hug. It was winner-takes-all against our title rivals in our home ground. It didn't get much better than that.

With mam and dad only attending the occasional game, and my brother living abroad, I didn't really have family supporting me from the terraces until Bronagh came along. But mam has offered so much more in terms of my outlook on life. Football wasn't her industry, so she was reluctant to ever get involved. Yet seeing her raise a family, work as hard as she did and travel the world – and then to see 'Crafty Carmel' in action – shaped me more than I could ever explain.

She is non-stop. If she's not hillwalking – she walked 26 kilometres over a mountain in Mayo in 2019, and she has climbed Ben Nevis – she is working long hours as a volunteer or she is planning her next big round-the-world adventure.

OUR PARENTS' SEPARATION was traumatic for my brother Neil and myself. Mam could see that, so she asked us to go to therapy. It was a turning point for both of us. While I would never stop yapping, it definitely helped me cope with the upset. Neil was the opposite to me... you'd struggle to get two words from him from one end of the day to the next. Therapy worked wonders for him. While the relationship between my parents dominated my upbringing, there were loads of good times too.

The family summers were so much fun. As dad was from Westport, we spent time there every year. And with mam from Castlegrove in Galway, just outside Tuam, we had weeks there, playing on the farm with our cousins; unforgettable times.

The one family holiday abroad was to Santa Ponsa in Majorca, when I was six or seven years old. That's where I learned how to swim. Well, I didn't have much choice. I was comfortable enough splashing around in the shallow end, but dad and Neil felt I was ready for the deep end. *No way*, I thought.

I remember standing by the deep end one day, sh*****g myself. I wanted to jump in but was paralysed with fear. Out of nowhere, dad and Neil appeared. They pushed me in. I waved my arms and roared at them to get me out, but they just stood there.

It was literally sink or swim. So I took off and never looked back.

While that was our only sun holiday as a family, I ended up going on loads of trips with mam. Just the two of us.

It started when I was in Second Year and the school organised a tour of France. It wasn't cheap, and there were only 40 spots. I went home to mam that evening and we had a chat, and we ended up deciding that we could probably get a three- or four-day trip for the two of us at that price. We both hated wasting money!

So we went onto the internet – dial-up at that time – and booked our own holiday to France.

We bought a cheap flight and flew in around 11pm, and hopped on a train from the airport. The carriage was empty, except for a few women. Just before the doors shut, a man boarded, and said 'Hi' to mam as he walked past and sat down behind us.

One of the women, who had been asleep, woke up and walked over to the man. They chatted briefly in French, before she sat down beside him and then gave him… some relief.

'Whatever you do, don't turn around,' mam whispered to me.

I was only 14 at the time!

We used to say we were like the odd pair, going on holidays together. We booked into a B&B in Paris and were stuck in a tiny converted attic. After a day out, we returned and found that our bags weren't there. We raced downstairs in a panic, only to be told that they'd moved us... but without informing us.

We both fell asleep on a tour bus, as it took us around Paris in the middle of February, while it was lashing rain outside.

On another trip we went to Barcelona. I wanted to see the Nou Camp. We went on the tour and got to the Trophy Room. Mam said, 'Pick up that cup there for a photo'. You weren't meant to touch them, but I grabbed the Champions League trophy, dreaming that one day I'd get to lift it for real. Someone else walked over and I handed it to him. Suddenly, security arrived and he was booted out!

We got to the little chapel in the tunnel. You weren't allowed in, but we snuck in and lit a candle.

When we got to our hotel, all the lights on our floor were out. We were told we'd be transferred to a sister hotel, The Plaza. It was basically a palace. We hit the jackpot... a five-night stay in luxury for the price of a budget hotel.

We went to Tunisia one time and that was an eye-opener. There were loads of old women there hooking up with young Tunisian lads for the week. It was mad seeing the women board their coaches to the airport at the end of their stay, their young lovers tearfully waving them off... only to wait for the next busload to arrive!

FOR THE FIRST few years of my life we lived in Tallaght, near where Tallaght Stadium now stands. Mam wanted out of there. She told me one story of how, before I was born, she had Neil upstairs with her when a gang started banging on the door, shouting to be let in. Dad was working down the country at the time, so she was effectively home alone.

Mam looked out the window and one of the lads had gone around the back. It was the middle of the night and she was scared silly. She rang one of the neighbours and he called another neighbour. They both came out with hurls and scared the gang off.

By the time I was born, her mind was made up. She wanted to move. Mam is a country girl at heart. We moved to Knocklyon when I was around three years of age and that move opened me up to a world of sporting opportunity.

There is a four-year age gap between Neil and myself. He played sports growing up and was a decent footballer. He possessed a good left foot. I looked up to him and played football with him for hours every day. Our back garden in Knocklyon was small enough, but we had a six-by-four metre patch of concrete, framed by walls at either end. We painted two small goals on each wall and played one-on-one against each other until sundown.

We had a basketball net as well, while there was a gaelic pitch just around the corner, where we kicked points against each other. It was great having an older brother, because I always had to play at a higher level. It really helped toughen me up.

And because he was older, Neil made a massive effort with me when our parents separated. I'd gone through a lot of shit when I was younger and lost a lot of friends around that time too. As soon as I reached my teenage years, all the lads I hung around with simply wanted to drink and hang around with girls and nothing much else, but I just wanted to play football. I continued to stick with them at first, but eventually a few of them shunned me. As for the others, looking back now I can understand why at that age they didn't stand up for me.

They had been my friends since junior infants, and it was crippling at first. But it made me tougher. And Neil made a massive effort to bring me out with his mates for games of football. Playing with lads three or four years older was great preparation for life in the League of Ireland.

They were a tough few years, transitioning from primary to secondary school. I was desperate to get out of Coláiste Éanna, mainly because of the situation with my old friends, but also because there was a small issue with some bullying. One close pal of mine went to Rockbrook Park and I wanted to join him there. But it was a private school and we were struggling for money at the time, so that was ruled out straightaway. Things did get better as the years went on and I ended up meeting some of my best friends there. Friends for life.

NEIL AND I still remain great friends. It was tough when he moved away to Australia. We had a trip – the three of us – to Boston and New York before he left Ireland.

Neil and I were like chalk and cheese, but we had a great relationship. After playing one-on-one football or basketball outside, we would play Pro Evolution all through the night.

I looked up to him, and still do. He's a genius. Literally.

His primary school wanted him to go on a Mensa programme. Mam said no. She felt it would pigeon-hole him socially.

Neil did his Leaving Cert when he was 16. He finished both maths papers in half the allotted time and walked out with an A1. No surprise then that he works in finance.

While I don't want my football career to ever end, there is one thing I'm looking forward to in retirement… seeing more of Neil and his family. Of all the sacrifices I've made to play professionally, missing out on visits to Bournemouth where they now live has been the toughest. You just don't get the time to take off for a few days.

And when he comes over to Ireland, I might get to spend a few hours with him before going training.

I miss our time together and can't wait to see more of Neil and his family.

You give up so much to play football… stags, weddings, family life. But it's not just the footballer, it's his partner and family too. In the end, however, you gain so much from this career, especially when you've won as much as I have with Dundalk. I'm lucky in that sense, as there are plenty of players who gave up just as much as me, but are without the medals or European football to show for their sacrifices.

Growing up, all I wanted to be was a footballer. Mam would ask what my Plan B was, just in case I didn't make it as a professional. I'd reply that I'd be a postman.

I could finish my route early in the morning and train after that, even if I was playing as a part-timer or amateur.

I WAS BACK to my primary school recently. They invited me to speak in 2019 – and to bring the trophies I'd won with Dundalk. That was a huge honour. It was also a bit of a laugh, because there were a good few Shamrock Rovers fans there.

'When are you signing for Rovers?' one asked. Fortunately, this was before the 2019 FAI Cup final. If I'd gone back after losing that penalty shootout, I'm sure they would have ripped me to shreds!

I've also been back to my old secondary school, where things did improve hugely as time went on. They were on their way to a Dublin semi-final and they wanted me to give a talk to all the kids involved in sport. I even took the team for a quick session before their semi-final against a Blackrock side with Andy Lyons – who now plays in the League of Ireland with Shamrock Rovers.

This was a massive honour. There's something special about going back to your school, and giving back. When I was a kid, I idolised the lads who came in to see us... the Stynes', the basketballers and, of course, Padraig Harrington and Paul McGinley. They were all superstars in my eyes.

I HAVE BEEN sports mad for as long as I can remember. My mam has a picture of me taken before I could even walk. I was on my two feet, holding onto our red setter for support with a ball at my feet. Apparently, I would kick the ball and Elsa, our dog, would race after it. I'm not sure if I ended up on my backside each time, but I'm told that this was one of my favourite pastimes as a toddler.

Once Elsa (who was named long before the movie *Frozen* came out!) got the ball, I'd crawl over, pull myself up and kick the ball again.

Basketball was another huge draw for me. I'd be an hour early to school every morning to get in a game before class. Our principal in Ballyroan National School was Gerry O'Brien, a basketball fanatic. He would head in early himself, supervising as kids from first class right up to sixth class worked off their breakfast in some pretty competitive games. Mr O'Brien's enthusiasm for basketball summed up just how much sport meant to everyone in Ballyroan National School.

Mr O'Brien dedicated his life to the kids and to basketball. It wasn't as if he was getting extra pay for it. Everyone would get a game. Every year, fifth class would go on a trip to Stoke-on-Trent for a mixed tournament. Mr O'Brien would take five boys from our school and five girls from a school down the road in Firhouse, pack them all into his little Hiace minibus and head for the ferry to Holyhead.

He was a great role model. He was serious when it came to schooling and sport, but he was always positive in his outlook. And it rubbed off on the rest of the teachers. They were all so personable. Ms Clear loved GAA. She took training, coached the team and even formed a B team so everyone who wanted to play, could play. Then there was Ms Halliday, who set up an Olympic handball team. Mr McDonald, a Rovers fan who loved all sports, took the hurling team, and even had us playing cricket! Once there was a bit of sun, we'd be outside playing sport.

It's little wonder that Ballyroan NS produced so many good sportspeople. One of my classmates and best friends in school was Dublin's multiple All-Ireland winner Michael Darragh MacAuley.

I was mad for gaelic football and hurling too. My gaelic football team was Ballyboden St Enda's. I played with MDMA, but we were friends long before that. We grew up together, from junior infants to our teens. We played basketball together and were both point guards. He was brilliant at basketball. He had a proper ring in his back garden, so I spent a lot of my childhood over there. Of course, I have followed his career ever since then and it's great to see how successful he has been with Dublin.

Not that I missed out on my own brushes with glory in Croke Park. I played in five finals at HQ between gaelic football and hurling. That included two schools finals in one day – one for the juniors and one for the seniors. In one hurling final at Croke Park, lining out for Ballyroan, we played Ballymun in the final. I was midfield and was marking a big fella, a real hardy kid. Jutting out of the band at the end of his hurl was a little nail. Here I was, a little posh boy, and I could see he was tough as nails.

After about 10 minutes, he caught me on the knee. I still have the scar. It was probably only a small nick, but in my mind blood was gushing *everywhere*. I wasn't in the game for the next five minutes, out of pure fear. Our manager saw how I was hiding and made a change, putting me in at full-forward. I ended up scoring 2-3.

I had another big day out in Croker when I was selected to play at half-time during the 1998 All-Ireland hurling final between Offaly and Kilkenny. I was in fifth class at the time and couldn't believe my luck, playing in front of 80,000 people on the biggest day of the hurling calendar. I still have my Kilkenny kit from that day. What an experience!

I ended up dropping hurling early enough but kept the football going for a while and played in some Dublin development teams. But my gaelic coaches always knew that the 11-a-side game was my priority. Anytime there was a clash between the sports, there was only ever one winner. I loved gaelic football, I loved basketball, but I always wanted to be a footballer.

I honestly have no regrets over choosing football, but as soon as I retire from professional sport I will be back on the gaelic football pitch. I even transferred to my local GAA club three years ago. Not that I had much of a choice.

My in-laws are heavily involved in Sean O'Mahony's in Dundalk. Bronagh's dad is club secretary, while her two brothers play there. One of them, John

O'Brien, is one of Louth's greatest ever footballers, or so he tells me! For years her dad has been asking me, 'When are you retiring, when are you going to play gaelic football?'

I remember talking to a fella in a local pub in 2019 and he was telling me how they were 3/1 to win the championship – but that a local bookmaker was offering odds of 2/1 if I started playing with them. I thought he was kidding, but the bookie confirmed it to me. Everyone in Dundalk knows that I'll be playing gaelic football when I hang up the soccer boots. So, yeah, the transfer from Ballyboden has been done, paperwork all signed three years ago.

I think it was part of the terms and conditions of being allowed to marry Bronagh!

It wasn't just my primary school that was a great breeding ground for future sports people. Barry Murphy, who went on to become a great goalkeeper at clubs such as Shamrock Rovers, Bohemians and St Patrick's Athletic, was a year ahead of me in Coláiste Éanna. He was a brilliant outfield player. We used to play in an 11-a-side astro league… he played centre-half.

It was only a year or two after I left school that I realised Dave Mooney – who had a great career with Shamrock Rovers, Longford Town, Cork City and a host of English clubs, including Norwich, Charlton and Leyton Orient – was also a year ahead.

Basketball was massive for me but eventually, midway through secondary school, I gave it up. I was captain and point guard for Coláiste Éanna. We were down in University of Limerick for an All-Ireland final against Monasterevin from Cork. The rules were, you had to play five players in one quarter, the other five in the second, and then in the third and fourth you could do want you wanted. This was so everyone saw a bit of action. We were getting trounced in the first quarter, but I came on for the second and pulled it back a bit. I felt I had a great quarter. We went on to win the final and, as captain, I lifted the All-Ireland trophy.

Next thing, the Ireland schoolboys team was being selected. I felt I was a shoo-in and others thought so too. But I wasn't even invited up for the trials.

I was told at one stage that it was because of my commitment to football. By that age, the basketball coaches were looking for everyone to give it one hundred percent focus. But it really pissed me off at the time. If I wasn't good enough, then fair enough. But I had just captained an All-Ireland winning team and had one of my best games in the final. I was convinced that I'd make a 20-strong selection at under-15 level. When it didn't happen, I started to lose interest.

AS FOR FOOTBALL, I played with Knocklyon up to under-11 under the brilliant coaching mind of Alan McGovern. When it comes to the success I've had, Alan deserves more credit than most. My biggest strength has always been my head – knowledge, organisation, reading the game, shape – and Alan taught me everything. As a defender, from a young age he was constantly teaching me about shape and where I should be. And not just me, but what an entire back-four should be doing at any point in a game.

I spent a year away from Alan when Knocklyon disbanded and I went to Leicester Celtic. We had a great year, getting to the All-Ireland semi-finals. I started that season playing up front and ended up making my way back to centre-half. Meanwhile, Alan moved to Verona in Blanchardstown, where he took on my age group. Once he rang me and asked if I wanted to rejoin him, I jumped at the chance.

Verona were in the same league as Leicester Celtic, but were mid-table. But Alan was involved with the FAI, he was coaching in the Irish schoolboy set-up, and as a coach I idolised him. I couldn't turn down the opportunity to play under him again.

Little did I know, when I agreed to the move, that their old manager had decided to go to Home Farm and he took a load of players with him. So, we ended up with sort of half-a-team at Verona. We had some great players, but we ended up getting battered and relegated that year. At the same time, Leicester Celtic were flying. And I know there was a bit of resentment from a few of the lads when I left. But I was happy at Verona, because I was working with Alan again. If I'd stayed at Leicester, I might have won a few more medals, but I wouldn't have gained half the footballing knowledge. Even if I wasn't playing well or we were getting battered, I was still learning.

And I was clocking up the miles too. The M50 was being redeveloped at this stage, so the trek to Blanchardstown was a grueller. I'd leave school at four, get home at half-four, get changed and head straight away to training for half-six, and I wouldn't get home until 10 at night. This was the routine two evenings a week.

Joan and Philip O'Neill would bring me over. They were great, and kind too when things were rough at home.

I returned to Leicester Celtic at under-17 – but only after a brief spell at the age of 16 when I trained with Shamrock Rovers. The sessions took place across from Aherne's Pub in Tallaght and I was desperate to sign for them. Unfortunately, they weren't interested. *Was it because I wasn't good enough? Or was it because of a debs invite?*

I WAS ASKED to go to a debs at Sancta Maria College in Rathfarnham.

Of course I said yes. I was only going into fifth year at the time, so I was delighted. Little did I know that it was a daughter of one of the coaches at Rovers. I got some shock when I walked in the front door.

I remember at the debs, someone said to me... 'See that fella... he's a footballer'. I didn't know him at the time, but it was Stephen Rice. He was at Coventry City. I got to know him later that year when I started dating a sister of Stephen's girlfriend. Who knows in what direction my career would have gone had I not accepted the debs invite. I could have been a Shamrock Rovers player, only the wrong girl asked me to her debs! Instead, after a few training sessions with the Hoops, it was back to Leicester Celtic for me.

After a year with Leicester, I went to St Francis, then played a few games with Lourdes Celtic before joining Bray Wanderers. John Curran from St Francis got in contact with the physio at Bray and he recommended me to Pat Devlin.

Pat brought me in for a look and quickly signed me up. I was just 17, turning 18 at the time and I was playing with the under-21s. I spent most of my first year there on the bench and watched on as a substitute as we beat St Patrick's Athletic to win the Enda McGuill Cup final on penalties.

But my big breakthrough came the following year when I was handed the captain's armband. But, unfortunately, that was as good as it got for me at Bray Wanderers.

· CHAPTER 2 ·

MY TIME AT Bray Wanderers all but came to an end in late-August 2006.

We went, as holders, to Maloney Park in Edenderry for an Enda McGuill Cup quarter-final against Kildare County. A goal down and with time running out, we were doing everything to chase the game. Of course Kildare were doing everything to hold onto their lead.

They used every trick in the book to wind down the clock, including booting the ball as far as they could into a big farmer's field next door to the pitch. With no spare ball available, play couldn't restart until it was retrieved. Add that to the feeling that lots of decisions were going against us and you'll have an idea of the frustration that was building – not just on the pitch, but also in our dugout.

Someone who I'd see again in the senior game, Phil Caschera, was the man in the middle that day in Edenderry. We were convinced he'd add five or six minutes of injury time at the very least. After all, it felt like we'd spent half the game fetching the ball from the next field over. Phil clearly didn't see it that way, because he blew the full-time whistle with what seemed like unreasonable haste. Cue pandemonium.

A bunch of us ran over to the referee and his assistants to remonstrate. It's fair to say we weren't too happy. *Who was first over to Phil?* Yours truly, of course.

Followed closely by my centre-half partner Willie Tyrrell, who went on to play for Kilkenny City, Kildare County, Longford Town and Wexford. Despite the almost blinding sense of injustice I just about managed to regain enough composure to realise that I was in danger of losing it and doing something stupid. I somehow dragged myself away from the situation.

By that stage, however, the whole team, the bench and the staff were involved in a big melee right in the middle of the pitch. Meanwhile, I had retreated to the dugout. Although I had the wherewithal to get away from the epicentre of the ruckus, I was still in a rage. The red mist hadn't gone away. So I took a swing at the side of the dugout and punched it with enough force that it cracked.

After what seemed like an eternity, we realised we weren't going to change any minds. Phil wasn't going to restart the game and reset his stopwatch. So, finally, things calmed down. We got changed and headed along to a local pub for some grub. Both teams and match officials were invited.

By this stage tempers had cooled and the conversation was normal once again – so much so that civil words were exchanged even between the aggrieved Bray camp and the match officials. Moments before we arrived at the pub, I was told that the referee had given me a red card for my role in the post-match scenes.

Fair enough. I was angry and upset, I felt we had been the victims of a great injustice. With all those emotions spewing out, I was probably over the top in what I said to Phil straight after the final whistle.

I'll take the punishment on the chin, I thought. *I'll learn from the incident… Try harder next time to keep my emotions in check. It'll only be one game on the sidelines.*

Two at tops… No big deal.

THE KILDARE GAME came at a pivotal stage in my career at Bray Wanderers. I was 18 and I'd been brought into the first team squad under Pat Devlin for a home game against Cork City. These were exciting times at the Carlisle Grounds. The objective that year was to qualify for Europe, although things didn't quite work out as planned.

Bray finished 10th in 2006, just one place above the relegation play-off spot. But the ambition was there and Devo was a seasoned pro. During the year, he brought me into his office. He told me he liked me at right-back, that I suited his style. He liked a big, strong defender who could hit the ball into the corners. That was typical of the football you saw in the League of Ireland back then.

I was buzzing after that meeting with Devo. Things were going great. I made the bench for a game at St Pat's too. While one eye was on progress into the senior set-up, another was on captaining the '21s' to back-to-back Enda McGuill titles. Kildare County scuppered that one, but at least I had a few more months to establish myself in the first team squad. Or so I thought.

It wasn't long before I realised that the Edenderry incident would come back to haunt me. Word soon got back to me that I'd been reported for something far more serious than I thought when I first heard that I had been red-carded.

According to Phil Caschera's report, I was done for putting my hands on the referee. I couldn't believe it. The linesman, apparently, with all that was going on, saw a jersey with the No 4 getting involved at a point when Phil felt he was manhandled.

I told anyone who'd listen that the linesman must have been mistaken. 'It must have been No 14', I argued. But no one was buying my defence of mistaken identity. All of a sudden I was facing a very serious disciplinary hearing.

The referee's report was just 158 words long. It began:

KILDARE COUNTY v BRAY
Enda McGuill Cup quarter-final,
Maloney Park, Edenderry – 30/8/06

I would like to report the following. At the final whistle I was approached by the whole Bray team, demanding to know why I hadn't played more injury time. I told them that this was at the discretion of the referee. I was then man-handled by Brian Gartland and William Tyrrell, who grabbed my wrist to see how much time was on my watch. During this I was being abused by practically the whole Bray squad, the reason I did not show any red cards was because I did not want to fuel an already volatile situation…

THE FAI WERE quick to move on Phil's report. It sparked a flurry of correspondence between the association and Bray Wanderers. FAI operations manager Michael Hayes wrote to the club secretary to inform him of suspensions to Willie Tyrrell, myself and some of our officials. All the paperwork from that time is still at home. My mam held onto it, along with loads of my medals.

Included in the paperwork was the letter from the late Michael Hayes that said we were… *Suspended with immediate effect from all involvement in football…*

This suspension remains in place, it continued, *until their cases are heard by the*

Disciplinary Commission at its meeting on Wednesday 13th September 2006.

That wasn't the end of it. One day later, and a second letter landed with the club. This time it was from Jack Kelly of the FAI Disciplinary Commission. Things were getting serious. It concluded that... *The matter will be considered by the FAI Disciplinary Commission at its meeting on 13th September 2006.*

As an 18-year-old who'd never been in trouble before, this was all swirling around my head. I was struggling to make sense of it all.

Within a couple of days, replies were sent to the FAI.

Next up, a week before the hearing, the club laid out our defence in a written submission. It acknowledged... *The referee was approached by a number of players and staff.* It continued... *As a club we have spoken with the two players involved. They are both devastated by what has happened. Brian Gartland has never been sent off to date in his career and William Tyrrell has an excellent disciplinary record.*

That's that, I thought. Surely those contributions would help smooth over this horrible misunderstanding. *We'll just turn up to the hearing, give our side of the story verbally, take a one- or two-game ban and move on.*

The reality was, we were only at the beginning of a long and painful process.

The hearing took place at 11am on Wednesday September 13. A day later the verdicts – and punishments – were delivered. I was... *suspended from all involvement in football until the end of the 2006 competitive season...* as well as being fined €200. My stomach dropped to the ground. I felt sick, dizzy. I couldn't understand it. Willie Tyrrell was hit with the same ban. Five days after the verdict, Bray Wanderers launched an appeal against the suspensions handed down to Willie and myself.

IF I'M BEING honest, I'd been uncomfortable with the way this had been handled by the club for some time. But when it came to the appeal, that's when my relationship with the club – Pat Devlin had left the club by then – was all but strained beyond repair.

Going into the initial hearing, I wondered if I should get my own solicitor. My mam told me that I needed one, as I was on the receiving end of such a serious accusation. The club assured me that their solicitor would handle it. I remember walking into the FAI's old Merrion Square building and sitting in front of the disciplinary panel. I gave my version of events, insisting that I hadn't put my hands on the referee. However, they sided with Phil Caschera and decided that my season was over.

When it came to the appeal, I was determined to have my own representation. Having sought advice from a number of people, including some involved in schoolboy football, I was all set to appeal the decision itself, rather than the severity of the punishment. But I was never afforded that opportunity.

I wasn't told when the appeal was taking place, so it went ahead in my absence. The first I heard of it was when, one evening in training, I was approached by a club official. 'Sorry Brian, that didn't go our way today.' That was it.

I was banned for the rest of the season.

The year ended on a brighter note. I was named Bray Wanderers under-21 Player of the Year. Finally, a sliver of hope. Maybe I could put the previous few months behind me and break into the first team. I was given a fairly modest contract, but all I cared about was making that step up. I had big ambitions at the time. I wanted to make the first team, get into the Ireland under-21 squad and earn a move abroad. That bubble burst within minutes of returning for pre-season training.

Eddie Gormley was in charge and he hadn't assigned me a squad number. In response, I asked to be sent out on loan. I was desperate to make the step up to first team football and I knew it wasn't going to happen at the Carlisle Grounds.

As for Phil Caschera, he ended up refereeing in the senior game. I was at Monaghan United when he took charge of one of our games. I approached him afterwards.

'Listen Phil, whatever's happened has happened, it's over, but you were wrong, I never put my hands on you.'

I'm not sure whether he believed me, but I'd waited a long time to get that off my chest. It had bugged me to bits for years. I often wonder where my career would have taken me if it wasn't for that day in Edenderry and the events that followed. *Would I have established myself in the Bray first team before the season was out?* I had my goals, my ambitions. I was already involved in first team squads and I was desperate to get some game-time.

Would that have been the catalyst for a move to England or an international breakthrough? It's all ifs and buts now. All I know for certain is that by early 2007 I was on the lookout for a new club.

PART **TWO**

My Trade

I love basketball (above, I'm lining out with a Dublin representative team at a tournament in France... I'm holding the ball in the front row, Michael Darrgh MacAuley is on my right shoulder). But soccer was my greatest passion and the decision to sign for Bray Wanderers (above, holding the under-21 cup) was an easy one in the end. With dad (right) in my Monaghan days.

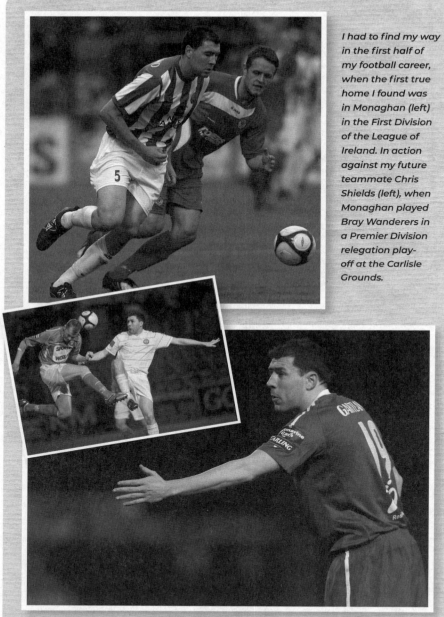

I had to find my way in the first half of my football career, when the first true home I found was in Monaghan (left) in the First Division of the League of Ireland. In action against my future teammate Chris Shields (left), when Monaghan played Bray Wanderers in a Premier Division relegation play-off at the Carlisle Grounds.

Before accepting Stephen Kenny's offer to join Dundalk, I had two really good years with Portadown in the Irish League that helped me further grow and mature as a footballer.

▪ CHAPTER 3 ▪

FROM LEAGUE CHAMPIONS to demotion in the space of a few short months, Shelbourne's fall from grace was spectacular. Between unpaid wages and winding up orders issued by the Revenue Commissioners, the fact that the club survived the winter of 2006 was a miracle in itself. But the future was bleak.

They were forced to give up their Setanta Sports Cup spot and in March 2007 they said they would not take part in that year's Champions League, a devastating blow considering the money earned by playing in Europe. Instead of defending their Premier Division title, they had to face up to life in the First Division.

Their squad was decimated. The management team that had brought so much glory to Tolka Park had gone. Shels hadn't a penny to their name and things looked grim for a side that had dominated the Irish club scene for the early part of the decade.

It was hard to believe that this was a side that was 45 minutes away from pipping Deportivo La Coruña to a Champions League group stage spot only two-and-a-half years earlier. They won league titles in 1999/2000, 2001/02, 2003, 04' and '06, and made it their business to snap up the best players from their biggest rivals. They looked set to dominate Irish football for years when, at the end of 2004, they pinched Glen Crowe, Bobby Ryan and Colin Hawkins from Bohemians, the other dominant force of that era.

But they finished third the next season, behind Cork City and Stephen

Kenny's Derry City. Although they won the league again 12 months later, the writing was on the wall at Tolka Park. Suddenly, they went from a club that was snapping up not just the best players from their rivals, but also bringing in former internationals such as Alan Moore and Curtis Fleming, to looking for favours from their old rivals.

Shelbourne's strife turned out to be my big break. They were desperate for players to fill out their squad ahead of the 2007 campaign. Just getting a team on the pitch was going to be a massive challenge.

AT THE SAME time that Shelbourne were going through massive upheaval, I was informing Eddie Gormley that I wanted out of Bray, that I wanted to make the step up to first team football, maybe find a club in the First Division and get some games there. However, I had signed a contract the year before and wasn't really in a position to make any demands.

Eddie told me he wanted me to stay at the Carlisle Grounds.

So that, it seemed, was that. I spent pre-season by the seaside. Just before the 2007 season started, Dermot Keely got in touch with Eddie and told him he was trying to put a team together. Eddie agreed to let me join Dermot at Tolka Park. Clubs all around the league were helping Shels out at the time, loaning out young players or releasing others, and Eddie was as eager to help as anyone.

I met Dermot at McGowans in Churchtown and signed straightaway. I'd barely read the contract. No one in my family or circle of friends had experience in negotiating deals, so I went alone to meet Dermot. I'm sure he couldn't believe his luck. He was a seasoned campaigner and I was a kid with virtually no experience when it came to talking terms. But I was on feck all money at Bray, so when Shelbourne threw a couple of quid on top of what I had been earning, I was chuffed with myself.

It wasn't long before my new-found confidence as a master negotiator (I left McGowans thinking I was a natural) was rocked. I spoke to someone at Bray who asked about my deal. I had been on around €100-a-week at the Carlisle Grounds, with an appearance bonus of €50 – but at Shels I was handed €150-a-week straight up. That extra cash was massive. I was in college at the time and living at home.

It wouldn't be long before the arse started to fall out of the Irish economy – it had certainly fallen out of the Tolka Park economy – so there wasn't that much money going around. But it wasn't as if I needed any more than that. With no financial commitments, it was all spending money. However, when I revealed the details of my deal, eyes rolled. 'They were definitely willing to give you more… if you'd asked for it,' I was told. But I was inexperienced when it came to contract talks. Not that I improved greatly later in my career.

DERMOT KEELY WAS back in the Tolka Park hotseat after a five-year absence. In between his Shelbourne reigns, he had spells at Kildare County, Derry City and Dublin City. And while he didn't win any trophies in those five years, Dermot was still one of the greatest League of Ireland legends of all time. In management he won four league titles, one each at Shamrock Rovers and Dundalk, and two at Shels. He also won two FAI Cups as manager. There certainly was no doubting his credentials. As a kid, the idea of working under such a highly decorated boss was really exciting.

As a player, he was a member of Rovers' famous four in-a-row side. He won the last of those as player-boss. He'd already won a championship with Dundalk, where he is still revered. Dermot also won five FAI Cups as a player and a handful of big Player of the Year awards. For a club in Shelbourne's predicament, they were getting a manager with one hell of a CV. And as a centre-half, the prospect of playing for one of the best and most feared defenders ever had me looking forward to my first day there like it was Christmas morning. However, as I soon discovered, this wasn't just a brand new challenge for me - the same could be said for Dermot, despite his vast experience. He was old-school and, suddenly, he was in charge of a really young team, packed with players in their late-teens and early-twenties. A lot of lads had come in from UCD, where the environment was completely different to a traditional Dermot Keely dressing-room. To survive under Dermot's style of management, you needed a really thick skin.

Experienced players such as Owen Heary, Mick Neville, Pat Scully, Paul Doolin and Pat Fenlon thrived under Keely's rule. But our squad lacked such robust and hardy characters. We had a lot of softer lads who just didn't respond well to Dermot's abrasive ways. Plus, you had a lot of players who had little or no experience of playing senior football. While it was a real eye-opener for us, it must have been incredibly frustrating for Dermot.

So, as soon as the mid-season transfer window opened, Dermot added some real steel to his side. He had lined up a load of players, including his son Alan, and Marc McCulloch and Stuart Malcolm, who both came in from Scotland. They would both fly in the night before each game, play and then head home.

Alan, Marc and Stuart were all defenders, so I found myself being edged out of the side. I didn't play much in the second half of the season. But the 20-odd games I played that year was more than I would have managed elsewhere.

The 2007 season at Shelbourne was tough, it was a real learning curve. We had some great people there, great lads such as Mark Leech, who had arrived on loan from Drogheda United. I grew up with Mark and was thrilled to see him walk through the door. Mark Rooney was another good pal. He was only 23 but he had experience from earlier spells at Dublin City, UCD, Drogheda and St Pat's.

I COULD HARDLY have dreamed of a better start to my Shelbourne career. In our first league game of the season we were up against Dermot's former side Kildare County. The game ended in a 2–2 draw, with Darren McKenna earning us a point with two minutes to go. Philly Gorman had put them 1-0 up from the penalty spot after just four minutes but then, 10 minutes later, I popped up with the equaliser.

To this day, I am gutted that there is no footage of the goal. In recent seasons every single goal in the Premier and First Divisions has been caught on camera – either by RTE or eir Sport, or by the club's media officer. In 2007, however, it was a different story. So, I suppose I could tell you that I found the top corner with a bicycle kick from the edge of the penalty box and there'd be no visual proof to the contrary. But here's how it really went down.

I can still remember it like it was yesterday.

I was up for a corner, standing on the penalty spot, when the ball dropped right onto my head. I probably jumped a little too early, because I was falling back when I made contact. I lost sight of the ball for a split-second as I hit the ground, but then through a forest of legs I saw it drop inside the far post. To this day I'd rate it as one of my best headed goals.

But again, you'll have to take my word for it. It could have been average. But that's how I'll always remember it. And I will never forget the euphoria I felt as the ball hit the back of the net. This was a brand new era for Shelbourne and I scored their first competitive goal. As I celebrated, the players piled on top of me. All I could see looking up was Jim Crawford's head.

EVERY NIGHT BEFORE a match, I visualise how certain plays or set-pieces might go. I am big into that. I'll go to bed and picture certain scenarios – and scoring is one of them. The night before the Kildare County game, I visualised myself scoring from a set-piece. The newspapers the following morning had a picture of the goal celebration and there I was at the bottom of it, with lads piling on. I don't know what I was thinking when I scored, but I ran to an empty stand instead of one that was packed with Shels fans.

Jim Crawford was probably the oldest member of our squad at the start of that campaign. He was one of the first over to celebrate that goal. Jim was brilliant, a really likable person and he was great for the younger members of the squad. He wasn't soft on us. Not that he'd hammer you, but he would have a way of letting a player know that he wanted more out of him. I'd imagine it was a strange new world for him, having played such a big role in Shelbourne's previous successes along with so many big-name and experienced teammates. Jim was in the final few years of his playing career at this stage. He was approaching his 34th birthday and suddenly he was in a dressing-room with a load of 18, 19 and 20-year-olds. Come to think of it, his final season at Shelbourne was probably the perfect preparation for his future role as Ireland under-21 head coach.

TRAINING WITH SHELBOURNE took part on something resembling a rough patch of grass near Dublin Airport, and tantalisingly close to the facilities at ALSAA. I remember lads going fist-to-fist at times during sessions – lads were nearly battering each other.

That was Dermot's way; he wanted us to train with match-day intensity. Dermot would tell us, 'I don't want to see any fannying about, so make sure you wear your f**king shin pads to training'. I remember thinking… *Do I really have to wear my shin pads?* As a young lad, relatively inexperienced in the world of senior football, there will be times when you are not sure if someone is serious or not. I turned up for the first session with a pair of shin pads, looked around at the rest of the lads, saw no one else was wearing them and quickly hid them in my bag. Dermot was just making a point, but I took what he said literally.

Shelbourne was as big a learning curve as I could have asked for. It was the perfect launchpad for a career in senior football. Real into the deep end stuff.

There were some great people there who kept the club alive during its darkest days, such as their dedicated and hardworking chairman Joe Casey. The club would not have survived without the loyal volunteers who gave up their time and money to keep it going. The kit man Johnny Watson was a great character, as was Stephen Fagan, a young lad who helped Johnny out.

There was a real family feel to the club. And the fans were great too. It must have been hard on them to go from watching an all-conquering side, competing regularly on the big European stage, to cheering on a bunch of kids who were doing their best in the rough and tumble of the First Division. But we were stunned at the levels of support we received early in 2007. We had close to 2,000 fans at our first two home games of the season – against Kildare County and Dundalk (a 2-0 defeat).

Naturally enough, attendances started to drop as the year progressed. But that had its positives too. It led to an environment where you got to know a lot of the people around the club, people who kept turning up for no other reason than their love for the club. It was a real eye-opener into how clubs survive against the odds. If it wasn't for some very determined people, only a handful of whom are named above, I am convinced that Shelbourne would have gone the way of so many other Irish clubs and drifted out of existence.

THAT YEAR OF survival was about loyalty and passion, and a big glamour friendly against Leeds United. Joe Casey, a big fan of the Elland Road side, called in a few favours to get this game on. Funnily enough, Leeds were in a similar boat to Shels. A few months earlier they had been relegated from the Championship, having been deducted 10 points for entering financial administration. Had they not lost those 10 points they would have stayed up by the skin of their teeth. But they still had some big names at the club. Dennis Wise was their manager and Gus Poyet his assistant. As a young lad with dreams of playing in England, I got a real kick out of seeing those two in the opposition dugout.

We lost the friendly 2-0 and afterwards both teams headed out to that famous Dublin nightclub Lillies.

One of my mates was a huge Chelsea fan, so he begged me to bring him along.

We both got chatting to Wise and Poyet, who were happy enough to mingle. Wise said something to me about being a centre-half who didn't like to play football, as all he'd seen me do earlier that day was hoof the ball away. Straight away I pointed over to Dermot Keely and snapped, 'I f**king do like playing football and I'm good at it too. See that manager over there? He's the reason why I kick the ball as far as I can whenever it's at my feet'.

That comment from Dennis Wise has stuck in my head ever since.

Growing up, I played a lot in midfield and up front, and I did so at a decent standard. I loved pulling off flicks and tricks. But when it came to organised football I was overcome by fear, I clammed up in possession. Managers would never encourage me to play the ball out. I was always fed the line Pat Devlin delivered at Bray, which was that I was a big strong defender who should hit the channels whenever possible.

Then with Dermot Keely, if you tried to play any bit of football at the back he'd shout, 'F**king boot it… what the f**k are you doing there?'

These were experienced managers and I was just a kid. I wasn't going to argue. I was afraid to try anything different. Of course, things have changed in the League of Ireland. Even a veteran such as Devo has evolved and he has Cabinteely playing some great football. But that's the way it was for me. I was obsessed with becoming a professional footballer and was convinced that the only way to do that was to follow orders to the letter.

So, there were always two types of footballer within me – one who did what he was told and another who, away from the pressure of organised football, would open up his bag of tricks and show a decent bit of skill… 'for a big guy'. When it came to the League of Ireland, something always held me back.

I had never been coached by someone like Dermot before. He was different, competitive. Naturally enough, having won so much in his career, he wasn't going to change just because he was in charge of a bunch of kids. Both as a player and a manager, he was involved with teams that were either winning trophies or competing for them. He would do anything to get a result and the League of Ireland – the First Division in particular – wasn't a footballing league at the time.

We were in a results business and the football was no frills, end-to-end stuff. Defenders *defended*. It was our job to stop attacks and get the ball up the other end of the pitch as quickly as we could.

The logic was simple – there's less chance of us conceding when the ball is at the other end and more chance of us scoring.

Years later I was back as Shelbourne, just before I signed for Dundalk. But it was a different Shels side. John McDonnell was now in charge and the way he wanted to play football was much closer to my own philosophy. I trained with them for a few weeks and played in a friendly against Peterborough. I was at the point in my career where I didn't care anymore what people thought, I just wanted to play and enjoy myself. Of course I still had ambition, but I was 26 at the time and felt that my chance of a career in England had probably passed me by.

Johnny encouraged his defenders to get the ball off the goalkeeper, whereas before it was a case of heading up to the halfway line for a long kick out. Players and managers are far more comfortable now with risk-taking. I had a great game that day. At that time in my life I was really enjoying my football. To be honest, even now, after years of playing the Dundalk way, the fear still creeps in every so often. On the other hand, you have some lads who are too laid back and they can be a liability. Nobody's perfect, I suppose. But as I always say to people, if I never made a mistake I wouldn't still be playing in the League of Ireland… I'd be in England or Spain earning millions.

IT WAS MY time at Portadown that helped to unlock more of the footballer in me. I went up there and I didn't give a damn. No one knew me, no one had ever seen highlights of my performances. Alan Cawley signed midway through the season and he was like, 'What's going on… Garts is doing Cruyff turns at the back!'

But the whole team was playing great football at the time.

I had Garry Breen beside me in defence, Keith O'Hara, ex-Charlton midfielder Neil McCafferty was there and Kevin Braniff too. He was an unbelievable footballer. These were all players who were comfortable on the ball and had no problem knocking it about. Alan was there for a few months. He drove a Volkswagen Buggy and I'd meet him just outside Dublin, we'd pick up Garry Breen in Dundalk and head up to Portadown for our games.

OLLIE BYRNE PASSED away while I was at Shels.

I didn't get to meet him, as he had taken ill before I arrived. The whole squad turned out for his funeral and I could see just how big a personality he was within

Irish football by the size of the turnout. I'd heard all the stories though, how in love he was with the club and how he'd do anything to help them. While he hadn't been in control of the club for most of that season, his passing felt like the end of an era.

But despite all that had happened the club between 2006 and '07, when Shels went from champions of Ireland to a mid-table First Division side, the atmosphere around Tolka Park was good. As a young lad, I was just delighted to be at a big club and to be getting my game under Dermot Keely. I just wanted to work hard and prove that I belonged, at the very least, at this level.

My old pal Mark Leech had scored the winner in the Setanta Cup final the year before and I'd always considered him to be a great player. We lived around the corner from each other growing up and spent most of the day playing football together on the green. I'd come home from school, put on my worst clothes and we'd run around in all types of weather for hours on end.

Kieran Hart, Leechy and I would travel over to Tolka Park together. We had some of the best under-21 players in the country at the time, so we were a confident bunch. But the First Division was an unforgiving place.

Results often didn't go our way and I was someone whose mood would be determined by how the last game went. If we didn't win, the weekend would be ruined. I have learned over time to control that, to move on from a poor performance or result. But in my early days I would sulk a lot after a defeat. I'd be in a real stinker over a bad display.

I remember one game when Niall O'Reilly was playing right-back for us. Niall was younger than me, probably 18 at the time. A friend of mine was at the game with their kid, who was five years old. That kid went home thinking the right-full's name was 'Nelly You Little Bollix'… because that's what Dermot kept shouting at him throughout the 90 minutes.

At this stage in the season crowds had dropped from 1,500 and 2,000 down to around 800, so you'd hear a lot of what was said from the dugout. But that was life under Dermot. If you had a thick enough skin, you'd learn to deal with it and toughen up. Others, though, would crumble under the pressure. It probably wasn't the best environment for young players, but for those who were able to take it, it set us up for life in senior football.

If Dermot gave you a bollocking, he would go right through you.

And I was on the receiving end of plenty of them, as we were conceding lots of goals. We kept seven clean sheets in 36 league games that year. Dermot was an old school manager and his style worked for him for years. Just look at his list of honours. I think he came back to Shelbourne as a favour to his old club more than anything.

He had a real soft spot for them and he couldn't say no in their time of need. Reflecting on that time now, I can see why he was so tough as a manager. He wanted his players to give the same type of commitment and play with the same kind of drive that made him one of the most successful stars in the history of Irish football. But he was dealing with a different generation to his.

If I'm being honest, I ended up hating Dermot for years. I felt his way of treating his players was out of order. But times have changed and I understand now that the game he played was different to the one I started out in. Thanks to Dermot I toughened up more in one season than during any other time in my career. I learned to deal with adversity, to take things on the chin and move on.

It has to be said that he was funny as well.

He was banned for one particular match, so he couldn't be in the dressing-room on the day of the game. So, one of the coaches put his phone on loudspeaker and placed it on the physio's bed in the middle of the dressing-room. All of a sudden, a voice boomed from the phone.

'You f**king bastards… YIS ARE SHITE!'

He addressed one of the players, who happened to be fixing his shinpad at the time. Dermot was having a go, but the player in question was largely ignoring him. Suddenly Dermot roared, 'And stop fixing your f**king shinpad'. It was gas. The lads were all looking around for a hole in the wall or to see if he was hiding under a bunch of kit bags.

Of course, things changed when players were let go in the middle of the season. I was told that I'd be kept on, so there I was, thinking I'd obviously shown enough. But during the second half of the season I was on the bench a lot, and in the stand a few times too.

These are things you have to deal with as a young footballer.

Going from playing every week to being dropped, can get you down. Your confidence can take a hit. Fortunately, however, I had done enough that year to earn another shot at first team football elsewhere.

· CHAPTER 4 ·

MY PHONE RANG one day in late-2007.

It was Mick Cooke, then manager of Monaghan United.

He wanted to meet me. They had gotten the better of us that season, beating us twice, including a 4-0 win, and drawing the other two clashes.

Despite that, he still wanted to sign me! So, I agreed to meet him at the Red Cow Hotel, just off the M50. Within minutes of our chat I knew I wanted to play for Mick. He came across straightaway as a lovely, genuine person and a really knowledgeable football man. The fact that they were training in Clondalkin at the time, just up the road from me, was a huge bonus.

I remembered how, four games from the end of the 2007 season with Shelbourne, we were away in Monaghan and they beat us 1-0. My future Dundalk teammate Darren Meenan scored the winner. I was on the bench that day and was really impressed by their performance.

The team was packed full of young lads and they played some decent football. So, when the chance to join them came up, I thought to myself... *Why not?*

Once again, it was all about the chance to get some more games under my belt in senior football. I won't lie and say that I had a load of options, but Monaghan really was an attractive proposition. And I was convinced that I would improve under Mick.

So I signed there and then.

I still wasn't very savvy when it came to contract negotiations and Mick was a shrewd man who had been through it all before. I knew Monaghan wouldn't pay that much anyway, so there was little point in haggling. But it wasn't about the money for me.

When I look back at my career, I probably should have been greedier when it came to contract talks. I didn't have enough confidence in myself or in my own value. Afterwards, I'd think back and say... *F**k me, I was in a great position last year to ask for more money.* Then sometimes I'd hear about the contracts other lads were on and realise how short-changed I'd been. But there is a balance to be struck between playing somewhere where you are happy, or getting an extra €100 a week somewhere else and being miserable from a footballing point of view.

Sure, that's €5,000 a year. But if I'm not happy, that five grand wouldn't mean a lot to me. Money was never the be-all and end-all for me. At the same time, though, I probably could have been a little more pushy.

MICK HAD ASSEMBLED a great group of lads and he was as good a manager as I thought he'd be.

Like I said before, I wasn't a big fan of playing under Dermot Keely at the time, and I never had a chance under Eddie Gormley. But Mick was a great man to play for. I had a feeling right from the off that he wasn't going to mess me over – and he never did.

I spent three years at Monaghan with him and they were some of my favourite times in football. He was a brilliant, decent person. The reason I'm harping on about this is because, believe it or not, men like Mick are hard to come by in football. Of course, you have to be ruthless to survive, particularly in management. But many lose the ability to be compassionate – and even fair – when they take their seat in the dugout.

And, as a young lad, it was nice to feel a sense of worth. At the same time, he was honest with me and told me straightaway that I'd be competing with some really good players for a place in the team.

WHILE I STARTED the first game of the season, I don't think Mick knew his best centre-half pairing yet. I didn't have a great game so I was dropped to the bench at home to Wexford. I remember sitting there thinking... *I better up my game here.* I got back in quick enough and pretty much stayed in the team for the next three years.

It was great craic at Monaghan.

There was a really good atmosphere in the squad. Mick had cultivated a really good environment. He was competitive and he knew this was a team that was getting better every year. Every player he brought in seemed to improve the side and there was a great mix of youth and experience. We had the likes of Aaron Mooney, Aidan Lynch, Dom Tierney and Cathal O'Connor... and Brendan Kennedy in goal. Aidan and Dom were so good to me. Two experienced players, but decent people with a great sense of humour. We car-shared to games, and their advice and encouragement helped me to grow as a footballer.

In my third year there we were right in the mix for the First Division title and promotion, as the end of the season approached. We played Waterford at home with six games remaining and Vinny Sullivan was up front for them.

He scored to put them two-up after just half an hour and that's how it stayed until half-time. I was really worked up in that game and was throwing my body in front of everything. At one stage I got a boot in the face as I went for the ball.

Moments later, Vinny clocked me right in the jaw.

It happened right in front of the fourth official and the two benches. I dropped in a heap. At this stage I had a dead leg too from a bad challenge. Safe to say it was a feisty game. There I was at half-time, laid out on the physio's table in this tiny L-shaped dressing-room.

Mick stormed into the room.

Maybe I was at fault for one of the goals, but I was sure I hadn't been as bad as some of the other players. And I'd taken a couple of big blows too, so surely Mick would take it easy on me. No chance. He saw me first.

'YOU... you little f**king bastard!' ... and he went on and on.

So I grabbed a bag of footballs and swung them as hard as I could.

BANG! I smacked Mick square in the face.

Next thing I knew, he jumped at me and grabbed me by the throat. I was still lying down, trying to grab him back, but before things could escalate any further, some of the other boys jumped up and pulled us apart.

Before we knew it, we were back out on the pitch for the second-half. How did the game end up?

We won 4-2. Philly Hughes got two, Cathal O'Connor scored and Sean Brennan got the other one. I ended up having to come off with the dead leg, but was delighted with the fight we showed in the second-half. And how it mirrored the fight we showed in the dressing-room at half-time!

Mick sometimes brought us to the Phoenix Park for training. That's where we had the next session after the Waterford win, two days later.

I turned up, slightly apprehensive, wondering what kind of reception I'd get from Mick. I approached the steps up to the little changing room near the cricket ground. Suddenly, Mick stepped outside.

He was standing at the top of the steps with a pair of boxing gloves on.

'Right Garto… let's settle this!'

That was it, the ice was broken, the half-time row was in the past and we had a good laugh about it. That's the type of man he is. I wouldn't have a bad word to say about him and I'm not sure anyone else who has played under him would have a view to the contrary.

WE HAD A decent team at Monaghan.

A young goalkeeper by the name of Aaron McCarey came in and played some games for us. He was only 17 and it was a real gamble to throw him into senior football. But we were struggling at the time for goalkeepers. Brendan Kennedy picked up an injury and Mick needed someone to cover. So in came Aaron and we kept six clean sheets in-a-row. It wasn't long before he was on his way to Wolves. Aaron ended up playing seven times for the first team at Molineux. He gained more first team experience at Walsall, York, Portsmouth and Bury, as well as Ross County in the Scottish Premiership. Not bad for a kid who started out playing behind me in Gortakeegan.

We were reunited at Dundalk – and I've rarely let an opportunity pass to remind him that he owes me a few bob from that career I got him!

Aaron was a big GAA player when he came to Monaghan and it really stood to him.

He was a real physical presence and whenever he came for a cross, you got out of his way. He held onto everything. You could see straightaway that this lad had talent. I would have given anything for a single one of the 10 under-21 caps he won playing for Ireland.

I'VE BEEN VERY lucky to have achieved so much in my career, but one of my fondest memories is Monaghan United's run to the 2010 EA Sports Cup final. It ranks right up there along with the league titles, FAI Cups and the 2016 Europa League campaign. Well, close enough!

After all, we were a First Division club at the time.

No one expected us to go so far. We caused a few big upsets along the way, beating Shelbourne, Tullamore Town and knocking out defending champions Bohemians on penalties. That Bohs side had Owen Heary, Conor Powell, Mark Rossiter, Ruaidhri Higgins, Killian Brennan, Mark Quigley and Aaron Greene in their starting 11. It didn't get much tougher than that.

We saw off Limerick 3-0 in the quarter-finals and a very strong Dundalk in the 'semis'. I remember having one or two chances from set-pieces, but in the end it was Cathal O'Connor who popped up with a late winner. We could hardly believe it, we were in a national final. Gortakeegan went wild that night.

We felt we really earned our place in the decider, as we'd eliminated some really strong teams. It wasn't a case that some of the bigger sides were resting players. And the Sligo Rovers side that we played in the final, they were full-strength too. It was a top quality side with the likes of Richie Ryan in midfield.

Richie was class. I loved him as a player in the League of Ireland. His little slide-rule and no-look passes were great to watch. Unless, of course, you were on the wrong end of them.

Our best hope that day in September 2010 was to keep things tight for as long as possible, and hopefully nick something. But that went out the window when Matthew Blinkhorn scored after just 14 minutes. To our credit, we stayed in the game. Sure, they were the better team, but that was always going to be the case, such was the strength of their side. As well as Richie, they had Gavin Peers, Alan Keane, Eoin Doyle, John Russell, Gary McCabe, Romauld Boco and Joseph Ndo.

We were rightly proud of our performance. If I had just a fraction more luck late in the game, we might have come away with more than just proud memories. With 15 minutes left, I rose to meet a corner. It flew past Ciaran Kelly in the Sligo goal, but it hit one of their players on the line. I think it was Eoin Doyle's shin that denied me a big cup final goal. I remember thinking at the time... *Lucky bastard.*

My dad was there that day. He got to a few home matches early in my career, although he didn't travel to many games down the country. But he was in Sligo that day. As were my mam and a few friends. I still have a picture of my dad and myself at the Showgrounds after the final.

It really was an incredible achievement, especially with the group of lads we had. It was such a tight-knit squad. And a trophy would have been just reward for Mick Cooke and the work he did at Monaghan. At the time, I had no idea what I was going to achieve further down the line. For all I knew, I might have missed out on my only chance to pick up a winners' medal. I'm sure that was the case for some of the lads on the team.

As for the club itself, less than two years later Monaghan United dropped out of the league. People might say it's only the League Cup, but what an achievement it would have been to bring a piece of national silverware back to Gortakeegan.

As it was, we brought a decent party back to Gortakeegan.

A few drinks were had on the bus back to Monaghan, before we headed into the town for a few more and then back to the club for a lock-in. You know it's been a good night when one of the residents near the ground pops up to let us know that a completely naked teammate is after running down the road.

I LOVED IT at Monaghan and was heartbroken when we didn't win promotion in 2010. We missed out on going up in the worst way possible.

We were going for the league with Stephen Kenny's Derry City at the time. They had been demoted the previous year, but they still had a Premier-class team. Stephen had stars such as Mark Farren, Ger Doherty, Eddie McCallion, Patrick McEleney and Barry Molloy in his side. They were far too good for that division. Oh yeah, and they also had a bright young winger by the name of James McClean. *Whatever happened to him?!*

Also in the First Division that season you had a really strong Waterford side. And at Limerick they were pumping money into the team to try and win promotion, bringing in some top-class players such as Joe Gamble and Stephen Bradley. So on reflection, we did really well to work our way into the promotion shake-up. It really was one of the most competitive First Divisions in years with Cork City, Shelbourne and Finn Harps also in the second-tier. I doubt there will ever be as strong a First Division again.

We were at home to Derry on the last day of the campaign – and it was all set up to be a winner-takes-all clash. They were a point ahead of us, but as long as we won our penultimate game away to Mervue, a win against the Candystripes would send us up as champions. We certainly would have taken that scenario at the start of 2010.

So, we headed to Terryland Park to take on Mervue full of confidence and belief that we could get the three points we needed to keep the heat on Derry. What happened that night summed up the ironic social media hashtag #TheGreatestLeagueInTheWorld.

We got off to a poor start and fell behind to a Dave Goldbey opener after half an hour. We recovered quickly enough though and equalised three minutes later through Aidan Collins. Once that went in, we battered them and did everything but score again.

Then, with an hour on the clock, we won an offside decision just inside our half. Shane Grimes ran down towards the corner flag to retrieve the ball and carry it back up-field. As he put it down, Aidan Lynch shouted to him, 'It's over here!'

So Grimesy knocked the ball over to him so he could take the free-kick from the correct spot. Suddenly, Rory Gaffney appeared out of nowhere and intercepted the ball, before making a beeline towards our penalty area.

By this point it was all happening in slow motion. Rory had half the pitch to run into and we were standing there motionless, wondering what the hell was going on? I remember looking at the linesman and the referee John McLoughlin, and nearly exploding with rage when they waved play on.

So we started racing back, but only after giving Rory a huge head-start, probably 30 yards or so. At the same time we were still roaring at the referee.

Rory slotted the ball home… 2-1.

Derry City won their game, so we could not overhaul them on the final day.

We were absolutely sick to think that a title chance had been taken from us like that. Social media wasn't big back then. If it was, I'm sure a clip of that goal would have gone viral within minutes of Rory scoring. We played Derry on the last game of the season and they brought a massive support with them, because they knew they were getting the trophy. We were utterly deflated at this point and lost 1-0, with the late great Mark Farren scoring the only goal that day.

Two games earlier, we were a point behind Derry City. They ended up seven points clear of us and we slipped to third, behind Waterford. Because of that, we had to travel to the RSC for the first game of the promotion/relegation play-offs.

We went down there and battered them, playing some great football and winning 3-1. The pep was back in our step after the bitter disappointment of Terryland. Next up was my first club Bray Wanderers, who had finished second from bottom in the Premier Division that season. Bray had lost their 'semi-final' against third-from-bottom Galway United, so were left to battle for their lives against us.

We were at home first and we destroyed them in every way but on the scoreboard. I remember walking off and Pat Devlin said to me, 'I don't know how that tie isn't over'.

Seriously, we smashed them, but we missed loads of chances.

We were still confident, however, going to Bray. Another stalemate, another scoreless draw after 90 minutes. Extra-time loomed. We were all knackered, but with two minutes to go we won a corner.

I got around to the back post, literally on the end-line, and I caught the ball with my left foot. It went behind the goalkeeper, off the post and back across the face of goal. It landed at the feet of Dom Tierney; he took a swing, but his effort was going wide until it hit Bray defender Chris Shields and deflected into the goal.

That was it. We were sure we were going up.

We all ran over to the side of the ground that runs alongside the DART line in celebration, to where the away fans were. The Monaghan supporters rushed towards the perimeter wall and suddenly it collapsed.

Huge cinder blocks started raining down onto the side of the pitch.

Dom and I were at the bottom of a pile-on and we could see the blocks falling in our direction. I still don't know how we managed to escape without getting a right clatter. The sideline was a mess and the game was stopped for ages while they moved the blocks away.

When it finally restarted, Bray sent a long ball up into our area. Wanderers striker Gary Shaw won a header and our goalkeeper Gabriel Sava went to catch it on the line. But in the worst weather conditions that you could imagine – wind and rain swirling around an open stadium – Gabi dropped the ball and it fell in front of Jake Kelly.

Six inches from goal, all he had to do was poke it home to send the tie to penalties.

THE SPOT-KICKS WERE as tense as I expected them to be.

But when Gary Shaw missed their third, and I scored our third, again we were looking good for promotion. However, Alan Byrne missed our last and it went to sudden death.

It went to penalty number eight and Paul Whelan stepped up for Monaghan. He smashed the ball off the crossbar.

Chris Shields, whose own goal looked to have sunk Bray, then had a chance to go from villain to hero, which he grabbed with both hands. Chris netted the winning penalty, Bray retained their Premier Division status and we were stuck in the First Division for another year. I have since become great pals with Chris at Dundalk and he has deservedly earned a reputation as one of the League of Ireland's finest midfielders. But spare a thought for poor old Whelo.

For ages after that, we'd tease him with taunts of… 'Come on, we'll hit the bar'. And whenever we'd be out for a drink, he would be on the receiving end of at least 10 shouts of… 'Whelo… it's your turn, hit the bar!'

His head must have been absolutely melted.

Paul is one of my best mates, and in 2021 I stood at the altar with him as he got married to Lisa. We've had a great friendship and a serious amount of laughs. Football has been so good to me, in allowing me to meet people like Paul.

I DIDN'T REALLY want to leave Monaghan United, but I felt I had to push on in my career. It was early 2011 and I was still young enough to believe that my ambition of a career in English football was still within reach. The arse had fallen out of the league here and there was no money in the game.

There were serious problems in Irish football at the time. All the headlines were on off-field strife. Brian Shelley and Steven Gray had taken Bohemians to court over unpaid wages. The game here was in a real mess.

I met with Martin Russell at UCD and immediately felt he was someone I wanted to play for. He told me that they were only able to pay two players – me and someone else – and I was offered €350 on a part-time deal, which I felt at the time was brilliant. After all, they were just down the road from home and I could practically train there full-time, as they had a high-performance centre. It would be a chance to get some proper professional training in, even if I was a part-time footballer. I loved the way Martin had his team playing, so I thought it would be a great chance to develop as a footballer on the pitch, as well as off it. But there was one snag. A lot of players had left, having finished their scholarships.

And with them only paying one other player, it would have been a real struggle to get some quality into the squad. I thought to myself… *We could end up with a really poor side.*

At centre-half, I could be on the wrong end of some serious hidings.

That wouldn't do me any favours in terms of catching the eye elsewhere. On reflection, Andy Boyle was a young centre-half whose career didn't suffer on account of his time at UCD. He had moved onto Shelbourne at that stage. Next stop for him was Dundalk. Andy was still really young when he moved to Oriel Park. He had just turned 22 when Stephen Kenny saw the potential in him and swooped.

It wasn't long before Andy showed how good he was, particularly when surrounded by other excellent players. At the time, though, I figured playing centre-half in a team that was constantly up against the cosh would not have reflected well on me.

Also, a few struggling Premier Division sides were in for me.

Then Pat Fenlon called.

I was delighted. Bohs were a big team. They were losing players, sure, but they still had Aidan Price and Liam Burns at centre-half. Mark Rossiter was there too.

They may have been struggling financially, but they still had some big names on their books. I was working for Littlewoods at the time, so I met Pat at eight o'clock in the Crowne Plaza Hotel in Blanchardstown one morning.

He told me he would love to sign me, but that he didn't know yet what he could offer in terms of a contract, as the court case with Shelley and Gray was still ongoing. I came away from the hotel thinking… *What was the point in meeting me then?*

I realised afterwards that he just wanted to let me know that he was interested, and to keep that in mind while considering opportunities elsewhere.

By this stage, however, all I could see in the League of Ireland was a transfer merry-go-round, with the same old players moving to the same old clubs. Managers seemed to be shying away from the younger lads, going instead for experienced players. It used to piss me off so much.

Every time I played a Premier Division club with Monaghan, I'd have a great game. I'd won a few Man of the Match awards in cup games against top-flight sides. But I felt like I was ignored when it came to possible transfers because I played for lowly Monaghan United. So I'd pretty much given up on getting a big club in the League of Ireland.

FORMER MANCHESTER UNITED defender Pat McGibbon had been coaching at Monaghan. He rang me one evening and asked me if I would meet with Portadown. I drove up, met their manager Ronnie McFaul and signed for them that night.

I probably shouldn't have been so eager, but that was my naivety in contract talks coming to the fore once again. However, Ronnie convinced me. He threw plenty of incentives my way. 'We can win this… we can win that. There's a bonus for this… a bonus for that.'

We were playing Bohemians in the first round of the Setanta Sports Cup. Beat them and we were in line for an extra £500. It was awfully hard to resist.

But the big thing for me was, playing football in the League of Ireland meant no summer holidays. But up north, the season finished in May.

I thought to myself… *The league has gone to shit down here… I'll just sign for Portadown… Play… Enjoy it… Train up there one night a week… Play Saturday and get a decent amount of cash out of it.*

In sterling!

I could still do a bit of coaching on the side in Dublin and continue to work in Littlewoods. When it all added up, it was a lot of money for a 24-year-old who was still living at home. So, I said I'd do it for a few months and then have a proper holiday. Play it by ear after that.

After I signed for Portadown, I had a look at the league table and saw they were second from bottom. I probably should have checked out that minor detail beforehand!

But after I signed – and I'm not claiming sole responsibility here – we won 11 games on the trot and got to the League Cup final. I did loads of extra training myself in Dublin. I decided to give up the Littlewoods job – the office environment just wasn't for me. Instead, I'd wake up whenever I wanted and head straight for the gym every morning. I'd do weights and a bit of cardio. I also acted as a personal trainer to a couple of mates as a favour.

I did a bit of coaching every Monday and Friday, and I was free every other day. If I wanted to do a bit of personal training, great. If not, then feet up. It was a good life.

I was on good money. And I had loads of free time.

I was playing five-a-side or 11-a-side on astro some evenings. I was flying fit. Training with Portadown was every Thursday evening. Then on Saturdays, I'd leave Dublin around 11am to head up for our match and I'd be back home by 6.30pm.

I had a great first year and a half, but I didn't really enjoy my last season there; I was counting down the months, weeks and days until my contract was up. But that's how football goes. I had never intended to be at Portadown for so long.

I had gone up for just a few months initially, but ended up staying for two-and-a-half years. And it was at Portadown where I had my first taste of European football.

After the run of 11 wins in-a-row, we finished in the top half of the table. We ended up beating Bohs in the Setanta Cup that time, so I pocketed that bonus. The next season we signed a few more quality players and we had a great side. But we were just off the title pace. When injuries hit us, the squad lacked the depth needed to sustain a successful challenge.

The people up there and the club were so good to me. I did have an outburst at the gaffer as the final season was being played out. Another player got sent off for kicking out, but Ronnie pointed the finger at me. 'F**k off… f***ing dinosaur!' I shouted at him. He shunned me, but forgave me that too!

During my time at Portadown, however, I had the holiday of a lifetime.

I went to the 2012 European Championships for three-and-a-half weeks. I wouldn't have done that if I was still playing in the League of Ireland. I went with three of my best friends from school. I'll never forget the memories from that trip.

▪ CHAPTER 5 ▪

IT WAS RONNIE McFaul who sorted me for tickets for all three of Ireland's group games at Euro 2012. He got them through the Irish Football Association. Those three and a half weeks in Poland with my three best mates – Rory, Shane and Dave – were some of the best times of my life.

We flew into Poznan three days before the first game against Croatia and pitched up in one of the fan camps in the city. We spent most of our time in the big square, singing, drinking and having the craic.

And the crowd seemed to grow bigger and bigger every night. On one occasion there was some trouble on the opposite side of the square between Croatian and Polish ultras, but we were fairly oblivious to it at the time. I do remember the police presence growing, but they hadn't much interest in us.

They were too busy trying to contain the trouble and making sure it didn't spread over to our corner.

They quickly sussed out what we were all about and were happy to let us carry on. In return for their light-handed approach, I cannot recall one incident where an Irish fan caused trouble. On the other side of the square, Croatian and Polish fans were still throwing bottles and chairs at each other – and at the cops.

It remained all about the craic in our little corner. And that was pretty much the way we were throughout the entire trip, regardless of how things turned out on the pitch.

THE FAN CAMP was great fun, but it was exhausting.

You could forget about sleep. It was so hot that condensation would form on the inside of our tent. The foghorn-like farting didn't help either.

Anytime I did fall asleep, I'd wake up a few minutes later in a puddle of sweat. So, after two nights in the fan camp, we decided that after the Croatia game we'd get the overnight train to Gdansk and check into a hotel.

Little did I know, when I made the last-minute booking, that I had set us up in the team hotel, just one floor above Giovanni Trapattoni and his squad.

THE CROATIA MATCH was a real disappointment.

We conceded early, but started to play a bit after that. When Sean St Ledger equalised, it nearly caused an avalanche of fans in the top tier. We were behind the goal at the far end to St Ledger's goal and everyone went absolutely nuts.

My three mates and I were dressed in green morph suits – so apologies to anyone who remembers being bundled over during the celebrations by people matching that description. It was my idea to wear the suits. I'd been to a few away games in Paris – including the infamous Thierry Henry handball match in 2009. It was at the World Cup play-off that we first wore the morph suits.

I'd been to Paris before and any time the Boys in Green played there, we ended up playing football under the Eiffel Tower.

After St Ledger scored, things went downhill pretty quickly and we lost that game 3-1. We were all gutted. But still, we had an overnight train to look forward to and a nice five-star hotel once we arrived in Sopot.

WE THOUGHT WE were being really smart racing to get the overnight train from Poznan to Gdansk, before heading out to our hotel in Sopot. But when we got to the station, we realised that the entire Irish contingent in Poznan had the same idea. We bundled our way through the crowded station and onto the train, which was jammed. The only bit of space was next to the toilet in the area between carriages, so we threw our bags there and used them as seats. Some of the lads couldn't sleep, but I had no problem catching some shut-eye once the train started to move.

By the time I woke up, my legs were in the air and my head was next to the floor. I'm not sure if it's what woke me, but the stench in our little compartment was revolting. On reflection, it could well have been us.

Those morph suits were unforgiving when it came to body odour. We were in some state when we arrived in Sopot the next morning. I'm not sure the staff in the Sheraton were too happy when we arrived at reception with our booking.

The lads have always regarded me as some sort of wheeler-dealer, someone who could always nab a decent last-minute deal. And once again I came up trumps – I managed to get us into the Sheraton for around €100 per room… per night. With two sharing each room, it was ridiculously cheap for such luxury.

We were in tatters as we checked in, still reeling – and stinking – from the night before. I wasn't really conscious of how I looked or smelled, until I got into the lift. Just before the doors closed, a couple of the Irish players joined us.

There I was, morph-suited, with a pair of white jocks over it, smelling like I'd spent the night swimming in beer, and I was standing next to some of my heroes.

But I was still buzzing. I was dying to say something to them about the game the night before. I opened my mouth, but nothing came out.

Literally silence.

I was so hoarse that I couldn't even muster a whisper. They looked and me, smiled and had a little laugh. I couldn't blame them. The state of me. I just stood there, next to a couple of guys who were living out my dream, dying to chat to them… to say anything. Before we knew it, the lift 'dinged' and they got off.

Just one more floor before I could hop into the shower and get a quick rest, before heading out to explore Sopot.

In the end, we did get to meet a few of the players around the hotel. Stephen Kelly would come down to the cafe in the lobby and sit with his family at the table next to us. He was very friendly and would stop for a chat.

I'm sure he was wondering how we ended up in their five-star team hotel, on the floor right above them. But it was a great part of the trip.

We'd be out on the town at night. Get up the next morning… wolf down a club sandwich. Head out for a few pints… watch the early game. Get back for a shower. A change of clothes… then go out again to watch the evening kick-off.

ON OUR FIRST full morning in Sopot, I woke up with a pretty bad hangover. I pulled back the curtain and opened the window to let in some air. Suddenly, there were huge cheers from below.

'What's that?' I asked one of the lads. I looked down and saw a huge crowd. They were looking back up and singing… 'OLE… OLE, OLE, OLE'.

Do they think we are part of the team? Why not?

Despite the drink and the temporary relaxation of my strict footballer diet, it's not as if I packed on the pounds. So through a fourth floor window all they could see was an athletic-looking fella in his mid-twenties. There I was, in nothing but my jocks, waving back down at the crowd. Every time I waved, they let out a huge cheer.

Walk away, walk back… wave… *CHEER!*

Walk away, walk back… wave… *CHEER!*

THE CITY OF Gdansk was only a short hop on the train from Sopot, which was a beautiful seaside town. The pedestrianised main street and square, which was right in front of the team hotel, was a magnet for Irish fans. It was a great holiday destination and an appropriate base for the Green Army, given the number of bars dotted around the place.

Ireland played their second match of the Euros – against tournament favourites Spain – in Gdansk, so we all made our way into the city and then out by tram to the stadium.

The city of Gdansk itself was beautiful. The Irish fans took over another square and once again the sing-songs kicked off. People were standing on any bit of wall or monument to get an elevated view of the festivities. It was all good natured, not one bit of trouble. It was the holiday of a lifetime.

There I was, 25 years of age, no commitments – no wife or girlfriend or kids. In my career in football up to that point, I hadn't had a summer holiday. This was years of pent-up holiday frustration spilling out in one amazing three-and-a-half-week session. Throughout the trip we got chatting to random people, had the craic and then moved on to the next group of randomers. There was some really good Irish wit on display in Poland during the summer of 2012.

If things weren't going well on the pitch, we were a shoo-in for the title of European champions of one-liners. I'm sure Bronagh won't mind me saying – as I hadn't yet met the love of my life at this point – but the women in Poland were gorgeous. I remember sitting with two lads from inner-city Dublin and they were hilarious. Pure Dublin wit. At one point, an absolute stunner walked past us pushing a pram.

MY TRADE ■ CHAPTER 5

Without missing a beat, one of them said, 'Do you need a father for that child?' The whole beer garden burst out laughing. She turned and smiled.

SOME OF MY fondest non-playing memories are of the adventures I've had on away trips following Ireland. The first one was Paris in October 2004.

It was the match in which John O'Shea missed a great chance to secure a famous win. I got in from my debs at around seven in the morning and had barely been asleep an hour when my brother woke me up. I knew we were going, I just didn't realise our flight was that early. But I shook off the fatigue and ended up having one of the best trips of my life. I had just finished school, and was a month off my 18th birthday. My first away game and I was hooked.

From that moment on, any time I had the money and had no footballing commitments, I was on the first flight out of Dublin.

When we drew France in the play-offs five years later, I knew I could make it. The League of Ireland was in the off-season, so no problem there. We put a little group together, me and a few mates, and away we went for the second-leg. The craic was absolutely nuts. We were booting footballs around under the Eiffel Tower, drinking cans of beer... no one I encountered ahead of the game felt the tie was over, despite France winning 1-0 in Dublin.

And then the game itself.

I firmly believe the players went out that day knowing they had nothing to lose... *Let's play the football we know we are capable of playing.* Robbie Keane opened the scoring.

The play came up our left, a low cross, great finish. *What a goal.*

Everyone around us went bananas. We had quality players, everyone seemed to be on song, the hosts were rattled. We were convinced we were going to the World Cup finals. Ireland should have won it in normal time. We had the chances to wrap it up. I still don't know how we failed to get a second goal.

Then came extra-time.

We were still playing well but the French got a free-kick, playing into the opposite end to us. The ball was floated in, there was a bit of commotion and it was scrambled over the line. Heartache. We saw the Irish players protesting, but hadn't a clue why.

Was there an offside?

There was a forest of players and a great deal of distance between ourselves and Shay Given's goal, so we couldn't see what was going on. Suddenly, texts started flying in. Remember, this was before Twitter or social media really exploded.

There were no WhatsApp videos going around then.

Handball… f**king handball… read one text.

Really? It didn't look like handball form our vantage point.

The final whistle went. I stood on my seat applauding the players, tears rolling down my face as they came up to our section. I'll be honest, I still get a little misty-eyed when I think about those few minutes. As performances go on the big stage, the display against France was as close to perfection as I'd ever seen from an Irish team.

It was a good half-hour after the final whistle by the time we left the stadium, still oblivious to what had quickly become a major international incident. The feeling at that point was still one of despair at the result, yet pride in the performance. We weren't going to South Africa, but these guys were my idols.

They were living my dream.

To see them so gutted and dejected, it broke my heart.

OFF WE WENT, back into town in search of a few drinks. One thing we noticed straightaway was that the crowds you'd usually see, even after a defeat, weren't there. Even the French seemed pretty subdued.

Any local we met commiserated with us, which I thought was surprising but nice. We had an early flight back to Dublin the next morning, so we decided we'd call it a night. I still hadn't seen the incident.

I woke up and decided to skip my flight. Another mate was booked onto an Air France flight later that day so I thought… *I'll hitch a ride on that one.* I've always been like that. There were other trips where I'd booked an early flight home and decided to stay an extra day or two. That's just my nature.

You only live once. If you are enjoying something, what's a few bob? I have always had a spontaneous side to me. When it comes to booking holidays, I've tended to go in one afternoon and ask what's available the next morning. I've always managed to get a great deal. Plus, there's the excitement of knowing that you are going on holidays, but not quite knowing where until the last minute.

At breakfast the morning after the France game and again out on the street, locals were coming up to us still… and apologising. By now I thought it was a bit over the top. I mean, we did play well, but come on. Eventually we passed by a bar with the telly on. They were showing highlights of the game. That's when I saw it.

Holy shit. I hit the roof.

I felt like I was reliving the incident, but the sadness and grief had been replaced with anger. I still get emotional when I think about it. I still think of the Irish players and imagine what it would have been like to go to a World Cup. This team was at its peak.

We'd held our own against reigning champions Italy in the qualifiers, went through our group unbeaten. We were one of just five teams in that entire qualification campaign to avoid defeat – along with Italy, Spain, Germany and The Netherlands. We were in great company. For those players it was their big chance.

For the nation itself, it would have been a wonderful lift at a time of economic gloom. And to hell with my own career, I would have gone to South Africa that summer.

So there I was, in the middle of Paris, sadness turning quickly to anger.

I barely said a word to my mate for the rest of the day, despite him getting me on his flight, and using up some of his air miles to buy my ticket.

GDANSK WAS AMAZING.

The game against Spain? Not so much. The less said about that match the better. I was gutted. I know Spain were brilliant, but the utter humiliation was just too much. This was the famous *Fields of Athenry* match, when just about everyone – apart from Roy Keane – hailed the spirit of the Irish fans, after the rendition of the famous old song during the closing minutes of the 4-0 defeat.

I have to admit, I wasn't in that particular choir.

We left just as the *Fields of Athenry* started. I just couldn't bring myself to join in. I was in no mood for a sing-song at that stage. All I could think about was getting on the tram into the city and then the train back out to Sopot, so that we could drown our sorrows with a few pints. I could hear the singing as we walked down the steps and exited the stadium.

There was zero temptation to turn back.

As much as it was a dream to play football and to pull on the green jersey, it was also an ambition of mine to support Ireland at a major tournament. But I never pictured it like this. I was devastated. Sure, Spain were ridiculously good at that stage. They were the reigning European and World champions. Being in the profession, of course I appreciated the gulf in quality. But whatever about being beaten, getting spanked like that really hurt.

It was a massive humiliation on the international stage. As a nation, we had never experienced anything like that before. At Euro 88, Italia 90, USA 94 and the 2002 World Cup, whenever we lost, we went down fighting. This was different.

BY THE TIME we got back to Sopot, the thirst had almost worn off.

Maybe an early night? Nah, I didn't need much persuading to head out. Those five minutes we shaved off at the end of the match turned into an extra hour in the bar, which was quieter than normal given most fans were still trying to make their way back.

We were in our morph suits once again but, because of the heat that day, we were only wearing them up to our waists. It was body-paint the rest of the way up. Although that ended up being a waste of time. It was so hot on the tram on the way out to the game, our sweat had washed away most of the green.

Everyone was crammed onto the tram, faces mushed against the windows. So we looked a right state by the time we got to the turnstiles. And when we finally got back into town, I'm sure we looked even worse, with the re-dried paint streaks giving us a green and Irish-tan-pink-style zebra look.

But we didn't care. We hit the pub and had a great night, drinking all our troubles away. When everyone else got back, it was carnage.

It was as if they'd moved Coppers to a picturesque costal town in northern Poland – but with no bouncers and just two poor bar staff. People were leaning over the bar and pulling their own pints.

NO JUDGEMENTS PLEASE, but by the early hours of the morning after the Spain defeat we all found ourselves in a strip club. It was basically the last place to serve, so it was a magnet for Irish fans. We walked in and the club was wedged.

Wall-to-wall green jerseys. It was a lot cooler at this point in the night, so I'd pulled the morph suit all the way up. All of a sudden, *The Rocky Road to Poland*, the official Ireland song for Euro 2012, came on. There wasn't a single girl on the podium by the time the lyrics kicked in, it was all Irish lads swinging off the poles and gyrating around the stages.

The place had gone mad.

People had even climbed up onto the bars. A few lads had been handing out masks – faces of Robbie Keane and Giovanni Trapattoni. There I was, in a full-body morph suit, white jocks and a Trapattoni mask, up on stage swinging out of a pole.

One of the lads tried to take a picture, but a bouncer ripped the phone out of his hand. The poor girls that night, none of the lads were interested in them. It was all about getting a late drink. But when *The Rocky Road* came on? Carnage.

A few hours later, as we were heading back to the hotel, a fellow in a suit was walking towards us. It was around six in the morning, the sun was rising and already it was far too warm to be dressed up so formally. As he came closer, one of the lads shouted out, 'Hey, Cabbage Man'! It was Fabio Capello.

He looked up, smiled and continued on his way. He's probably wondering to this day why he was called Cabbage Man. Unless, that is, he's listened to Mario Rosenstock's impression of him on *Gift Grub*.

It's funny how many interesting people you bump into on Ireland away trips. I met a fellow in Poland who works for *Fox Soccer*. Keith Costigan is from Malahide and, like me, had spells at Bray Wanderers and Monaghan United. He ended up going to the U.S. on a soccer scholarship, to Augusta State University. Keith played a bit with Portland Timbers before moving into commentary. He calls Seattle Sounders games.

I've kept in contact with him and I watch him every so often alongside former Newcastle defender Warren Barton on Fox Sports.

I also saw John Delaney in our hotel bar. I was introduced to him by Pat Duffy, but we didn't really chat. Despite being the FAI CEO at the time and me having played in the League of Ireland, he didn't seem too interested in talking to me.

It was during our time in Sopot that Monaghan United suddenly dropped out of the league. I was in the hotel at the time and I remember getting a text from a couple of Monaghan supporters. I still had some friends playing there. It remains a vivid memory, seeing FAI officials at the bar, seemingly without a care in the world, while back at home one of their clubs had just gone out of business. If anything, it was an instant validation of my decision to sign for Portadown in the Irish League for a few months.

And it also influenced my decision to re-sign for them after that summer. That certainly wasn't my plan when I made the move. I was only going to head up for three months and then head back to the League of Ireland. But Portadown looked after me really well and everything seemed more stable in the north.

Then, in the middle of the season, a club dropped out of the league and no one outside of a small circle of people in Monaghan seemed to care.

I loved it at Monaghan United. We had a great dressing-room, a brilliant manager in Mick Cooke and it was a homely club. The sad part, however, was that their exit from the League of Ireland didn't come as a huge surprise to me. It was a small club, after all. And during my time in the league they weren't the only club to go out of business. Kilkenny City had gone… Dublin City had gone… Kildare County had gone… Sporting Fingal had gone.

Then you had Derry City with the dual contract situation and their demotion to the First Division. Cork City would have disappeared if it wasn't for a very loyal and devoted set of fans. And, of course, my big break in senior football came at Shelbourne after their brush with extinction.

How was Monaghan United, a small club with a very small, but brilliant fan-base, expected to survive? That's why I signed up north. Of course, I wanted to stay in the League Of Ireland, but it was the right decision at the time.

THE DAY AFTER the Spain game, we packed up and said our farewell to Sopot – and to the glamour of life in the team hotel.

But we didn't want to head straight back to Poznan and to the fan camp. The drop from five-star luxury to a steamy, condensation-filled tent in the middle of a sea of cans and bottles would have been too much to handle. Also, we were convinced that the games of foot-tennis with the locals were going to spill over into violence.

They just didn't get the Irish humour. We'd celebrate each point as if we'd won the European Championships. Prior to leaving for Sopot, we could see that their patience was quickly running out. The novelty of the fan camp had worn off pretty quickly too. The fields were crowded with tents.

You were nearly walking over tents to get into the fan zone area, which was massive. There was a big dome with bars and giant screens, with football matches shown throughout the day and night. We went in there once, but it wasn't for us.

It was too dark and the weather was far too good to be stuck under a roof.

Torun, on the other hand, was great craic.

We stopped off for a couple of nights and managed to book a couple of cheap hotel rooms. There were no games in Torun, so there was no shortage of accommodation.

As it was on the train line between Poznan and Gdansk, it became a base for lots of Irish fans, including several *You Boys in Green* members who set themselves up in Torun for the duration and travelled from there to the matches.

For some reason, it was common enough on our trip for me to be mistaken by the locals as a member of the Ireland squad. It happened on the train from Gdansk to Torun.

I was wearing a white FAI polo shirt and a Polish lad approached me. He had very little English, but my mates egged him on. At one stage they told him I was John O'Shea. Why John O'Shea would have swapped the team bus for a cramped old train ride, I still don't know.

But all of a sudden, this stranger's wife and child were on the phone and he wanted me to talk to them. They had very little English too, so there I was, awkwardly saying, 'Hello' and going bright red at the same time. The more embarrassed I was, the more the lads egged the local on. By the end, everyone on the train was in bits laughing.

Our new Polish friend didn't seem to twig though. He took his phone back and seemed chuffed with himself as he headed back to his seat. Then, while we were in Torun, one local got me to sign his cap. My mates loved putting me in situations like that. They loved making things as awkward as possible for me.

We had a great time in Torun. Things weren't as hectic, as the numbers of fans there were dwarfed by Poznan and Sopot. It was a nice change of pace. We chilled out for a couple of nights before heading onto Poznan for the Italy game. I'll be honest, I don't remember much about that one, other than Gianluigi Buffon walking around applauding everyone after the final whistle.

I know we lost 2-0, but after that it's a haze.

We knew what was coming, so we had a few drinks in us by kick-off. Being back in Poznan was great, though. From a touristy point of view, the buildings, the colours, the big square in the centre of the city, it was like nowhere I had ever been before. I loved it. It's still on my list of places to head back to.

WITH IRELAND'S EURO 2012 adventure at an end, we decided we'd have one last hurrah before going home. The chances of us catching a flight out of Poland were pretty slim anyway, given the mass exodus of Irish fans in the days after the Italy game. So we decided that we'd get in one more city before heading back to the real world.

None of us had ever been to Berlin before, and it wasn't that far away, so we decided to spend a few nights there before flying back to Dublin. We booked ourselves into a nice hotel there. We needed some chill-out time.

Travelling to Berlin, however, was going to be a problem. The trains were as packed as the flights out of Poznan. It would have cost us €50 to get there by rail, so we decided we'd haggle for a taxi fare. As chief negotiator, I got a quote of €200 from one of the first drivers we approached. Between four of us, that was the cost of a train ticket. *Great!* The lads were ready to hop in. But no, me being an absolute dope, I had to see if I could get it for cheaper than that.

Suddenly we were being told it would cost €300, €350…

Eventually the lads had enough. They ordered me to find the driver who'd quoted us €200. I raced between the taxis, hoping he hadn't picked up another fare. To my relief, he was still there, at the top of the queue. What a result.

And he was driving a nice big Mercedes, so the trip to Berlin was even more comfortable than the train. *The only downside?* He was a mad racist! It was one of the most awkward three-hour drives of my life. We couldn't wait to get out of the car.

Probably the highlight of the whole trip for me happened while we were in Berlin. I roomed with one of my best mates, Rory, throughout our time in Poland. Rory is basically the nicest guy in the world. Too nice at times. So much so that it actually pisses me off! I don't think I've ever heard him say or do a bad thing to anyone.

You could do or say practically anything to him and he wouldn't bite back. So, to work him up to the point where he started throwing punches at me in a taxi one night was possibly one of the greatest achievements – and proudest moments – of my life.

We shared a room together for the three and a half weeks we were away. Now, I'd be giddy enough, I love winding-up people and I'm constantly talking rubbish. That night, we decided we'd give it one more big session before flying home, so we headed to a nightclub in east Berlin, down by the Wall.

It was an industrial yard, an old rail depot with loads of stone arches. Under each arch was a different DJ. Because the arches were so thick, the sound didn't travel from one into the other.

We had a great night. We said, let's splash out.

We put in €50 each to buy a bottle of something – I can't for the life of me remember what. They gave us a table, so we sat there drinking and listening to the music. Every so often, girls would come over. I figured most of them just wanted some free drink, so eventually I took the hump. Near the end of the night, one girl came over and she clearly had no interest in any of us.

I told her to buzz off, that she wasn't going to get any free drink from us.

I didn't stop there. It was really bugging me for some reason, so in the taxi back to the hotel I kept slating her. And that was it. The tipping point. Three and a half weeks listening to me non-stop and on our final night… he snapped. And it was over someone we'd never seen before and would never see again.

He turned around and punched me.

How did I react? Did I hit him back?

No, my response was to burst out laughing. That only wound him up even more, so he kept throwing digs. I'd never seen this side to him before. On the gaelic football pitch he was always fierce competitive. He could look after himself, no problem. But off the pitch, he was gentle to a fault.

Yet, there he is in a taxi in the middle of Berlin at some ridiculously early hour of the morning, battering me.

When we got back to the hotel, I decided I'd leave him alone in the room to cool down, so I went and found a late bar, then got a hot-dog in an underground station nearby. I tip-toed back into our room.

If I'm being honest, I deserved it.

In fact, he was probably two weeks late in lashing out. I'd be the real messer of the group. I'd be fairly strong-minded as well. If the lads wanted to do something and I didn't, I wouldn't be one for compromise. I'd just head off and do my own thing.

Would I want to be stuck in a hotel room for three and a half weeks with myself? No chance!

■ CHAPTER 6 ■

IF FOOTBALL DIDN'T work out for me, there was always Hollywood!

I won't lie, I did fancy myself as a bit of an actor. And I did once make an appearance on the big screen. No, not the one in the cinema. I'm talking about the giant screens at the Aviva Stadium. Eamonn Donohoe, formerly of RTE, roped me into featuring on the opening credits for the very first game at the redeveloped Lansdowne Road.

The opening scene saw a random Ireland fan (me!) sitting at the DART crossing, looking devastated, in as cheesy a way as possible, as the old stadium was being knocked down. Cut to the end and I'm in a sleeping bag outside the new ground.

An alarm clock goes off.

'It's time for the Aviva Stadium.'

For the craic, Eamonn brought along a pink sleeping bag, which he forced me to use. Friends still remind me about that particular prop.

That wasn't my first acting job. I'd done some more serious stuff, albeit as an extra, on shows such as *Fair City* and *Love/Hate*. And then there was an infamous advertisement for a Dublin hotel. That's probably where my on-screen career peaked, so it's fair to say the acting work was never going to make me rich.

I got into it through a man called Martin Guilfoyle. I knew him through basketball. I was a few months too old to play under-16 in the Community Games, so I coached the team, which included Martin. Then when he was too old, he came onto the coaching staff with me. He was big into extras work and convinced me to sign up for what was basically a text service. Once an opportunity came up, you'd get a message. You would reply with a 'yes' or 'no', and if the job interested you, then wait for a call. On other occasions, you might go for a casting for an ad shoot. I did a little bit of extras work here and there, hoping to land some of the better paid jobs.

I loved it. It was interesting to get a glimpse behind the scenes of some of Ireland's biggest television shows. Martin also loved that side of the business. He is now a DJ and signed with Sony, and has a big social media following. It obviously went well for him!

If you look closely at old episodes of *Fair City*, you might see me sitting in the background in McCoy's pub or the cafe, or working out in a gym. I remember the casting call for *Love/Hate*.

They wanted a couple of muscular fellows. I got an email asking me to send in some photos. They were very specific in terms of what they wanted – me in a pair of shorts and nothing else. My mam, of all people, took the pictures in our kitchen; me in a little pair of shorts, tensing like hell, because I really wanted the job.

Looking back at it now, it's quite embarrassing. But I got the job. Then, for all the hassle and embarrassment, I was on screen for no more than a split second, while a hit was carried out in the gym. *Love/Hate* was massive at the time and it was great to be on set, watching some really good actors at work.

I did a few other bits and pieces, but as the football, training and coaching got busier, I let the extras work slide. I ended up saying no to all the extras stuff and concentrated on casting opportunities. Not that I ever landed a killer role… unless you consider the Wynn's Hotel ad a stepping stone to a Hollywood career.

THAT CAME ABOUT through a girl I was seeing at the time.

Her friend was in advertising and she knew I had done some work. The money wasn't great, but I said I'd do it anyway. Sure, at the very least it would be another thing to stick on the CV. And I was told that it would be on prime time TV. *Great!*

The thing with this kind of work is, you could be asked to do some mad stuff – and you can't say no. I was told to dress smart-casual, that the idea would be me and my girlfriend/wife checking into the hotel. I arrived in a pair of jeans, a t-shirt and blazer.

My 'girlfriend/wife' was already in reception by the time I got to the hotel. She was really good looking and really well dressed, which made me feel a little underdressed. Two other lads were there, dressed as porters. We all made our way to a room off the reception area, where the director talked us through what we were going to do. The instructions were… check in and go to the lift, and when we get to the room, my 'wife/girlfriend' goes in first, with one of the porters carrying her bag. She sits down on the bed and, suddenly, the door swings open again.

It's the second porter – and he is carrying me! I could see the fellow playing the second porter eyeing me up, looking at the size of me. He had a look of terror in his eyes. As for me, there went my vision of a suave, sophisticated appearance on prime time TV.

The first few takes were write-offs. He tried to carry me and open the door at the same time and it looked really awkward. So I suggested that if he carried me a certain way, I'd kick the door open. But he really struggled to hold onto me. The poor fellow looked like he was going to collapse at any moment.

I tried to help him by wrapping my arms around his neck, but that just looked even weirder than the original concept. Then there was the fact that he was getting weaker and weaker with each take. By this point we were both laughing at the situation. It was getting harder and harder to get through a take with straight faces.

At one point, I managed to kick the door open and just as we were going through, he did a big fart. We were both laughing so hard that he nearly dropped me. Finally we nailed it. But I'd say his arms were in bits for days after the shoot.

My next instruction was to sit on the bed beside this good looking girl. *Great, at least I'll look kind of cool in the final shot*, I thought. But they even managed to ruin that for me.

'We need a bit of a cheesy smile,' I was told.

My head was nearly gone by that stage. I wasn't getting paid nearly enough for this crap. So there I was, trying to look half-cheesy but still a little bit cool at the same time. But they kept saying, 'No, cheesier… cheesier'.

The ad ran every Saturday at half-time during the 3pm Premier League game on Setanta Sports. Every single time it aired, without fail, I received loads of text messages slagging me about it. That, unsurprisingly, was the end of my acting career.

PART **THREE**

One Last Shot

Joining Dundalk was the best decision I ever made in my football career, as I made friends for life in the town, and also got to meet the most important person in my life, my wife Bronagh. I did not think I would be getting the chance to lift trophies (like our first FAI Cup win in 2015) and have the chance to share such days with my mum Carmel and brother Neil.

I got on the scoresheet a few times that same season, including one against Cork City at Oriel Park. Celebrating (right) with Andy Boyle... I'm pointing to the Heavens thinking of my dad who was no longer with us.

Challenging big teams in Europe was a central part of the Dundalk story. Ciaran Kilduff celebrates (as I have a word in his ear) after scoring our first goal in the UEFA Europa League Group D game against AZ Alkmaar at the AZ Stadion. I win the ball against Fred Friday in the same game (top right) and celebrate at the finish.

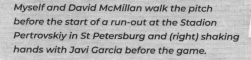

Myself and David McMillan walk the pitch before the start of a run-out at the Stadion Pertrovskiy in St Petersburg and (right) shaking hands with Javi Garcia before the game.

· CHAPTER 7 ·

THINGS HAD GONE stale for me up north. I couldn't wait for the 2012/13 season to finish so that I could start the search for a new club. After packing it in with Portadown, Johnny McDonnell gave me the opportunity to train with my former club Shelbourne. I was there for a few weeks, but there was no talk of a contract offer.

So when my old Monaghan United boss Mick Cooke asked me to head up for a few sessions at Drogheda United I jumped at the chance, especially as they had a European game coming up against Malmö. Unfortunately, to sign me, Mick had to move a couple of players out in order to make some room in his budget. Not that I was going to bust their budget. But the players he wanted to shift didn't want to go… because they had a European game coming up against Malmö!

Why would they? There were bonuses on offer for their exploits in the Europa League.

While this was dragging on and on, I went back to Shelbourne and played a friendly against Peterborough. I had a really good game and afterwards Johnny Mac sat me down and offered me a deal. He said he could only give me €200-a-week. I told him I couldn't sign for those terms. So I went home, my future as up in the air as when I drove out of Shamrock Park for the last time.

Happily, the next morning was an eventful and life-changing one.

First up, Johnny phoned and said he could up the offer to €300-a-week. That was definitely more acceptable from my point of view, but I didn't commit to anything. When we hung up, I saw that I had a missed call from Mick Cooke. I rang him back and Mick said, 'Listen Garts, I'm just trying to free up some space here, but I really want you to sign'.

He wanted me to hold out just a little longer.

Again, I didn't give him a commitment. When I got off the phone from Mick, I had a voice mail from an unknown number. *Who the hell could this be?* I listened to the message and it was Stephen Kenny. *What did he want?*

I rang him back and he told me that he was short of centre-halves at Dundalk. He was only six months into the job at Oriel Park and he was eager to strengthen his squad after a strong start. He said he knew me from his time as Derry City manager, when they were competing with Monaghan for the First Division title. He told me he'd kept an eye on me ever since and that he wanted to sign me straightaway.

It certainly was flattering. I'd admired his teams, their classy style of football. But I was living in Dublin and had done the whole travelling thing with Monaghan and Portadown. I was ready for an easier life when it came to football. I was 26 and was thinking it was time to put other stuff first.

Football would have to take a back seat to work, I thought... *A proper job, something that I could put on a mortgage application form and not get laughed out of the bank.* I was ready to give up on the dream, to be a little more pragmatic. My chance of securing a big move over to the UK, I thought, had well and truly passed by now. I'd pretty much convinced myself that even the dream of signing for a top, title-challenging League of Ireland club was gone. The older you get, I suppose, the more pragmatic you become and the louder the doubting voices in your head grow.

FOOTBALL HAD ALWAYS been my priority, but it was time to focus on earning a few extra quid, money I didn't think I could now make in the game. Certainly at the level I was at. This was all in the back of my mind when Stephen called.

Also, I had this determination that I wasn't going to rush into an agreement, regardless of who was making the offer. I had signed so many contracts in the past without giving them much thought, or without putting any effort into negotiating better terms. So I was eager not to commit to anything without having a chat with my mam, my dad or my brother. I'd become a little more streetwise about contract talks.

I told Stephen I'd need some time to think about it, that I'd get back to him and we ended the call. As far as I was concerned, I would take a few days to think it over. Anyway, I had other pressing concerns, such as the need to get a haircut.

I popped down to Frankie's Barbershop in Rathfarnham. I always got on well with Frankie. He was the type of barber that would chat all day with his customers. He knew I played football. He always asked how I was getting on. So there I was, next up for a haircut and suddenly my phone rang. I answered… it was Stephen Kenny again, barely an hour after we'd ended our previous call.

When I had told him I needed time to think about it and that I'd get back to him, he said, 'Yeah, no bother'. He clearly had a different idea of just how long I needed to mull things over.

Straightaway he said, 'Well, did you think about it?'

I blurted out, 'What?'

I hadn't a chance to talk to my mam, or anyone else for that matter – Frankie included – about the offer on the table from Dundalk. But Stephen wasn't going to let me hang up without another effort to cajole me into signing. I stepped out of the barbershop. We ended up talking for a good 45 minutes – on top of the hour-long call earlier that day.

While on the call, I could see the lads inside looking out and having a good old laugh. Every so often, Frankie would pop his head out the door and tell me I was next, and each time I'd have to wave someone on ahead of me.

Stephen wanted an answer.

He told me he wanted me to sign, that they had a game in a couple of days and that he had pencilled me into his plans. I'd have to sign that day in order to get the international clearance through in time.

I'll be honest, I liked his persistence. It was flattering. But I had this thing firmly in my head that I wasn't going to rush into anything. Again, the money wasn't great. What was on offer at the time, and you have to remember that Dundalk had narrowly avoided relegation the previous season, was €300-a-week and a part-time contract. It was the same as Shelbourne, but with extra driving.

I knew I'd be on the road up and back a few times a week for training and games, and that was quite off-putting. Shels, on the other hand, would have been the easy option. I'd done the over-and-back to Tolka Park before. But Shels were bottom of the table, while Dundalk were already flying high under Stephen.

After a good three-quarters-of-an-hour I finally managed to fob him off and get my hair cut. Once again, I didn't commit to anything. Instead I went home and later that night I had the chat I'd wanted to have with my mam. 'I'll sleep on it,' I told her, and maybe get back to Stephen the next day.

I LAY IN bed. I couldn't sleep, thinking about the various conversations I'd had that day.

Dundalk or Shelbourne?

Or wait it out for Drogheda?

I was finally drifting off when my phone started ringing. I knew who it was before I looked at the screen.

'Hello Stephen.'

I still don't know why I answered it. But there we were, chatting away, having pillow-talk! Again, I insisted that I wasn't ready to sign.

However, Stephen's persistence finally paid off when I agreed to join Dundalk ahead of their game away to Derry City. *F**k it*, I thought, *I'll give it one more shot, one more move with glory in mind rather than a steady mortgage-friendly income.* What harm would half-a-season at Dundalk do in the grand scheme of things? But I wanted a bit of security too, so while the rest of the lads were on one-year contracts, I said I'd only sign if I had the option of another year. I said to Stephen that I was going to prove my worth, show him that I was a top player, that I could compete at the top of this league and win titles.

I knew then that I had to back up those words with my performances.

AFTERWARDS, I HEARD that Johnny Mac thought that I'd used Shelbourne to get a better offer. It wasn't like that. I had been training there for three or four weeks without being offered anything, but loving the sing-songs in the car with Leechy!

And it's not as if I hadn't asked several times what the story was.

If an offer had come earlier, I probably would have signed. But by the time Johnny came up to me with a deal, I was already looking elsewhere. I just wanted to get back to the League of Ireland.

I had happy memories of my previous time at Shelbourne. So it was never a case of using them to alert other clubs of my availability.

I SIGNED ON Monday and trained with Dundalk that evening. I was too late in signing to be part of the Derry game. Dundalk won 1-0, with Tiernan Mulvenna getting the goal in injury-time, a result that really put them in the title mix.

My first appearance was from the bench on July 12 in a 3-0 win at home to Bohemians. Patrick Hoban grabbed a hat-trick, while I replaced Dane early in the second-half. I made my first start away to Cork City on July 19. Ciaran Kilduff, my future teammate, scored an absolute beauty of a bicycle kick inside the first few minutes for them, before I popped up with an equaliser. I scored again, but the goal was disallowed. There was no one near Cork goalkeeper Mark McNulty, but he hit the deck and the referee gave a free out.

It was an eventful first start. Cork went ahead again, but Stevie O'Donnell rescued a late point from the penalty spot.

There we were, up there with some top teams challenging for the Premier Division title. I didn't really think too much about the fact that the squad had very little title-winning experience. When I went up north, I tuned out of the League of Ireland a little bit. I knew where my friends were playing, stuff like that, but I wasn't overly familiar with the lads at Dundalk. I knew there were some good players there, the likes of Keith Ward and John Dillon. There was also my old teammate and pal Darren Meenan. Stevie O'Donnell had been around for a while and he was a big name. I knew that he had a few league titles from his time at Bohemians and Shamrock Rovers. And he played a big part in Rovers getting to the Europa League group stages in 2011. Mark Rossiter had played for Sunderland and was a double-winner with Bohs. Richie Towell was starting to make a name for himself. But it wasn't the type of squad that many people expected to see challenging for the title.

I remember turning up for training early on and seeing Simon Kelly arrive. He's a local lad, a centre-half who had just come home from Australia. I didn't realise he was coming in when I signed. I thought, *They are after bringing in another centre-half!* The first thing you do when you join a club is you eye up the competition for your place. I suppose seeing Simon there gave me a kick up the arse and made me work even harder to impress Stephen Kenny.

My first few months at Dundalk were brilliant.

I couldn't have been happier. We ended up pushing St Patrick's Athletic for the league and we went from strength-to-strength. Ultimately our failure to see out the challenge boiled down to the fact that we only had a couple of lads with league-winning experience, whereas the St Pat's team was packed with serious quality. But the hunger to do well and the attitude really impressed me. The craic in the dressing-room was great and the tempo in training was like nothing I'd ever experienced before. There was a real mix of personalities in the camp.

Probably the biggest disappointment was the FAI Cup semi-final defeat to Drogheda United. The game was absolutely nuts.

PLAYING IN AN FAI Cup final had become a huge ambition of mine.

In November 2012 I attended the FAI Cup final between Derry City and St Patrick's Athletic. Derry won 3-2 after extra-time and there were more than 16,000 fans at the Aviva Stadium. I remember sitting there, watching the game, the crowd, experiencing the buzz and thinking to myself, *I want to get back down to the League of Ireland, just for the chance to play in one of these occasions.* The Aviva Stadium, using the same dressing-room as the international side, playing on the same pitch as the *Boys in Green*, and all in front of a huge crowd… the flame was lit.

That dream was in my head for the next 11-odd months. I couldn't wait to face Drogheda in the semi-final.

I'LL NEVER FORGET that game. It was one of the most frustrating matches of my career. By the 30th minute we were down to nine men.

We were a goal behind thanks to a penalty that never should have been given. Darren Meenan was the first for an early shower. He was shown a straight red card. A few minutes later Chris Shields followed him.

Anthony Buttimer was the referee that day and it was his view that Chris brought down Declan O'Brien inside the box. It was never a foul, but we were punished on the double. Penalty conceded and another man down.

We couldn't believe what was happening. Gavin Brennan scored from the spot and with nine men it was always going to be difficult to mount a comeback. The game finished 1-0 with Drogheda happy enough to sit on their lead. I don't remember them really threatening us after that, even though they had a two-man

ONE LAST SHOT ■ CHAPTER 7

advantage. We had one chance on the break; Tiernan Mulvenna nearly scored, but very little else of note occurred aside from that.

If you lose a game, fair enough. But the way we lost that one and given what was at stake – a place in the FAI Cup final – it was hard to take. We were gutted. My dream of playing in *the* cup final would have to wait a little while longer.

STEPHEN KENNY WAS so disappointed not to make the cup final in his first season in charge at Dundalk. He's a born winner and any chance for silverware that passes him by is a blow. It was a great experience to play under him and I learned so much about Stephen and his style during those first few months.

I could see straightaway his enthusiasm for the game, and the energy and passion that he had for his job. He had different ways of doing things, which is something the senior Ireland players have learned in recent times. From my own time in football, Stephen was quite unique when it came to managing a team. Any player who came into a team meeting feeling lethargic tended to dance out of the room at the end. Stephen always brought a strong energy into the group.

We'd have meetings ahead of training and he would get really animated while getting his point across. He would start running and jumping around the room. Whether it gave you a laugh or not, it was always infectious, and it helped set the tone for the players.

I remember how excited he would be whenever something came off in training, be it a passing move, a set-piece or a finishing drill. He'd be right there in the thick of it having the craic. Stephen would get so excited on the training ground. If a piece of play came off, he'd nearly be off celebrating himself, arms in the air.

'Yes, yes… magic, I love it!'

You'd have a laugh about it, but it was all about encouragement. It was a completely different environment to any of the groups that I'd been in before.

But there was another side to Stephen. In contrast to his happy, cheery training ground persona, Stephen would *lose it* in a second. He would go from one extreme to the other. There was that harder side to him, one that you never want to be on the receiving end of – some lads would get it more than others when he'd lose it.

Players such as Chris Shields and myself, we were regulars for Stephen's version of the old Alex Ferguson hairdryer treatment. Then there were a few lads in the squad who seemed to be exempt, no matter what they did. Stephen tailored

89

his treatment of each player to suit their personality. He knew who would react positively to a blast and who would retreat into their shells.

Ronan Finn? He was Stephen's golden boy!

As for myself and Chris, Stephen knew we could take it, that he would get more out of us by delivering a timely rocket up our behinds.

One of the first bollockings I can remember from Stephen was aimed at Stevie O'Donnell after we played St Pat's in Inchicore. A win would have put us three points clear of the Saints with five games remaining, but they ended up getting the result and opening up a three-point lead on us.

Pat's were 2-0 ahead when Stevie was sent off with 15 minutes to go. He had just returned from a ban and was shown a straight red for an off-the-ball push on Ger O'Brien. He was such an important member of the team that it was a huge blow to lose him. That ended any chance of a comeback in that match and we ended up losing the next game away to Limerick, with Stevie missing out through suspension.

Stephen Kenny tore into him after the Pat's game, while the rest of us just kept our heads down. No one wanted to make eye-contact with the manager when he was in that kind of mood.

As for what Stephen was best at, getting us up for a match, I have never been able to put my finger on exactly how he does it. But the way he'd fire us up was like no other manager I'd ever come across. It's often been said, I know, but we would have run through brick walls and walked across hot coals for him.

He just had this knack, this Stephen Kenny magic.

And because of the intensity he brought to the dressing-room, which we then brought onto the pitch, suddenly we were in contention for the Premier Division title. A year after the club not only faced a relegation play-off, but looked to be in serious financial trouble, we were the surprise package gunning for league glory.

Inside the squad, we were happily going along with the flow. We were buzzing; picking up win after win and gaining in confidence with each result. The lads had been on a good run before I signed, but things really picked up late in the summer. Beating Derry away in the last game before my debut really marked everyone's cards. The atmosphere at Oriel Park was electric after that Brandywell result. We were having great craic and there was plenty of messing – it was a great mix of players and personalities, and we all got on really well. But we knew when to get serious too. A huge amount of energy and focus went into training. The tempo was frightening, like nothing I'd ever experienced before.

Stephen made us work really hard on finishing. We'd spend ages at the end of each session taking shots on goal. I loved that part, because it wasn't just for the strikers and midfielders, the defenders got in on the act too.

Off the training pitch, Stephen was equally focused on the little details. I remember going one day for a team meeting in the Clarion Hotel at Liffey Valley. We had a meal there before heading upstairs to the meeting room.

On the top table was a bowl of after dinner mints.

Ganno was launching them to lads in their seats when Stephen came in and grabbed the bowl.

'I hope you haven't eaten any of them,' he said.

And he was serious! It was just after dinner mints. But that's the way he was. In any team I was at previously, you might get back on the team bus after an away game with a can of Coke or a bag of crisps or a chocolate bar. Not at Dundalk. Stephen just wouldn't allow it. So you had a situation where players were trying to smuggle chocolate or sweets onto the team bus and eat them down the back without getting caught.

WHILE WE ONLY finished three points behind St Pat's in the final table, they won the title with two games to spare, when they beat Sligo Rovers 2-0. It was disappointing that we didn't push them to the final day, but even then I don't think we realised what we were building at Oriel Park.

I certainly had no idea what was coming.

All I knew was that I loved my time so far at Dundalk. I looked forward to every training session, every game. The way we played, the slick passing game, I never believed that I would get to play such a style in the League of Ireland. Stephen gave us the freedom to be creative, to express ourselves on the pitch.

He brought together a great mix of experienced players and young lads with points to prove. And it clicked. Everyone wanted the ball, no one hid during matches. As a centre-back, I had spent most of my career in Ireland with managers shouting at me from the sidelines… 'Just clear it!'

I wasn't encouraged to play it out from the back. Instead, I was told to hit the corners. I had never enjoyed organised football as much as with Dundalk.

And with Darren Meenan on set-pieces, I was getting plenty of goals too. His deliveries were laser-guided. He had over 30 assists one year! He could pick me out in a crowded penalty area nine times out of 10.

Crucially, everyone bought into Stephen Kenny's ideas. Even when we went on a team bonding trip at the end of that first summer together, everyone behaved without exception. We went kayaking and zorbing in Carlingford and when it came to the evening time, there was a strict no-drinks policy. That set the tone for me. I can honestly say I don't remember anyone going out for a few sneaky ones that night.

I had been on team bonding sessions before and it was all about going out on the piss. But this was Stephen's way. You can't afford to go out on the lash if you want to reach the top, if you want to be the very best that you can be. And while Stephen is a really nice guy, there was always that element of fear there.

You didn't want to cross him.

That is a crucial ingredient for any manager and it's a difficult balance to strike. You need your players to both respect you and be fearful of the consequences of going against your orders. Stephen had that. I don't think anyone wanted to test the boundaries with him.

Stephen had started to plan for the next season long before the end of the 2013 campaign. He came to me to discuss my situation around mid-October and asked if I was going to take up the option in my contract to stay for another year. I said to him that I wouldn't, that I wanted to stay but that I needed better terms. We parked it until the season ended and then I headed off to Thailand on holiday.

When I came back, we sat down again.

We were still going to be part-time – Dundalk only really went fully professional, with training taking place in the mornings, in 2018 – but the money went up. I ended up signing a contract for the 2014 season worth €450-a-week.

While I didn't sign after the initial talks with Stephen, there was no danger of me wanting to leave Dundalk. The bond in the dressing-room was so tight. I didn't want to be dragged away from that environment, from the joy of playing the type of football Stephen had us playing.

THINGS MIGHT HAVE fizzled out in the challenge against St Pat's, and in the FAI Cup, but we were determined to finish the season on a high. We wrapped things up with a draw away to Bohs, a 4-0 win against Cork City and a win away to Bray. I'd never finished as high as second place in the League of Ireland before. At Portadown, we were runners-up in the north, so I had experienced plenty of near misses. We were pipped for the First Division title at Monaghan, we lost out then on promotion in the play-offs and we were losers in the EA Sports Cup final. Same old story up north, where we ran out of steam against Linfield. I lost a League Cup final up there too. So, this was another case of so near, yet so far both in the league and in the FAI Cup.

Then, a sign that things were turning a corner. For me, at least.

The focus turned to our end-of season do. We started off at Oriel Park and then headed into town for my first night out in Dundalk. We ended up in Ridleys nightclub and it was upstairs there that I first met my future wife Bronagh. She was a local girl. It was the start of me truly putting down roots in Dundalk.

As the players all went our separate ways for the close-season, there was a feeling that we could take things a step further in 2014. I'm not sure it was ever said out loud, but there definitely was a quiet confidence within the group. That St Pat's team was brilliant; they played such stylish football and the squad was packed with experience. Yet, we knew we weren't that far off them.

The season had just finished, but we couldn't wait to get started again. No one was having itchy feet, everyone wanted to stay and play for Stephen Kenny. No one would ever want to miss a single training session. One or two of the lads didn't return, but Stephen brought in some top quality with the likes of Sean Gannon arriving. There was real optimism over that close-season.

I was never happier in my career as a footballer than I was at the end of the 2013 campaign. But that joy was short-lived, as things at home took a turn for the worse.

· CHAPTER 8 ·

IT WAS DURING my first pre-season with Dundalk that I learned the full extent of dad's illness. He had complained of feeling ill a few months earlier, so Caragh him to his doctor, who diagnosed an infection and prescribed some antibiotics. When they didn't do the trick, dad was sent to Tallaght Hospital for tests. It was early November 2013 and a scan revealed a small growth. They wanted to keep him in overnight. By that evening he was on a trolley. With no bed available, they sent him home and said they would call him back in to remove it.

I had a three-week holiday in Dubai and Thailand booked long before dad got sick. He told me I shouldn't worry, that I should go ahead as planned and that he would keep me up to date while I was away.

During the first two weeks he texted regularly, letting me know how he was feeling and generally coming across as pretty positive. But the messages dried up by week three. As soon as I got home, I went over to his house.

Caragh answered the door. 'He's not doing too well,' she said. I took one look at him and my stomach dropped. He looked like a ghost. Dad was really pale.

I'd never seen him look so run-down.

He told us he had just received a letter from the hospital. They missed a big growth behind his bladder. He rushed back to Tallaght Hospital. That was just the start of our problems.

Dad was sent to the urinary ward, but straightaway I knew that wasn't the right location for him. The nurses there were overworked. No one seemed to specialise in the pain medication and treatment that dad needed. One day his medication would be too high and he would start to hallucinate, and the next it would be too low and dad would be in agony.

One minute I'd be told that he was going for chemo and the next I'd be told he'd have radiotherapy instead. Eventually he went on a course of chemotherapy.

I SAT WITH dad during his first session.

I went in clueless, with no idea what it would entail. I certainly didn't picture him just sitting there with a drip attached to him. Chemo is such a big deal. This just seemed so trivial. If you can picture the scene in *Breaking Bad* where Walter White is going through his first session, it just doesn't seem to match the gravity of the situation. The chemo ward was basically a bunch of chairs scattered around the place. There were others there, all sitting in silence, all looking bored, counting down the minutes until their session ended.

Dad was brought into a little cubicle, maybe because it was his first time there. He was quiet. I'd imagine he was scared.

If he was, he certainly wasn't going to admit it.

It wasn't long before dad's hair started to fall out. I remember telling him to either shave it off or cut it short, as it was going anyway. He wasn't too impressed with that suggestion. In the end, dad managed just one session of chemotherapy. After that, he was never strong enough to go again.

As I mentioned already, I was in pre-season with Dundalk at the time and was desperate to make a strong impression ahead of my first full season at Oriel Park. But I was exhausted and I wasn't looking after myself properly. I was doing some personal training at this time, taking a few lads in the Phoenix Park early each morning. Then I'd go from there straight to the hospital, where I would spend a few hours with dad. From there, I'd head to the gym for a session, then back to the hospital for another short visit if I had the time. And then I'd be on the road to Dundalk for training that evening. I'd be back by my dad's bedside for half-nine and spend a few more hours there. That was the routine, day after day.

I kept my dad's situation pretty much to myself. It's just the way I've always been. I've never wanted people to feel awkward or strange around me. Also, I just don't know how to talk about stuff like that. *Where do you start?*

ONE LAST SHOT ■ BRIAN GARTLAND

It's not as if talking is going to change anything. You just have to get on with life. I didn't want people feeling sorry for me. Nor did I want to have to talk about it all the time. Even some of my closest friends weren't aware of dad's cancer until very late on. That worked for me. I was spending so much time with dad and when I wasn't with him, I was thinking about him. So it was nice to meet up with people and talk about normal, everyday, non-cancer related things.

It was stressful enough having to deal with it when I was in the hospital, trying to catch a doctor who might give me a straight answer about dad's condition. I must have been told of a hundred different treatments that they were going to put him on.

When he finally got moved onto the cancer ward, his pain was managed far better than on the urinary ward. At this stage he was in the care of a palliative care nurse. She knew exactly what and how much to give him, so that he'd be comfortable. I managed to speak with her one day and finally got some answers about my dad's condition. I told her, 'I don't want any bullshit, I just want to know where he's at'.

She was straight up with me. She said, obviously in a much more professional way, that his condition was a real puzzler. It was different to the common cancers that they treated on a daily basis. Basically, the doctors were unsure what to do with dad. She told me that he was a long way down the road and that he was on his way to the hospice. Someone else had told me he was going there to build up his strength, so that he would be able for some more treatment. I was naive enough to believe that. But he was only going to the hospice for one reason. Maybe they did believe that he could get stronger, but dad wasn't long in the hospice.

For the first few days, he was in a room with four others. I was amazed by the care that he was given, the pain relief, the comfort they provided. In what's a very difficult time for patients and their families, I don't think dad could have been in a better place. Eventually, he ended up moving into a private room. I suppose that's when we realised that he was nearing the end.

ONCE DAD WAS moved into a private room, I practically moved in with him. I slept on an inflatable bed. It was hardly ideal in terms of recovering from gruelling pre-season training sessions, but I wanted to give as much of my time as possible to dad. We hadn't moved to full-time training yet at Dundalk, so the sessions were every Monday, Tuesday and Thursday. It was still very full-on.

I came back from Thailand that December in pretty good shape. I suppose that was down to my vanity. I didn't want to throw on the kilos on holiday because I'd just met Bronagh, my future wife, and I'd only gone on one date with her before the holiday. We went on more dates when I came back, but I didn't talk to her about dad's situation. I really liked her and I didn't want to be throwing stuff like that at her so early in our relationship.

I started to put on some weight when I moved into dad's room. If I wasn't with dad, I was in the car driving here and there. I wasn't cooking my own food. Mam would make some dinner, but I'd just grab a few mouthfuls on the run. Otherwise, I was eating out of a motorway garage or a takeaway. I remember Stephen Kenny saying to me, 'You enjoyed that holiday a bit too much!'

I just smiled and told him I'd work hard to shed the excess weight. He didn't know about dad, or that I was sleeping on a blow-up bed on a hospice floor, or that I was living off a combination of McDonalds and deli rolls. I didn't want to tell Stephen, I didn't want to be making excuses so early in my Dundalk career. I didn't want a fuss being made. I just wanted to get my head down and work as hard as possible.

But I wasn't looking after myself at all. I'd grab whatever was handiest, be it a chipper or McDonalds. Normally, I wouldn't eat stuff like that. The only time I've had McDonalds since dad's passing was on Dane Massey's stag in Amsterdam (unfortunately, I've signed a non-disclosure agreement, so I'm not allowed to reveal anything about that weekend!). But while I was spending time with dad I was a regular visitor to the 'Golden Arches'. And I'd be eating late at night too.

I suppose the mental stress was driving me to eat more. I have always tended to eat emotionally. I found myself grabbing chocolate bars, crisps, stuff like that.

My body fat ended up being quite high in pre-season and I was under pressure to cut it quickly. Stephen Kenny knew I had a reputation for training like hell and being disciplined in-season, but letting loose during the weeks off. I was always very good when I had to be. I used to go out twice a week while playing for Monaghan United, and even in the early days at Dundalk. But I didn't drink. I would be the designated driver.

All my friends were delighted – they never had to get taxis. Chris Shields once said to me that I seemed to know a lot of pub and club owners in Dublin. Not a good look for a footballer! But that was down to the fact that I wasn't pissed every time I went to the pub. I could have a conversation with these people and actually remember it.

Reputations are hard to shake, though, and I was known for having a bit of a party lifestyle. I was big into organising nights out. Stephen would have known about that. And the fact that he didn't know about my dad probably meant he was suspicious as to why I was carrying a little extra timber in pre-season.

A FEW WEEKS into training, I finally told Stephen's assistant manager Vinny Perth that dad was in hospital. I wasn't as close to Stephen as I became later in our time together at Dundalk and I didn't want to burden him with the news while he was busy planning for the season ahead. I didn't really get into the detail about the seriousness of dad's situation, so Vinny tried to be as positive as possible about it. But it got to the stage where I needed someone to know, just in case I was in really bad form one day or I couldn't turn up for training.

One week before dad passed away, we were training, playing five-a-sides and Pat Hoban went to tackle me as I shot. He caught my ankle full on and it was quite a bad injury. I missed the first game of the season as a result, the 4-1 defeat to Drogheda United.

Anyone who has ever kicked a ball – from five-a-side to the professional game – will tell you there is no greater escape from worries and stress than playing a game of football. Once you are in the thick of the action, you simply can't think of anything else. And that's what training and playing was for me around the time of dad's death… it was an escape. I didn't want to miss a single session.

An added bonus was the atmosphere around Stephen's squad. Aside from the draw of working under Stephen and with such a great group of lads, you knew that if you skipped even one session, someone else was ready to step in and take your place.

The biggest example I can think of from those early days at Dundalk was when Mark Rossiter, just a few weeks into the season, was Best Man at his brother's wedding in Sligo. The ceremony was the day of a game, and Mark left for Oriel Park straight from the church. His speech was played on video later in the hotel, but after driving to Dundalk Mark pulled a hamstring in the game. A young lad called Sean Gannon came on, played the remainder of that game and never looked back. Ganno is one of the best I have ever played with. He was capable of making it at any standard in the game.

But Mark's sacrifice was typical of what we did *all the time*. Our personal lives came second to our footballing lives.

That's just how football works and that has always been in the back of my mind during my time at Dundalk. You don't want to miss a single day's training.

So, when I got injured the week before the season started, I still went up every evening. It was a great release. I needed to get out for a few hours and talk to people about normal stuff. I'd arrive, get some treatment from the physio and head back to the hospice.

Football has always been my saving grace, a great way to channel any frustration or built up anger. I'd run my legs off in any session, but even more so when I was stressed. I'd rather dive head-first into physical activity than talk about issues. At the same time, I am quite good at talking as a result of my teenage therapy sessions.

I always had a million and one things going on. I suppose I got that from mam. I'd take on stuff that I shouldn't, and then throw some more stuff on top of that. That's probably why my time-keeping has always been so poor.

When I think back to those days, I'd be in the Phoenix Park for seven in the morning and I'd get home late at night. And I'd pack about two days' worth of activity into that time. It was the mental fatigue that got to me more than physical tiredness during dad's final weeks. That's why I lost my discipline in terms of my diet.

BY THE TIME dad passed away, everyone on the team was aware of what I was going through. I told them there was no need for them to turn up to the funeral, but the entire squad and backroom staff still showed. While Stephen insisted on it, the lads really wanted to be there and needed no cajoling.

That was really touching, because many of them were still working in day-jobs at that stage. They already had to take time off work for football, so this was an added burden on their professional lives.

The day before the funeral, Des Dunleavy, the player liaison officer, came down as the club's representative. Looking back now, it's probably the done thing, but at the time it felt like he was going beyond the call of duty. He was there in his Dundalk crested suit. It was really appreciated by the family and it summed up the atmosphere that Stephen had fostered at the club.

Dad had wanted a humanist service at his funeral. I had no idea what that entailed, so I did a bit of research and ended up at the Humanist Association of Ireland on St Stephen's Green. I was told that you could play whatever music you wanted. It was easy enough to come up with a playlist.

Next up, I was advised that I would have to say a few words about dad at the service. That was going to be tough. *What on earth do you talk about at your dad's funeral?*

I'd be standing there with loads of people in front of me, including the entire Dundalk squad. This was a new enough team, we were still getting to know each other, so that added even more pressure. Then there was the situation between mam and dad's partner. *Who would sit where?* In the end, we came up with a seating plan that satisfied everyone. But that was another issue that I could have done without.

Then, on the morning of the funeral, there was the embrace between the two loves of dad's life. That was a huge weight off my shoulder.

When it came to the funeral music, dad loved Mary Black's *No Frontiers*, so that was a no-brainer. *The Parting Glass* was another one. And as for the final song, dad was a big fan of the Traveling Wilburys. He had a great sense of humour, so I felt *End of the Line* would be a fitting finale. I know it sounds a bit morbid, but I still laugh about it. I just thought… *Why not?* He loved the Traveling Wilburys and he loved that song. I did debate it for a while and I wondered what people might think. But the more I listened to the song and read the lyrics, the more convinced I was about it. It summed up dad perfectly. No matter what you do, no matter where you come from, we all end up in the same place.

STANDING UP IN front of everyone and talking about dad was the hardest part of the service. I had to talk about his life, so that included mam and Caragh, which wasn't easy.

I did have a word with mam beforehand, told her that I couldn't speak about dad's life and not mention his partner. She understood.

The line I came up with was, 'Some people are lucky enough to have the love of one person, but my dad was lucky enough to have the love of two women in two different periods of his life'.

It was important to acknowledge both of them.

Dad had gone through a bad patch with drink and depression, and separating from mam was best for everyone. Mam got her life back, dad got his act together. And my brother and I forged stronger relationships with him.

After the separation he got back into the taxi business, which was great for us! He would start his shift at around five in the morning. Happily, that was around the time that I'd roll out of whatever club I was in.

Trying to get an early morning taxi in Dublin back then was near impossible, so the hotline to dad was a lifesaver. Neil knew the ranks that he'd sit at and he'd always make a beeline for them. Even if a club finished up early, I'd get a bit of food and head to a casino until his shift started.

I'd go in with around €30, the equivalent of my taxi fare home. If I lost it, grand. I was getting a free ride home anyway. I'd be there playing roulette, betting €1 on each spin, until dad would arrive to take me home.

MY BROTHER IS never one to show his emotions – and even in the build-up to the funeral he was fairly stoic. He was living in England at the time when dad passed away and came home for the service. I'll always remember him sitting there beside me when dad's coffin went behind the curtain. He burst into tears. I put my arm around him and we just sat there crying together. We'd been through a hell of a lot growing up, but I'd never felt as close to him as in that moment.

Because I kept myself so busy organising dad's funeral, I didn't really take any time to mourn his passing. I was flat out setting up the arrangements... the coffin, the removal, the afters and the ashes. *What do we do with the ashes?*

Once the funeral was over I dived straight back into the football.

I didn't give myself any time to grieve. Neil and I went down to Westport a year after dad passed and went on the lash together. I suppose that was us, 12 months on, kind of dealing with our feelings. Even now I have a little playlist with dad's favourite songs.

If I'm in the car I'll put it on and I'll smile or have a little misty-eyed chuckle. There would be times when I'd be on the road on my own, I'd put on the playlist and I'd be in floods of tears! There are a couple of songs – the ones I used to listen to with dad – that get me going.

That's how I deal with things. I prefer to do it on my own.

Sometimes it feels like I'd be burdening others by sharing stuff like that. I'd always be worried that they would feel awkward around me.

A FEW MONTHS later we played Sligo Rovers in the Setanta Sports Cup final. It was the last one before the competition was disbanded.

The game took place in Tallaght Stadium and the last 10 or 15 minutes were played in monsoon conditions. I was up near the front of the coach as we made our way to the ground from our base at the nearby Green Isle Hotel. What came on the radio just before we arrived at the stadium? The Traveling Wilburys... *End of the Line.*

I'd never heard it on the radio before. *It couldn't just be a coincidence, could it?*

It had to be a sign. Surely dad was looking down on us that day.

Yeah, right. We lost that game.

I remember looking up at the sky afterwards and thinking... *You bastard! You got my hopes up.*

Paul O'Conor scored for Sligo after 13 minutes and that was that. No one could play any football once the heavens opened up. The game probably should have been abandoned. We were all sliding around the place and the ball was getting stuck in ankle-deep puddles. All the photos of Sligo's celebrations were of the players diving through the water.

After getting over the disappointment of losing the final, I did have a little laugh about it. Dad had a sense of humour. *Was this one last little prank?*

Speaking of pranks, one way that I deal with stressful situations is to crack a joke, a little gallows humour. You see, dad's ashes are still in my house. It's about time we did something with them. *But what?* We still haven't figured that one out. That's a decision I've kept putting off. One thought I had was to bring them down to Westport, where his parents are buried. But we aren't down there often enough.

Dad loved photography. He was self-taught. During his early-morning shift he would take a break around sunrise, head over to Sandymount and snap some amazing photos. I got one printed and framed for his partner. I've been meaning for some time to get one framed for our own wall.

He loved that part of the Dublin coastline. Scattering his ashes there is another option. As for the gallows humour – and I realise that some people might find this particularly distasteful – but I managed to turn the indecisiveness over what to do with dad's ashes into a practical joke.

WHILE I WAS moving house, getting ready to settle down in Dundalk with Bronagh, I placed the ashes behind the driver's seat in my car. One day a few of my Dundalk teammates were in the car. Fearghal Kerin, our physio at the time, was there too.

He was sitting in the back seat with his feet on the box. I turned around and said, 'Fearghal, remember my dad died?'

He was, like, 'Yeah'.

I said, 'Did you ever think you'd be using him as a foot-rest?'

'What?!?'

'What's that beneath your feet Fearghal?'

'Ah for f**k sake!'

The other lads in the car didn't know what to do.

'Ah Jesus Brian, you can't be doing that.'

If you think I'm bad, check out Bronagh's family and their sense of humour. This one sums it up. I was lying out in our back garden one day relaxing, the sun beating down, some music playing. Bronagh was upstairs and she came to the back window.

She shouted down, 'Do you ever think your dad is looking down on you?'

Just as I was about to give a solemn and honest response, she said, 'He's looking down on you right now… his ashes are on the window-sill'.

I definitely think it's time to do something with them, because they have become a prop for jokes at this stage.

· CHAPTER 9 ·

IT'S ONE OF my all-time favourite goals... 35 passes and a brilliant Sean Gannon finish from a tight angle.

At least that's Ganno's version of events.

If you were cynical, you'd wonder if he meant it, or if he was trying to knock the ball back into the centre of the area.

Regardless of whether it was intentional or not (and Sean insists it was), what a way to announce ourselves as serious title contenders – a 4-1 win away to the reigning champs. It was quite the turnaround after our nightmare start to the 2014 campaign.

THE BEGINNING OF that season was a turbulent time for me, with dad passing away. On the pitch, there were a few weeks where I couldn't even let off steam on the training ground, because of the injury I picked up during pre-season. I missed out on the season opener against Drogheda United, a game we were all looking forward to. After the previous year, when we ran a really talented St Patrick's Athletic side close in the title race, expectations around the club were high.

There was a real buzz in the town and a great atmosphere inside the dressing-room. We couldn't wait for the league to start again. Of course, we were also out for revenge after the shock and injustice of our FAI Cup semi-final defeat. That one still hurt.

So there we were, ready to get off to a flier, all set for revenge…

And then we got spanked 4-1.

Eric Foley, Philip Hughes and Declan O'Brien fired Drogheda into a 3-0 lead. Even when Patrick Hoban pulled a goal back, we barely had any time to think about a dramatic comeback. Within a couple of minutes, 'Fabio' O'Brien had put away their fourth. We were stunned. I'm sure Drogheda's players were too. No one had predicted this outcome.

Looking back on that game, it was probably a good kick up the arse. I can say that now, but at the time it was hard to put any kind of positive spin on a really bad at the office.

We were a confident bunch, we knew we had a strong team and that if we produced the same work ethic as the previous year, we'd be in with a shout once again for the title. But there were no airs and graces. We all knew where we came from. Some of us were sent packing from the UK, while others, such as myself, had bounced around various clubs without seriously contending for the top honours. So there was no cockiness in the squad. Certainly not after a result like that.

The lads worked their backsides off like never before in the next training session. Making the best of a bad situation, we figured it was as good a time as any to be tanked 4-1 by our nearest neighbours. Loads of time to hit the reset button.

We were shell-shocked, but we didn't panic.

If anyone in the club needed reminding, it was evidence that nothing would come easy in this league. And if we wanted to be champions, if we wanted to be the best in Ireland, we would have to scrap for every single point.

Did we learn from that game? Check out our reaction. We overturned a home first-leg defeat in the Setanta Cup quarter-final against Coleraine, then we clocked up Premier Division wins over Limerick, Sligo Rovers and Shamrock Rovers. We really kicked into gear. Then after drawing against Bohemians, next up was a trip to St Pat's, our arch-rivals from 2013.

And that goal.

We were 3-1 up going into injury-time. Greg Bolger had already seen red for St Pat's, so there were gaps in their side. Not that anyone expected those holes to be exploited in such style. It started with a foul by Ian Bermingham on Sean Gannon. Richie Towell took a short free-kick to Daryl Horgan, who passed to Darren Meenan… back to Towell…

to Horgan… and back to me. We were moving their players everywhere we wanted, we felt like we had them on strings. They were chasing shadows. I played the ball to Gannon… he moved it to Chris Shields, who played a couple of one-twos with Andy Boyle, before passing to Horgan, who was popping up all over the pitch.

WHILE THEY WERE a man down at this stage (Killian Brennan was also sent off deep into stoppage time), we bossed the game pretty much from start to finish, particularly in the second-half after we bounced back from Chris Forrester's opener. Thanks to goals from John Mountney, Horgan and David McMillan, we were in the driving seat. So, sure, it was easier to move the ball about with a numerical advantage, but this had been one of our finest displays as a group to date. And to do it against a great footballing side such as St Patrick's Athletic, the champions, it sent alarm bells ringing throughout Irish football.

Horgan brought Dane Massey into the move and he sent it back to the omni-present Horgan, who knocked it to me. I pushed it wide to Gannon and he found Meenan. Again, it came back to me and I moved it into Shields in midfield.

ST PAT'S HAD beaten us well the year before, so there was a bit of bite coming into this game. We travelled to Richmond Park determined to send a message to them – and to the rest of the league.

Stephen O'Donnell passed to Horgan… to Boyle… back to Horgan… and back again to Boyle… then to me… and up the right to Meenan… to McMillan… all the way back to me… and once again into midfield where Shields had plenty of space. To Horgan… Boyle… Shields… Boyle… and then Towell moved it left to Horgan. He sent a cross beyond the far post and into the path of Gannon, and his first-time volley lifted the ball over the head of Pat's goalkeeper Brendan Clarke and inside the left-hand upright.

THIRTY-FIVE PASSES, 102 seconds. Ganno and Darren Meenan inter-changing all the time. Horgan coming off the line and into the middle. Pat's barely within five yards of the ball at any stage of the move, it was glorious.

As a group you appreciate that type of goal more than a 30-yarder into the top-corner, because the whole team is involved. Especially when it comes away from home against the team that pipped you to the league title the previous season.

Less than one month earlier we were licking our wounds, having been beaten 4-1 by our local rivals in the first game of the season. So, to turn it around, to go to Inchicore and do that, there was such a buzz about the place. I remember that goal going viral, being watched by people all around the world. That added to the feeling that we'd done something special. I think it was Damien Richardson on co-commentary that night and he joined the chorus of people talking us up as proper title challengers.

Horgan was in unreal form, Richie Towell was flying around the place, and there was a great shape and balance to the team. Plus, there was more maturity to us than in 2013 in terms of controlling games. It was clear to everyone that we had moved up a level – and that game against St Pat's was the clearest sign yet that we were on the rise.

But we knew we would have to continue to raise our standards. Once you are tagged as title contenders, the scrutiny grows. As soon as you let your performance levels drop – even by a fraction – people are ready to call you out. Suddenly, the focus on Dundalk was more intense. We could see it on social media and in the mainstream media. It just fed into our desire to give everything in training, and to keep working as hard as possible on and off the pitch. Any slight drop in standards and it nearly felt like a crisis. The Pat's game was ground zero in terms of a change in the perception of Dundalk FC.

I FIRMLY BELIEVE Dundalk, under Stephen Kenny, kicked off a revolution in the Irish game. We set new standards, which forced other clubs to either change their approach or get left behind.

It wasn't much different to how Arsene Wenger changed the attitude towards nutrition and conditioning in English football after he arrived at Arsenal in the mid-90s. It was because of this high bar we set ourselves that we were able to finish the game against St Pat's in such style.

I was big into my health and fitness before I moved to Oriel Park, but never before was I in a squad where so many other players shared that same passion. John Sullivan, Richie Towell, John Mountney, Patrick Hoban, Darren Meenan, they were all in really good shape. We had a culture in the squad that demanded we trained, ate and looked like proper athletes.

There was no spoken competition between us, but in truth we were driven by each other to get fitter and stronger, and everyone at the club knew they'd be left behind if they didn't embrace that culture. So, we would train as a group under Stephen and his coaching staff, still on a part-time basis, and separate from that we'd each head off to our respective gyms.

My days were packed from one end to the other.

I'd go to the gym early in the morning. Myself, Richie Towell and John Sullivan trained in the Carlisle Gym together. Then I'd do a few hours' coaching, before heading up the M1 to Dundalk for training in the evening.

Lads wanted to look better, be more athletic, stronger... fitter.

It started with a core of players in the dressing-room, but it spread right throughout the squad. All that work culminated in what we achieved in 2016. You just need to look at pictures of Ronan Finn when he signed for Dundalk and when he left at the end of the 2016 season. He was a different person; he filled out, he was stronger, bigger and leaner. Then there was Daryl Horgan. He was an absolute machine. His work ethic, his drive, they were frightening. All the extra work he did set him up nicely for his move abroad and his elevation to the senior Ireland squad.

This was how we laid the foundation for the successes we had at Dundalk. The players drove that on. We made the decision to be motivated enough to work really hard outside of our regular training sessions.

And it wasn't just the extra sessions in the gym; it was nutrition, what we were eating, how we were living, what we were (or were not) drinking. We had our nights out, don't get me wrong. But they were always at the right time. As I said, I'd always been into my fitness and conditioning, but I had never been in a squad where so many players paid such close attention to their physical development. In a game of little margins, I am convinced that it played a huge role in our successes at home and in Europe.

Our fitness coach would advise on nutrition and give us workouts, but without a full-time set-up, he had to rely on each player to be disciplined enough to stick to his regime. There was a general ban on bread and on pasta, which sounds strange in a football environment. But that was the mantra and, again, it was up to us to stick with it. It was the train low, play high method. Limit your carb intake during the week, come into each training session off a low-carb diet, and then load up on carbs in the build-up to each game.

Sure, we were part-time, but we were encouraged to live like professionals. Anyone who didn't stick with the programme would have been quickly found out, because it felt like we were reaching new levels of fitness every week. We were offered an environment in which we could thrive as athletes and as hungry young footballers – and many of us with points to prove – we grabbed it with both hands.

IF THE DROGHEDA match was a kick up the backside, then the St Pat's game was proof that it worked. We followed that result up with big wins against Derry City and UCD, and a Setanta Cup semi-final win over Shamrock Rovers. We had huge belief in ourselves, but it always came back to the fundamental issue of hard work. No matter how talented you are, if the other team works harder than you, forget about it. We took that attitude into our next meeting with Drogheda United and we beat them 7-0 at Oriel. That was more like the Drogheda we expected to face on the opening night.

That was more like the Dundalk performance that we knew we were capable of producing. They were a solid team a few years earlier, but we really didn't rate Drogheda and felt the 7-0 was far more reflective of the gulf between the two sides than the freak result back in early-March. And it wasn't just Drogheda, we felt at that stage that we could go and steamroll lots of teams.

And that's what we did when it came to that traditional April/May bottleneck, with games coming thick and fast. I always felt we showed our class when we were playing two games a week. A lot of the sides we faced couldn't handle the fixture pile-up, but we had the strength, depth and talent in our squad to cope, as well as our conditioning. We chalked up some big wins in that period against Cork City, Sligo Rovers, UCD and Bohs before the mid-season break.

At that time we saw Cork as just another team. We certainly didn't think of them as potential title rivals. There was no hint of what was to come, the years-long battle between the two clubs for the league and FAI Cup. We battered them at the end of 2013, winning 4-0, and we were leading by the same score after just 50 minutes of our latest meeting.

I looked forward to games against Cork because I thought at the time that they were handy to play against. I felt the way they played was too old-school to earn them a crack at the title. Their game suited Andy Boyle and myself down to the ground.

They favoured the long ball and we would eat it up for breakfast. We loved those physical battles. And when it came to the other end of the pitch, we had too much pace and power for them. It showed in the final score that day, with two goals from Patrick Hoban and one each from John Mountney and Richie Towell sending us back to the top of the table.

MY RELATIONSHIP WITH Andy Boyle at centre-half clicked right from the start. We were the perfect fit for each other. We felt so impenetrable as a unit that anytime we conceded a goal, it felt like a disaster, a proper crisis. The coaching staff never had to do any serious work with us, as our understanding seemed to come so naturally.

One in front, one behind. That was the system.

By this stage, most teams were playing one up front, so if the ball was coming down my side, I'd be out front and Boyler would be behind. That way we won so many balls that we were able to snuff out attacks before they began.

Strikers had no time to get control of the ball and bring others into play. And if the ball went over the top, whoever stayed behind would be there to sweep things up.

The way teams were going in attack really simplified the game for us. I grew up playing against two strikers and in that scenario you couldn't gamble by pushing out in front. If you did and got rolled, suddenly it would be a two-vs-one situation. But with the majority of teams now playing one up front, I'll be honest and say we found it a doddle.

Of course, the understanding that Andy and I had made things a lot easier. The game seemed really straightforward in our heads.

As for our full-backs, we would both encourage them to bomb up the pitch. I'd constantly tell Sean Gannon to go, that I didn't need him. If he was too deep, I'd roar at him to push further up the pitch, whereas a lot of defenders would be reluctant to leave themselves potentially exposed. But we were an attacking team, that was our style. If Sean and Dane Massey on the other side were high up the pitch and we lost the ball, we would be in a better position to turn it over in an area where we could get back on the attack straight away.

And if the other team cleared it long, we were still two-vs-one against their striker, so either Boyler or myself could just pick it up and restart the attack ourselves.

Playing alongside Andy was a breeze.

We didn't spend hours on the training pitch working on issues such as shape. It was as if we could read each other's minds. If one of us made a mistake, there was no yelling or pointing fingers. That was never the way between us. We would turn to each other, give a little fist-bump and a word of encouragement, and we'd switch on once again. It was always a partnership, the two of us in it together.

We would stand or fall as one.

We get on well off the pitch too. Not that we are best mates or anything like that, we wouldn't be on the phone to each other all the time. Boyler is quiet enough, whereas I'd be a little louder, a bit of a messer. There is no drama with Boyler. What you see is what you get.

When he returned to Oriel Park after a spell in England, I was happy to see him come back. Apart from the times he kept me out of the team, of course!

AFTER THE 4-0 win against Cork, we went to the Carlisle Grounds and beat Bray Wanderers 3-0. Then it was onto Tallaght Stadium for the Setanta Cup final against Sligo Rovers. Another chance to claim my first winners' medal, another runners-up finish. I remember thinking at the full-time whistle... *Jesus Christ, not again!* Sligo were a good team, but we were better than them. They had a fantastic player in Joseph Ndo, but collectively we were much stronger. They lost Ndo in the first-half through injury, but they were 1-0 up at that stage. It was just one of those days, lashing rain, them taking what was probably their one clearcut chance. The conditions made it near impossible for us to play our style of football and make a comeback.

I was sure beforehand that we would win – and that our first trophy as a team would be the perfect way to kick on and win the league. To this day, that defeat still eats away at me. If we'd won that game, I would have every medal going. But there's a little Setanta Cup-shaped hole in my collection. It would be nice to point to a gold medal from every domestic competition in which I've played.

After that final, we had people coming up to us saying, 'You need to lose one before you can win'. Apparently you need the experience, the pain to drive you on.

But I don't really buy that. If we'd beaten Sligo that day, I'm pretty sure it would have done little to change the path we were on as a club. The funny thing is, we went and battered Sligo 3-0 in the league just three games later. When I say funny, I mean *annoying*. Really annoying. It was great to get the three points, but it wasn't going to change the colour of our Setanta Cup medals.

THE NEXT GAME after our league win against Sligo was an EA Sports Cup quarter-final against Derry City. I wasn't in the squad for that one. The manager wanted to shuffle things around in that competition. In each round he took out five or six players and brought in some young lads. Despite this, we still managed to beat Premier Division opposition, such as Derry at the Brandywell and Bray Wanderers away in the previous round.

Whatever magic Stephen Kenny had weaved, we had a style of play where you could interchange personnel, yet the level of performance wouldn't drop. We won 2-1 in Derry, with David McMillan and Kurtis Byrne scoring – and future teammate Patrick McEleney grabbing a late consolation for them.

I wasn't involved again in the semi-final, a 5-0 win against Wexford Youths, but I was back in when we fielded a strong team for the final against Shamrock Rovers. We knew how important it was as a group to win a trophy, and the boost it would give everyone at the club. Plus, we were desperate for revenge.

While we were continuing to march on in the league, I was keeping one eye on the FAI Cup. I was convinced this would be our year. We picked off Sligo Rovers and Galway United in the early rounds, and then drew Shamrock Rovers in the quarter-finals. I played the first game, a scoreless draw in Tallaght Stadium, but missed the replay through suspension, thanks to an accumulation of yellow cards.

We were 1-0 up going into the final 10 minutes at Oriel Park and then Karl Sheppard raced onto a ball that dropped behind our defence and finished well. When you are on the pitch, everything happens so quickly, but watching on from the stand it was as if it happened in slow motion. It's a horrible feeling for a footballer when you are unable to do anything to affect a game.

Their winner came with just two minutes remaining and it was Sheppard again, this time cutting in off the end-line and beating Peter Cherrie at his near post.

Another year without an FAI Cup final.

I was gutted. I was so sure, with how well we were playing and the fact that the replay was at Oriel, that we would have too much for them. I can still picture Sheppard's winner vividly. I was sitting in the main stand and he scored into the goal to my left. Sheppard rolling us on the end-line like that really surprised me, because we were always so strong at the back. You could count the number of defensive lapses that year on one hand – and if there was a mistake, there always seemed to be someone else there to cover. Not this time, unfortunately.

I sat there, head in my hands, knowing that my chance of a trip to the Aviva was gone for another year. It was just five days later that we faced them again at Oriel, this time with the EA Sports Cup trophy up for grabs.

Dane Massey scored twice that day – including a cracker of a free-kick that he still hasn't shut up about. He was on direct free-kicks for years after that one. I'm not sure he score too many though! We won 3-2, with Patrick Hoban scoring the third. The game was a sell-out, with a temporary stand put up behind one of the goals. That just shows what it meant to the club. It was Dundalk's first trophy in 12 years – our first trophy as a group.

And it was my first winners' medal!

It was a huge deal for everyone involved. But fast-forward three years and we win the EA Sports Cup against Rovers in Tallaght. I'm on the bench for that one. One of the younger lads, Carlton Ubaezuono, played in some of the earlier rounds but wasn't in the match-day squad for the final. So I gave him my medal. I hadn't played in any of the earlier games, I was an unused substitute in the final. I'd won league titles, FAI Cups, I'd played in European group stage matches. Of course I was delighted that we won another final, but it didn't have the same impact as the first one. That's just the way the goalposts moved for me.

And I'm so grateful that my career went in such a direction that I could feel that way about a 3-0 EA Sports Cup final win away to Shamrock Rovers. The League Cup, as it is in most countries, is very much ranked the third of the three big domestic trophies. But make no mistake, the first one in 2014 was massive for us.

I do remember, however, how we were given a bit of a wake-up call that night, as we celebrated our first piece of silverware.

WE WERE GOING around town as if we'd won the league when some fella came up to us and told us that it was just a measly League Cup. 'You need to win the league if you're going to be remembered around here!' he said.

Dundalk were in the doldrums in the years before Stephen Kenny's arrival. It wasn't that long ago that the club was nearly relegated, nearly put out of business. But there were plenty around town who remembered when the club was the best in the country.

And for them, nothing less would do than restoring Dundalk FC to the pinnacle of the Irish game.

I remember thinking… *Jesus, let us enjoy this win.*

It was huge for us as a group and it was a monkey off my back to get a winners' medal in something… anything! But at the same time we were quickly reminded that if we didn't go on and win the league, it wouldn't be long before we'd have the fans on our backs.

FROM THE MOMENT I joined Dundalk, it was hard to escape the club's proud history in Europe. There was talk of big nights against Rangers, Liverpool and Ajax, and famous draws against Celtic, Porto and Tottenham. European nights were massive in the town and there was great excitement in the build-up to our 2014 campaign. Little did we know at the time, however, what was to come on the European stage.

I wasn't exactly new to the experience myself. I'd played in Europe with Portadown a year before my move to Oriel Park. We played a team called KF Shkëndija of Macedonia in the first round of the Europa League – we drew 0-0 in the away leg. That game was played in a neutral venue as they were banned from playing in their own ground. My outstanding memory of that game was the heat. It must have been 35 degrees. We won the home game 2-1 and drew Croatian side Slaven Belupo in the next round.

This was a complete disaster, right from the moment we realised our goalkeeper couldn't travel for the first-leg, because he couldn't get the time off work. We had no wingers, so we ended up playing three strikers. The result? A 6-0 defeat. Again, the heat was a killer. We were playing in something like eighty percent humidity.

My central defensive partner scored an own goal inside the first minutes and we were chasing shadows for the rest of the game. We lost again at home, this time 4-2, but all I remember from that game were a couple of passages of great play by Kevin Braniff. Maybe it was the scoreline, the hopelessness of it all, but he was unshackled and he produced some outrageous showboating.

Kevin was a phenomenal player. He nutmegged one of their lads on the halfway line and sent an amazing 60-yard diagonal pass right to the feet of a teammate. Then, 10 minutes later, he nutmegged another player and sent a 60-yard diagonal in the other direction. When he wanted to be, Kevin was one of the best players I'd ever played with. He had talent to burn. As for that campaign, it was great to progress a round, but we were licking our wounds for a while after a 10-2 aggregate defeat to the Croatians.

Europe was treated differently by teams up North. Games in Europe were treated as a 'holiday', and I remember a Crusaders' player didn't travel one year because he actually had his holidays booked. I was astounded. This is in total contrast to teams in the League of Ireland – and then there was Stephen Kenny's intent when it came to European games!

WITH THAT EXPERIENCE – and a few harsh lessons – in the bag, it was time to turn our focus at Dundalk to the Europa League. We were drawn against Jeunesse Esch of Luxembourg in the first round and eased through that. Richie Towell scored twice in the away leg, so by the time I scored the opener early at Oriel Park the tie was done and dusted. We grabbed a couple more goals, before they got a second-half consolation. It finished 5-1 on aggregate to Dundalk – next up was Hajduk Split.

Another trip to Croatia? *Oh no*, I thought. I was still having nightmares about my previous visit.

It could hardly have started any worse in the first-leg at Oriel Park. They blitzed us in the early stages and took the lead after just nine minutes. They had to wait until late in the second-half before doubling their lead, but by the final whistle we were all but written-off ahead of the return game. Poor Dane Massey, I'd say he still has nightmares about their right-winger Jean Evrard Kouassi running at him. This fellow had lightning pace and was always first to any ball in behind our defence.

Stephen Kenny made several changes for the second-leg and there was no mistaking his ambition. He wanted to win the game. He wanted to progress. But when that man Kouassi scored midway through the first-half in Split, it was curtains. *Or was it?*

Despite falling 3-0 behind on aggregate, we felt comfortable in the second-leg. We controlled the game from the start, we were expansive, we moved them about and every single pass seemed to find its man.

We were opening them up, creating opportunities. And then, with around 25 minutes remaining, Patrick Hoban scored. Eight minutes later Chris Shields found Kurtis Byrne with a great first-time pass and Byrne, who had only just come on as a substitute, put us ahead on the day with a lovely finish.

Suddenly, with 15 minutes plus stoppage time remaining, we needed just one more goal to progress. We had them on the ropes, they were dazed and you could see the fear in their eyes. They were panicking, they were making mistakes.

If we could just land one more blow, it would surely go down as the all-time greatest comeback by an Irish club in Europe. We left everything on the pitch in our effort to score a third goal, but it wasn't to be.

It was heart-breaking, but I remember being told afterwards that getting through to the next round could have bankrupted the club! Next up was a trip to Kazakhstan to face Shakter Karagandy, and the potential logistics of that trip had the owners sweating. Even with the UEFA prize money, it would have been such an expense to try and get there that, from a purely business point of view, it wouldn't have been worth it.

St Patrick's Athletic played them a few years earlier and it was a case of planes, trains and automobiles to get to the away leg.

As players, however, we were heartbroken. We were gutted.

But at the same time, we were so proud of our performance. I stood on the pitch after the final whistle with the rest of the lads, thinking… *Holy f**k, we've just gone and beaten Hajduk Split in Croatia.* The home fans behind the goal, who were absolutely nuts throughout the game, throwing things like fish heads onto the running track between the stand and the pitch, stayed behind and clapped us off. It was surreal. But they were genuine football fans.

While they were disgusted with their own players, they appreciated our performance and the effort we put in. Now, had we got the third goal, they might not have been so warm towards us. Reflecting on that campaign, winning 5-1 in the first round and then going out in such heroic fashion, it ultimately added another layer of confidence and experience to our group. We had just battered a big European team.

I can honestly say that we found a new gear after that game.

AFTER THE WIN in Split, we were back to league action three days later with a 5-1 win against Bray Wanderers. Then it was down to Cork for a game against a side that had truly emerged as serious title contenders. This was our chance to open up a six-point gap at the top of the table, two-thirds of the way through the season.

The stadium was bouncing, with over 5,500 fans packed in. We got off to a flying start when Richie Towell scored after just 14 minutes. Our lead lasted until seven minutes from time when Darren Dennehy equalised. But there was one more twist. Within moments of that sickening blow, I experienced one of the most euphoric feelings of my career.

I went up for a free-kick, managed to hold off a defender, controlled the ball with my thigh and, head down, lashed it towards goal. I looked up in time to see the ball squeeze under Mark McNulty. We were right in front of our fans at the St Anne's End. To this day I don't know how many were there, although it seems like everyone I talk to in Dundalk was at the game. The block reserved for away fans was certainly full.

I'll never forget that moment. I raced towards the Dundalk supporters and I could see they were going ballistic. There were metal bollards in front of the stand and I saw a few fans rush forward, one falling face-first into a bollard. Suddenly, a load of lads piled on top of him. I've bumped into this fan since that game and he proudly sports a scar from his fall. Anytime we meet, he tells me it was worth the pain!

That was an unforgettable moment. As far as we were concerned, we were going to win the league. There were still 11 games to go, but digging out a win in Cork, just minutes after they had equalised, and with their fans urging them to push for a winner, had us convinced that we would finish the job. To score the winner in such a crucial game, there is no better feeling in football than the moment the ball hits the back of the net.

And to do it at Turner's Cross, one of the great Irish stadiums, made it even more special. Everything about the place, the atmosphere, their fans, the pitch, the four-sided all-seater ground; there are few better places to play – and, of course, win.

We have had so much success since that game – and I am very lucky as a centre-half to have enjoyed plenty of big moments – but the goal at Turner's

Cross was the first big one for me. It was up a level compared to any goal I'd scored before. I was on cloud nine for a while after that.

That game, for me anyway, marked the start of the Dundalk-Cork City rivalry.

CORY CITY WERE consumed with thoughts about Dundalk, whereas we didn't give a damn about them. We were beating them, cruising, winning title after title. We loved going down to Turner's Cross. There was no better feeling than walking into the Shed End after the warm-up and having their fans throwing dogs abuse at us.

Every time we stood in the tunnel there before a game, I had a big smile on my face. I loved it.

'You fat bastard,' they'd shout at me.

The best way to shut them up was to win… and we did it time and time again. We knew we were in their heads and we relished the rivalry.

Their manager at the time, John Caulfield, was a madman on the sideline. But whenever we made eye-contact in the tunnel before a match, we'd smile at each other.

'How are things… best of luck,'… that kind of thing.

Not that I'd be close to him, but I respected him. I'd like to think he respected me too.

I'd scored a 90th minute winner at Turner's Cross for Monaghan United in 2010. Tommy Dunne tried to sign me at the end of that season. I was in Littlewoods when the call came. He offered me huge money at a time when Ireland was in the middle of a huge recession. Accommodation was thrown in too. I'd have been living in an apartment with some of the other lads.

But I didn't want to move down there. My brother had moved away and my mam was on her own. There were a few options in U.S. at the end of that year too, but I couldn't leave. She would have been grand, but the guilt would have killed me.

The offer from Cork was so good that it took me about three years at Dundalk before I was on that kind of money. And that's without accommodation.

Cork were in the First Division at the time and I knew they were going to win the league the following season. Graham Cummins ran amok in that division and Tommy told me I was the only defender who could handle him. I remember thinking Cork was a massive club, but I ended up signing for Portadown.

Turner's Cross was a proper football stadium and it always seemed to be packed. The pitch was beautiful too. I just loved it… the buzz, the excitement, the crowd.

And I loved how they were so consumed by us!

Things changed at the end of the 2016 season, when Cork beat us in the FAI Cup final. We were on the coach back to Dundalk when Stevie O'Donnell's phone started ringing. The Cork lads were on the other end of the line… singing, jeering. Daryl Horgan had joined us from Cork and he recognised the number.

I remember thinking… *They've won the cup and all they can do is ring our skipper? How childish and petty is that?*

We always considered ourselves above that kind of crap. You never saw us attacking other players or clubs in the media.

Then that night, a video of their goalkeeper Mark McNulty slagging us in a bar went viral. In fairness to some of the other Cork players, you could see them stepping into the background, as if they didn't want to be associated with it.

I wasn't a fan of McNulty after that. I didn't know him at all, but thought… *He's the oldest in the team and he's behaving like that?*

Look, in the end it just stoked up the rivalry between the two dominant sides in the Irish game at that time, so no harm.

But at the same time, I could hardly believe how comfortable they were with showing how much we were in their heads.

IN EACH SEASON, there are moments that stand out as major turning points. That Turner's Cross win was obviously a big one. Another was in a league game in mid-October against Shamrock Rovers.

They had already done us in the FAI Cup, while it was our turn to beat them in the EA Sports Cup final. Now, they could potentially knock us off course in the title race. It was the third last game of the season and tensions were running high.

There was a lot of bite in the games between ourselves and Rovers, particularly after Stevie O'Donnell suffered a bad injury in a challenge with Shane Robinson in an earlier meeting. Shane didn't intend on hurting Stevie, obviously, but the immediate aftermath of the challenge had left a bad taste in our mouths. I will always remember him stepping over Stevie after making the tackle. I didn't like it.

Fair enough, you make your challenge, you injure someone, that happens all the time in football. But we felt Shane was disrespectful. He might not have meant it that way, but that's how we viewed it within our dressing-room. And it certainly added to our motivation whenever we faced Rovers after that incident.

The league game was a really tight, intense affair with plenty of heated challenges coming in from both sides. You could see that they were eager to stop us winning the league. It was only a couple of seasons earlier that Stephen Kenny, less than a year into the job, got the bullet at Tallaght Stadium. It was a strange move by Rovers at the time. He didn't get anywhere near the time needed to make his mark on a squad that had been well-established under Michael O'Neill.

The game was still scoreless heading into the final 15 minutes, when Rovers won a penalty. A defeat would have been really damaging to our title prospects. Ryan Brennan stepped up to the spot. He struck the ball. It flew over the crossbar. Relief. Not long afterwards, the final whistle went. It was a crucial point.

Next up was a trip to Bray Wanderers. This was a typical evening in the Carlisle Grounds – stinking wet and windy. They went 1-0 up. David Cassidy in the first minute. We weren't switched on. Dean Zambra latched onto Jake Kelly's cross, his shot was saved by Peter Cherrie and Cassidy was quickest to react. That's how it stayed until half-time, despite us having most of the play. Just before Patrick Hoban equalised, they hit the crossbar through Dean Kelly. In those conditions, it could well have been curtains at 2-0 down. But three minutes after that opportunity, we got the goal we desperately needed when Hoban finished from Darren Meenan's cross.

We pushed for a winner and left ourselves exposed as a result. A late goal-line clearance from Richie Towell denied Bray a winning goal. The draw was enough to keep them in the Premier Division.

For us, the result meant we were one point behind Cork City in the table going into the final game of the season. Two draws in-a-row put our title hopes in serious trouble.

Nothing less than a win against the Leesiders on the final day of the season would do.

▪ CHAPTER 10 ▪

THIS MIGHT COME as a surprise, but the week leading up to the biggest game of most of our careers – the visit of Cork City – was one of the most enjoyable of my career. There were no nerves.

We were all buzzing in training, which was strange, seeing as we had just messed up in the previous two games, blowing a really strong position. But there we were, bouncing around in training, having the craic, but working really hard too.

We were one hundred percent certain we would get the win we needed.

In the dressing-room, we were convinced it would have made no odds if we were a point ahead of Cork. It would not have changed a single thing in terms of our approach to the game. We only knew how to set up to win games. We were going for three points against Cork regardless of whether we were ahead of them or behind.

THE EXCITEMENT AND confidence lasted throughout that week.

There was no arrogance or cockiness, but we knew we were a better side.

Much better. We had proved that when we beat them 4-0 at Oriel Park earlier in the season, and again at Turner's Cross. Now we were back on our own patch – we were in no mood to throw away the league title in front of our own fans. The temporary stand was up and the game was quickly selling out.

Match night arrived and we took to the pitch in full belief that we could dictate the game from start to finish. I had lots of the ball in the first-half, and had the freedom to do some damage with it. They went man-for-man with our three in the middle, as they had done in all previous encounters.

Anticipating their game-plan, I told our midfielders to spread out whenever I had the ball. The Cork midfielders were literally acting as their shadows, so every time they split, I was able to roll the ball to Patrick Hoban's feet. Straight from central defence to centre-forward. A clear path.

It was like the Red Sea parting right in front of me. They were so preoccupied with stopping our middle three from playing that they left the door open for a more direct precision route into their final third.

In saying all that, Cork still managed to create some decent openings in the first-half. Garry Buckley and Billy Dennehy went close in the early stages. We lost Chris Shields after just 10 minutes to injury, but Ruaidhri Higgins wasn't a bad replacement to come off the bench. Their best chance of the half fell to Mark O'Sullivan.

The ball fizzed in low and he sent his effort wide. He should have scored. He made a great dart across the box and it was an excellent ball in.

It was a real let-off for us. It was 0-0 at the break.

While the game – and the title race – was on a knife-edge, we were calm in the dressing-room. We knew what we had to do and we were confident we would get the breakthrough. And we didn't have long to wait.

Within minutes of the restart, Higgins played the ball to Richie Towell. I'm still not certain if he controlled it with his hand, but he sent it on to Stevie O'Donnell and the skipper scuttled his shot along the ground and past Mark McNulty in the Cork goal. What a moment for Stevie, in his first start in half-a-year. As he wheeled off towards The Shed in celebration, I was one of the first to get to him. The feeling was unbelievable. It was relief, sure, but we knew this moment would come.

We also knew how Cork would react, that they would try to bombard us with long balls. I was in a war with Mark O'Sullivan, the two of us battering each other for the entire game. It got even more intense after Stevie's goal.

Throughout the second-half we kept our focus, everyone reminding one another to concentrate, to stay switched on at all times. Just one slip up could cost us the title. I don't remember too many specifics after our opening goal.

Not until the 82nd minute anyway.

We got a set-piece. Defending a lead in these circumstances, many teams might have kept their centre-backs in their own half at this point. But not Dundalk. I raced up to their penalty area in anticipation of the delivery. The ball came in.

John Mountney helped it on. It bounced to me... *Touch... Place...* and I watched as the ball sailed into the corner of the net. That was it!

We were going to be champions.

I'd dreamed of a moment like this my entire life, scoring a crucial goal like that. It was all part of my visualisation technique ahead of matches. I'd see myself putting the ball in the net, keeping a clean sheet, winning the game, scoring the winner and celebrating. And on that glorious night it came true.

Well, everything but the stylish celebration. A brutal celebration, more like. It was another one of those moments where I didn't have a clue what to do. I started to run towards The Shed. Then I remembered, mam and Bronagh were probably in the main stand. So I did a 90-degree turn and raced in that direction.

There is a picture of me running and pointing up to the sky. I thought of my dad at that moment. *That one's for you, dad.*

Halfway over to the main stand, I realised I didn't have a clue where mam and Bronagh were. It's mad the thoughts that go through your head in a moment like that. At one stage, I was thinking... *Jaysus, this must be the first time in my life that the lads can't catch me!*

I laugh anytime I watch that celebration back. I guess things like that never came naturally to me, knowing how to react to scoring. I can't really explain the buzz that takes over, the lack of control. It's one of the greatest feelings in the world. But I am glad that I thought of my dad in that moment.

That's something I'll treasure for the rest of my life.

WE STILL HAD to keep our heads for another eight minutes, plus whatever stoppage time referee Neil Doyle was going to add on. *Back to work.*

Forget about that goal, just make sure Cork don't get one.

They had already brought on another striker in Rob Lehane. They kept pumping the ball forward. But we held out. Then the final whistle came.

Then the tears. I think I embraced Peter Cherrie and Andy Boyle first. I saw my mam and some of my mates, so I went up to them and had a moment there.

Then I spotted Bronagh and headed up to her.

This is what it's all about. Fast forward six years to the Emirates for what should be one of the biggest games of my life, a Europa League group stage tie with Arsenal. Don't get me wrong, it was massive, one for the highlights reel, but there was something missing. It just wasn't half the occasion it should have been.

You create these moments not just for yourself, but for everyone associated with the club. You do it for the fans, the people who are there long before any player arrives and long after they leave.

There was such a great sense of togetherness on occasions such as that first title win in 2014, or a big European night. You want to give the people who support you through thick and thin something to remember. We didn't have any fans at the Emirates and it felt a little hollow as a result. But that night in Oriel? One of the best of my life, because I got to share it with the people for whom I cared the most… and the people who cared the most about the club.

AFTER THE TROPHY presentation and the celebrations in the dressing-room, we stayed a while at Oriel Park before heading into town and then back to the Crowne Plaza, where we were booked in for the night.

At five in the morning, I had a mad idea.

One of my best mates was getting married in Glasgow later that day. Months earlier, I had booked a flight that morning for myself and Bronagh. Just in case. But I had warned my mate that I might not make it, that there was a strong chance we'd be playing a title decider the night before his big day.

And so it transpired.

Yet in the early hours of the morning – and with lots of drink on board – I turned to Bronagh and said, 'Let's get ready, we're heading to the airport in an hour!'

The flight was due to take off around eight o'clock. I had a suitcase in the car, thinking if we'd missed out on the title, I probably would have gone straight to bed and could have done with a day in Glasgow. We raced up to our room.

Poor Bronagh had all but lost her voice from all the singing and shouting, so she was in no position to protest. Not that she would have tried to stop me. That's one of the best things about us as a couple, she doesn't mind all the spontaneous stuff that I throw at her. Or did, before we had kids!

We ordered a taxi.

I tried to get 40 minutes' sleep while she was doing her hair and getting ready. We got to the airport and I was still well-on. I can only imagine what everyone else thought when they saw me, club tracksuit still on and a title-winning medal around my neck! We went through security. *Time for another pint,* I thought.

We bumped into a few of my mates who were travelling over on the same flight. One pint, two pints… that was basically us on the drink for the day.

We had been going out for around a year at this stage, Bronagh and I, but between dad falling ill and passing away, and then getting straight back into the football, she hadn't a chance to meet many of my friends. So there she was, with her voice practically gone, meeting loads of the lads and their partners for the first time. The poor woman was sitting there while I was jumping around the place on cloud nine, dancing like mad.

We were on it for the night, but I was determined to catch a flight back home the next morning. I wanted to get back to the title-winning celebrations, which were still in full flight in Dundalk. Somehow, we dragged ourselves to the airport, only to find out that our flight had been delayed.

We plonked ourselves down next to the gate, but that was probably the worst thing we could have done. We were like zombies, eyes glazed over. We were so tired that we didn't notice people boarding our flight. They didn't call out our names, so by the time we approached the desk we were told that the gate was closed.

We argued our case, told them that we were sitting there the whole time. We were either going to convince them to let us through or we were going to get chucked out of the airport. For a while, it looked as though the latter would happen.

I probably wasn't being very diplomatic. 'You didn't call us on the intercom', I said. 'You never changed the screen to say our flight was closing.'

I could see the queue of people waiting to board the plane just 15 yards past us. I was desperate to get on the flight, because I didn't want to miss out on the celebrations back at home. You don't often win these battles, but somehow we convinced the staff at the gate to let us through. We got home and were back in the thick of the celebrations that afternoon. They went on for a week.

The night we won the title, the wedding and the next few days in Dundalk… somehow I made it through that time without Bronagh reconsidering our relationship!

• CHAPTER 11 •

THE 2014 TITLE celebrations were epic.

It's a good thing we had a few months off to recover. On that occasion, it was the right time to let rip. But we weren't always such solid judges of the appropriate time to party. After our trip to Luxembourg earlier that season, Stephen Kenny slapped a ban on us staying overnight after European away games.

Why? On the day of the game, I went for a walk around the town with Andy Boyle. At that stage, we didn't know if we would be let out for a few drinks after the match. Stephen would be strict enough, but surely we'd get the opportunity to head out for one or two pints?

I didn't mind the fact that he was quite uncompromising when it came to alcohol. A lot of people think it's overboard, that we should be given the freedom to let our hair down. But that can lead to problems, to a culture of unprofessionalism. I was delighted to be working under a manager who – unless it was the right place and the right time – had a zero tolerance policy towards boozing.

But our first European away game as a group? A nine-day gap between that game and our next? No flight home until the next afternoon? Sure, what harm would it do to have a few drinks in a quiet town in Luxembourg?

NOT SURE WHETHER we'd get the green light from the gaffer, Boyler and I popped into a nearby shop and bought a naggin and a few cans, and we hid them in a bush outside our hotel. And we weren't the only ones.

Others smuggled their drink back into the hotel in their gear bags, walking past Stephen in the lobby hoping he wouldn't hear the bottles clanking off each other.

After the game, which we won comfortably, we went to Stevie O'Donnell, the skipper, and asked him to approach Stephen about a night out. We were all sitting around, wondering if we would get the green light. Eventually we were told we could go, but that we had to be back by midnight.

Harry Taaffe and the club doc were to go with us. They were placed in charge of getting us back to the hotel before curfew.

This was a Tuesday night in Luxembourg, the place was like a ghost town. But we had great craic together. A call was made back to the hotel and the midnight curfew was pushed out to 1.30am.

The drinks were flowing, we were buzzing from the result and lads were well on it by now. It was 2am and we were still out, but the bars were all closing. We were out on the street. It was carnage.

Lads everywhere.

Someone gave me a little push, just a bit of messing. But I staggered back a little and fell onto a taxi behind me. It was an old Mercedes. My backside landed on the Mercedes sign on the bonnet and knocked it off. I turned around and a taxi driver got out of his car. He was going mad.

I had to take out whatever cash I had and give it to him.

Poor Harry was trying to round everybody up to get us back to the hotel, but he might as well have been herding sheep. He'd get a group of us together, have us penned in, but then he'd have to go for another few lads and the first group would be off running around again. Two of the lads had their tops off.

Meanwhile, I led another little gang on the hunt for a chipper. Of course, nowhere in the entire country of Luxembourg was open and serving food at this hour of the morning. So the poor doctor chased me down the street, me shouting back at him, 'There's no way I'm getting into a taxi until I get some food'.

Eventually, and I still don't know how, we ended up back at the hotel.

We woke up the next morning with heads thumping. There was a video going around of one lad looking like the Undertaker from WWE… lying on his bed and then suddenly sitting up, just like 'The Dead Man' after he'd been knocked to the canvas.

We got down to the lobby in time to see the hotel manager lose it with some of the club staff. We wondered what was going on? It turned out a bit of damage was done in one room when one of the lads smashed his head off the toilet seat.

And then there was poor old Steve Williams' bill.

A load of steak dinners and drink – expensive bottles of wine – had been ordered and charged to Willo, our goalkeeping coach's room. Stephen Kenny was going mad. But we could barely contain our laughter.

Eventually, it was all straightened out and we got on the bus.

We were flying home from a German airport. It was a bit of a distance away, and it wasn't the easiest bus journey to get through, given the varying degrees of hangovers throughout the squad. *What else could go wrong?*

Didn't the bus driver take us to the wrong airport! Everyone was going ballistic at the poor fella. He had to turn around and take us to the right airport. Stephen sat up at the top of the bus, fuming.

We never stayed over after a European away game again.

Not intentionally, anyway. We did lobby for an overnighter after the final 2016 group game against Maccabi Tel Aviv, but the plan was to fly out immediately after the game. Somehow we missed our slot and had to stay over. We had a few drinks that night. But if you were ever wondering why there was such resistance to us staying on after the Tel Aviv game in 2016, I'd imagine it had a lot to do with that night of carnage two years earlier.

WE'VE HAD SOME mad nights out though.

We worked our backsides off to achieve the success we had at Dundalk, but it certainly wasn't a case of all work and no play. Even the most serious, committed and professional (and I'd like to think of myself as being in that category) among us liked to party when the time was right. And at that early stage of our time at Oriel Park, the mid-season break in 2014 seemed like an appropriate opportunity to blow off some steam.

So a group of us planned a four-night trip to Portugal.

David McMillan was one of the travelling party. The night before we headed off, we played St Pat's at Oriel Park. During the game, Davy gave Derek Foran a half-shove. It was nothing really, but Degsey hit the deck, rolling around holding his face. The referee sent Davy off.

The game finished 0-0.

We had beaten them 4-1 on their turf two months earlier, so it wasn't the result we were after. Afterwards, Stephen Kenny stormed into the dressing-room. He laid into Davy over his red card. Then Davy delivered a line that had the rest of the squad a stitches.

'Stephen... I am absolutely devastated.'

It was the voice, the tone and the fact that he really was devastated that made it comedy gold.

We headed off the next day to Albufeira and Davy was in the depths of depression. He was in rotten form, as you would expect. Getting sent off like that, it's not a nice feeling. It puts you on a real downer because you feel like you've let the team down.

The plan was to snap him out of his misery – and no better man to do that than Marc Griffin. He celebrated his birthday in Portugal. On his big day, we kitted him out with an armband and told him, 'Right, you're captain for the day... whatever you say goes'. In hindsight, that probably wasn't the best idea.

Griff was great craic, but he could be a nut job!

But that was the rule for the day. We based ourselves in a bar at the top of the strip in Montechoro from 11am, playing shot roulette with rums, Aftershocks, absinthe, sambuca and a couple of waters in the middle of it. We were rotten by lunchtime. Griff had us doing shuttle runs across the road, from kerb to kerb, or doing push-ups in the middle of the street.

That's not easy when you are struggling to even stand up straight.

Daryl Horgan is one of the most dedicated professionals I have ever played with. He is so serious about his training, about what he puts into his body. It's no wonder he has made it to the senior international side. But for those four days he decided to go toe-to-toe with Griff. Some of the other lads, myself included, would get to bed for a bit of a kip, but others were determined to drink right through the night.

Some of the other lads, Chris Shields, Pat Hoban and John Mountney were over with their partners. They were staying an hour away, enjoying a far more relaxing break. The plan was to meet them the evening of Griff's birthday for a bit of food and a few drinks, but by the time they arrived we were in rag order. We could see them saying to each other... 'Holy shit, what's going on here?'

Poor old Mounts wasn't really a drinker. This was his first night on the lash. So, two pints in and he was almost as hammered as the early-starters.

We were having a great night, but the mood quickly soured when we returned to our apartment. I was first in and saw that the sliding door to the balcony had been forced open. The bathroom was a mess too. The shower curtain had been ripped from its rail. Deodorants, hair gels and aftershave bottles had been thrown on the floor. I raced into my room to look for the cash that I'd left behind. It wasn't there. Nor was my watch. I yelled out to the rest of them... 'We've been robbed.'

'Ah for f**k sake,' said Mounts.

We rang down for security. Within minutes they knocked on our door. I can only imagine how incoherent we were, with everyone shouting over each other. We were all messy, telling security that *this* was missing... *that* was missing.

They went around the apartment, examining everything. Eventually they left and said they would get back to us later in the morning.

It was just after 4am, so I decided to get into bed for a few hours' sleep. As I was getting ready, I came across my cash and watch. I'd just forgotten where I'd left it. Mortified, I didn't say a word. The poor security guards were probably back in their office at this stage sifting through hours of CCTV footage.

I woke up a few hours later and Mounts was looking pretty sheepish. He sat down and explained the 'break in'.

He told us how he came back to put his missus to bed. She'd had enough and needed to get some sleep. But as he wasn't staying in the apartment, he couldn't get in. He hadn't thought to ask for a key. So he climbed over our ground floor balcony railing and managed to crack open the sliding door.

Mounts went into the bathroom to try and splash some water on his face. He lost his balance and grabbed onto the shower curtain, taking it and everything that had been on the sink with him.

That explained why the place looked like it had been thrashed. A broken door, the bathroom a mess, stuff thrown everywhere...

Mounts said something along the lines of, 'Ah Jesus lads, I feel terrible'. His first night drinking and he caused carnage!

We came back from the holiday and were straight back into training. We only had five days off during the two-week break, but if Stephen Kenny had his way we wouldn't have had a single day away. He knew what we were capable of doing.

I missed the first day back as I had a chest infection – no doubt brought on by our exploits in Portugal. So I didn't have to do the dreaded bleep test, which was mandatory any time we came back from a break. I got over just in time to see Daryl Horgan sitting down with a towel over his head, and his head in his hands.

He looked like death warmed up. Remember, he was one of the fittest lads in the group. But he dropped out after only seven rounds. He was knackered. Next up was a training session on the grass pitch behind Oriel Park and poor Horgs was horrendous.

He couldn't kick the ball.

Anytime he tried to dribble, the ball would bounce off his knee or shins. He wasn't used to the kind of antics we got up to in Albufeira and was in a heap for the rest of the week.

The rest of us couldn't stop laughing.

Stephen Kenny didn't see the funny side though. I was 27 at the time but was one of the oldest in the squad, so Stephen turned around to me and asked, 'What did youse do to Daryl? He's absolutely f**ked!'

Those few days in Portugal – and the aftermath – really ate away at Daryl. He was disappointed in himself and he really beat himself up over it, because he was always such a dedicated professional. He never shied away from hard work, whether on the training pitch, in the gym or even when it came to how he lived his life… what he ate and drank (or didn't drink!). He was the best in the country as far as we were concerned, but he was never happy with himself.

He always looked for more from his performances. Horgs got better and better during his time at Oriel Park. And I'm convinced that his few days of boozing in Portugal contributed to his progression as a footballer!?

There was an impression out there that we were a team of angels, real good guys, no messing. We did work our backsides off and we earned every piece of silverware that we won. But when we let our hair down, we left it all on the dance floor, just as we left it all on the pitch week after week.

PART **FOUR**

A Higher Calling

I made friends for life in the Dundalk dressing-room, and I also found a brilliant central defensive teammate In Andy Boyle (above, before the FAI Cup final against Cork City in 2016). We became a dream partnership on the field.

Getting to captain Dundalk was a proud moment for me (left, I lead out the team against Rosenborg in the Champions League second qualifying round in 2016). Everything we achieved was down to the excellent management skills of Stephen Kenny (left, with the league and cup trophies on our homecoming to Dundalk in 2018).

The highs and lows in football are always present. I celebrate with Dane Massey against Cork City at Turner's Cross, but feel the pain (above). And once a team tastes that winning feeling it never wants to stop... I lift the SSE Airtricity League Premier Division trophy alongside Patrick Hoban and the lads (below) at the end of the 2019 season.

▪ CHAPTER 12 ▪

THE WRONG TRAINING top and 'biscuit night'. Just some of the memories of the time I finally realised my FAI Cup final dream.

November 8, 2015.

We beat Cork City to win the league and cup double. We had already seen them off by 11 points in the race for the Premier Division title.

I don't remember much about the cup final itself, other than the fact that it was a tense affair, a tough game to watch. That's largely because Cork's game-plan was to try and stop us. From an attacking point of view we weren't at our best. But we were solid throughout.

They didn't look like scoring, but they took us all the way to extra-time. That's when our class won out in the end. Richie Towell scored the winner.

It had to be Richie. He went from strength-to-strength that year. He was phenomenal. Richie had already scored the crucial goal against Shamrock Rovers to clinch the league. When the ball landed at his feet in extra-time in the cup final, just outside the six-yard box, he wasn't going to miss.

Others were out on their feet at that stage, but thanks to his focus on fitness and conditioning, he always had the potential to make an impact at any stage in a game. Once he scored, we just had to see the game out. While I don't remember much else about the game, I've got great memories of everything that happened before and after my first FAI Cup final.

CIARAN KILDUFF JOINED Dundalk from St Patrick's Athletic midway through the 2015 campaign. Before St Pat's, he was at Shamrock Rovers, and during his time at Tallaght Stadium he went on loan to Cork City.

It was the week of the big Aviva Stadium showdown against the Leesiders and we were training on the grass pitch beside Oriel Park. While this was only a few years ago, off-field operations at Dundalk were still fairly basic. We still had to do things such as bringing our training gear home and washing it ourselves.

We were in Umbro kit, as was the case with most League of Ireland sides. From club to club, the tops were pretty much the same, bar the crest. So there we were, in the middle of our warm-up, when Killer took off his sweatshirt. It didn't take people long to spot the crest. It was a Cork City training shirt!

He was running around, in the shadow of Oriel Park, wearing our cup final opponents' top. Killer couldn't get his sweatshirt back on quickly enough. I don't think Stephen Kenny spotted it. If he did, he certainly didn't let on.

Killer still had the top at home from his time at Turner's Cross and grabbed it on his way out the door, not bothering to check the crest.

Getting to the final was a dream come true. After two years of heartache in the FAI Cup with Dundalk, progress to the decider was fairly straightforward this time around. We beat Shelbourne 5-0, Galway United 4-1, Sligo Rovers 4-0 and Longford Town 2-0. As with our first league win 12 months earlier, winning the FAI Cup for the first time was a special feeling.

The excitement in Dundalk was unrivalled in the week leading up to the final. It was even bigger than the build-up to the title decider a year earlier. Direct trains were put on by Irish Rail to Lansdowne Road, buses were organised and people were harassing their bosses, looking for time off work the next day, just in case the celebrations that Sunday night went into extra-time!

Family and friends could talk about little else. All roads led to the Aviva.

Then there were the cup final suits. We weren't on massive money at the time, maybe €500-a-week max. So it was a real treat to get a fitted suit from one of the shops in town. Then there was the buzz of getting the suits delivered and staying overnight in a nice hotel beforehand.

It was hard to get much sleep the night before the final.

Again, it was all about visualisation for me. I had lots to think about that night. I knew what was in store for me, coming up against Mark O'Sullivan once again.

So I visualised winning headers, being strong, winning shoulders, getting in little digs, some sneaky pushes. One piece of visualisation that hasn't yet worked for me at the Aviva is scoring. I've played it over and over in my head, the ball coming in, me rising above everyone else… GOAL. Then the celebration. If you visualise something, you'll want it even more. You chase that feeling.

My head was racing the night before the final. I had to calm myself down, pull myself back a little. I needed to get some sleep.

Another big part of the night before the game was the craic with the lads. This was 'biscuit night'. A load of us rambled into one bedroom, kettles working overtime, everyone with their own cup, a teabag and a bit of grub, which was thrown into the middle of the bed. There were jellies, biscuits, chocolates…

The lads were all sitting round having chats, slagging each other, slagging the opposition. Well, slaughtering the opposition!

We woke up on the morning of the final, had breakfast together, got suited and booted, and hopped on the bus to the game. That first trip to the Aviva Stadium was unforgettable. The fans lined the streets outside the ground, cheering and banging on the side of our bus as we drove past. We were heading to a fantastic stadium, the kind that you dream of playing in as a child.

Everything about it was state-of-the-art… the dressing rooms, the facilities, the pitch. I remember jogging out for our warm-up and there were loads of fans already in their seats. The pitch was immaculate. Then it was back into the dressing-room for one last team-talk, before lining up in the tunnel next to the Cork City players. We could hear both sets of fans.

They were in full voice. We were used to playing in front of 3,500 on a good night at Oriel Park, so to see more than 25,000 was mind-blowing, as was the roar when we emerged from the tunnel. There were flares everywhere, smoke, fans wherever you looked. The Dundalk supporters were going nuts. It was early November and some of them were there with their tops off. The support we got in every FAI Cup final was consistently brilliant.

Lining up for the first time for the national anthem, shaking hands with the President, knowing it was going out live on TV… spine-tingling. I tried to absorb as much of the atmosphere as possible. Once the ceremonial stuff was out of the way, there could be no more distractions from the task at hand. So before tuning out of the atmosphere and onto the game, I had a quick look around for my family and friends. They were all located in one block. I looked up and saw a load of my mates there… 10 or 15 lads, all wearing a big topless photo of me on t-shirts, with love hearts all around it. They were close enough to the dugout that the backroom staff and substitutes had a great view of them.

I had to fork out for 50 or 60 tickets for the final – at €10 a pop. You don't really mind spending that kind of cash on family and friends for an occasion like the FAI Cup final. Having them there was part of the joy and buzz of the day. Although by the end of it all, my head was absolutely wrecked at having to get all those tickets. I put a system in place for all subsequent finals, where requests had to be in a week before the game.

I had to knock it on the head. People were ringing, asking for tickets, looking to sit in certain sections… when I should have been concentrating on preparing for the final. But I wanted to accommodate every single request.

AFTER THE FINAL whistle and the trophy presentation, I made my way over to friends and family. We had a moment together before I rejoined the lads on the pitch, as we walked around together with the trophy.

It was a phenomenal feeling. The celebrations moved into the dressing-room. Then we showered, changed and boarded the bus back to Dundalk – via Tesco in Ringsend. We all bundled into the supermarket and loaded up on drink for the journey home. It wasn't long before a sing-song broke out.

No better man for such an occasion, especially when celebrations are in full flow, than Stephen Kenny. Once the singing starts, you are guaranteed to find the gaffer right in the thick of things. He'll have been dragged in… but then he'll be banging out his party pieces. He does a great version of *Something Inside So Strong*. He's a good singer; mad into his music. Another Kenny favourite band would be Arctic Monkeys. The lads all loved it whenever Stephen broke into song. When the time was right – and he always seemed to know when it was appropriate to let his hair down – Stephen was great craic.

I remember buying tickets for U2 at Croke Park in July 2017. The closer we got to the gig, I realised we'd have a game against Shamrock Rovers the following night. I was gutted, I couldn't justify going to a gig ahead of such a big game. But Stephen was dying to go. He was the manager, he didn't have to get the same rest that we needed ahead of a match. So I sold my tickets to Stephen. I think they were €300 each! I had to show him the receipt.

'I'm not ripping you off, gaffer, honest.' The tickets were like gold dust. He had a great night at Croker, while I had an early night at home.

I've often thought he'd be a good interviewee for someone like Dave Fanning, someone who would steer him away from football and towards his passion for music. He'd be great for a *Desert Island Discs*-style show.

THE FAI CUP win sealed the club's first double in nearly 30 years. Winning back-to-back titles was sweet, but where we won the Premier Division was even sweeter.

It has always been an obsession of mine, trying to figure out where and when we could win the league. Even as far back as when the fixtures would come out, I'd look at the first few games and then flick ahead to the final few weeks. I wouldn't care too much at that stage for anything in between. As far as I was concerned, we would be in the running for the title, no matter what.

So where could we wrap it up? Against Cork?

Bray Wanderers? Galway United?

Or against Shamrock Rovers? Away to Shamrock Rovers?

A trip to Tallaght was pencilled in tantalisingly close to the end of the season. Our fourth last league game of the campaign. With so much needle between the two sides, with Stephen Kenny's sacking still fresh in the memory, winning the league in Tallaght Stadium was the dream scenario.

We were a strong group, we all stuck together. If you attacked one, you attacked everyone. And we all knew what it would mean to Stephen after the brief time he had at Rovers. And so it came to pass. Once we realised that we could actually win it in Tallaght, a few weeks before the game that was all we could think about. We just needed to pick up results in the weeks before that game. And so we did, winning 2-0 at home to the Hoops, drawing against Sligo Rovers, thumping Drogheda United 6-0 and winning away to Limerick.

There was a great buzz in Tallaght that night.

Stephen's passion and his team talks would come through even more so than usual on an occasion such as a title decider. That night the gaffer was even more worked up than normal. You'd swear he was getting ready to tog out himself. But like Stephen, I could only watch on as the game unfolded. I was suspended, so I had to make do with a seat in the stand. I was gutted that I couldn't play.

The game was taking place just down the road from my first house in Tallaght. A load of my mates, huge Rovers fans, still live around there. I'd love to have been on the pitch that night. But on the bright side, I was down near the away support and the atmosphere was unreal.

Danny North gave Rovers the lead, but Richie Towell – *who else that season?* – scored a penalty with five minutes to go. That goal, and Cork City's 1-1 draw against Drogheda United, confirmed our status as champions for the second season in-a-row.

The feeling we got thanks to the dramatic way we won it in 2014 will never be beaten, but winning it in Tallaght was still a brilliant feeling. We always knew we could do it. We were that confident, we were that consistent, picking up win after win after win, that there was never any doubt in our heads. It wasn't arrogance.

We knew that we had to work hard for every single point. But we were also having fun. We were playing football with smiles on our faces, even going into big games like that. Once again, there were no nerves.

We hopped on the coach afterwards and headed away from the ground. I remember stopping off in my 'local' in Dublin, The Blue Haven where my mate who is manager sorted us out. The off-licences had closed, so we cleared the place out of bottled beer and polished them off by the time we got back up the M1.

ASIDE FROM WINNING the league where we did, we were also motivated by the desire to wrap it up as soon as possible. We'd won our FAI Cup semi-final the week before the Rovers game, so the closer we got to the final, the less time we would have to celebrate our success.

With three league games remaining, we were able to give it a good lash. If we'd left it until the last day of the season, it would have been early to bed and straight into cup final mode the next morning. So we pretty much went on the beer for a week and then got our heads on for the last few weeks and our trip to the Aviva.

For all the hard work and professionalism in our team, when we partied and had the craic, there was no holding back. It was nuts. It would go on for days. Nothing, not a single trophy win, was ever taken for granted. Everything was celebrated.

The mentality at Dundalk was, once we won something it was in the past… it was all about winning more and more. We never got tired of winning. We absolutely loved it. But we always made the time to mark our successes with one hell of a party!

The hunger to keep on winning was something we all had as individuals, but it was fuelled by the manager. Stephen Kenny was a world-class motivator, such a great and relentless driver of this side. He was always going on about creating a legacy, about not being happy with just one title… or two titles. He always had us thinking about the next league or the next trophy.

He would constantly talk to us about breaking records.

If something popped up in the media – like we were X goals away from a season best or Y points away from a league record – he would encourage us to go out and beat it. If we scored five goals, he wanted six the next week.

He wanted to break the record for clean sheets, for final points tallies.

There was no ceiling to what we could achieve as far as he was concerned. This drive for uniqueness gathered momentum. Every year our standards rose, the demands from the dugout grew. It was brilliant motivation.

Stephen would set goals for individual players. He'd tell the likes of Daryl Horgan, or Michael Duffy after him, that, 'People are paying to watch you, they are coming in just to see you play, you are electric… so exciting!' He'd say, 'They are paying their hard-earned cash just to see you, so don't disappoint them, go out and entertain them!'

And he was right, punters were paying in every week to see players such as Horgs and Duffy do what only they could do. And with Stephen's words ringing in their ears, they'd be out there going on mazy dribbles, trying to give the crowd the kind of entertainment they came to see. When you look back at Daryl Horgan in 2015, and especially in '16, he was ridiculous. I didn't appreciate how good he was at the time, because we were going from game-to-game. But he was outstanding. That's because Stephen had this way of getting the best out of players, of getting into their heads and helping them reach their potential.

I LEARNED A lot from watching and listening to Stephen. He'd start off a team talk and you'd be wondering… *Where is he going with this?* But by the end you'd be so motivated to get out onto the pitch and give the performance of your life. We loved playing under him. His enthusiasm was infectious. There was nothing false about it. The joy he had when we came off the pitch after a big win, he'd make you feel 10-feet tall.

2015 was a big year for the team. Ronan Finn came to us and he was outstanding. He brought something different to our midfield. But we were yet to see the best of him. Finner saved that for 2016. Gary Rogers came that year too. What a legend he turned out to be. He brought a huge degree of experience to the side. Stephen Kenny always made sure he signed great fellas, really nice guys as well as excellent footballers. Shane Grimes also came back to the club that year. He was another great lad with an incredible attitude.

That was one of the keys to our success. That's why it was so enjoyable to be in this squad. A good attitude off the pitch and serious dedication on the pitch – they were two boxes that had to be ticked before you could sign for Stephen Kenny's Dundalk.

Ciaran Kilduff joined midway through that season and he slotted in without any hassle. Straightaway he was one of the fittest in the group. His cousin Paul Robinson is one of the country's top runners and Ciaran would always do a bit of training with him. Killer's 5k runs were unbelievable.

Then there was Finner, who was a machine on the dreaded bleep test.

Of course, we didn't know it at the time, but this was all building up to what we achieved in 2016. We couldn't have done it without the kind of characters Stephen signed. He did bring in some lads with unbelievable ability, but they didn't have the attitude. Personality mattered as much as talent.

It was great to see Stephen add to the squad, because in 2014 we were operating off a very small group of players. That wouldn't have been sustainable as things progressed. Looking back now at the additions he made in the run-up to 2016, and seeing the work-rate, the fitness and character he added to the side, it's little wonder we achieved what we did. Adding lads like the ones mentioned above to the great dressing-room we already had meant no one could let their standards drop.

It's easy to see now what Stephen Kenny was doing.

IT WAS SCORELESS at Oriel Park against BATE Borisov.

Five minutes to go. We were 2-1 down on aggregate.

I turned to the dugout, caught Stephen Kenny's attention and asked if I should go up top. *Let's send up the big man, test them with a few balls into the box,* I thought.

It's the old Irish way, tried and tested by generations before this side. But he shook his head, told me to stay in my position. That just wasn't his way.

It was the first time I truly understood his philosophy, and that he was a man of unshakable principle. We always stuck to Stephen's way of playing and it served us well. In the League of Ireland, we faced that scenario on plenty of occasions – a goal down, time running out. And on the majority of those occasions, sticking to our principles worked out for us. But this was a different calibre of opponent.

Stephen wanted us to stick to what we were doing. He believed that was our best chance to score. It didn't happen for us against BATE in 2015, but there were so many other occasions when the crucial goal arrived.

I might have believed that throwing a big centre-half up top for the last few minutes and lumping the ball into him was the way to go, but Stephen had a different view. Sure, we might have scored. But equally they were so sharp that they could have exploited the gap in our defence and put the tie out of reach.

That moment, when he shook his head, has stuck with me to this day. It marks Stephen out as different to every other manager I have played under. Other gaffers would tell you to get up there and hope for a lucky bounce or break, but not Stephen. The game kind of petered out without any chances of note being created in the closing moments and that was the end of our 2015 European campaign.

One round and we were out. There was no safety net this time. No parachute into the Europa League qualifiers.

It was clear from the start of the second-leg at Oriel Park that BATE were happy to settle for a scoreless draw. All they were interested in was shutting us out, holding onto their first-leg advantage. They took one look at the pitch and decided that they'd done enough in their home game one week earlier.

THE STADIUM IN Borisov was class. It was miles out from the city in the middle of the woods. It was my first time heading over to that side of the world and I found it a drab old place, but fascinating nonetheless. We were in Croatia the year before, but this was really the beginning of me exploring different places through football.

While we don't get too much time to sightsee on European away days, the travel and experience is one of the perks of the job. At Dundalk, we have always made the most of whatever free time we are given.

There was always a group interested in checking out the sights, the architecture, the museums and cathedrals. Most of the squad was fascinated by that sort of stuff. Not that there was much to look at in Borisov, but the stadium was amazing.

They had an outstanding player in Vitali Rodionov, a Belarus international who had scored 10 goals for his country by the time we came up against him. He was a real handful... strong, quick movement. His biggest contribution that night, though, was when he dropped Dane Massey with an off-the-ball headbutt. We had clear footage of the incident. The late Harry Taaffe was videoing the game and he caught it on camera.

The referee hadn't spotted it, so we sent the footage to UEFA. We were convinced he would be suspended for the second-leg. He wasn't. You'd always hear how UEFA's big decisions would never favour the small club in an argument, but this was our first time experiencing a footballing injustice on this scale. The small clubs never get their way.

We conceded early on in Borisov, despite making a good start. Even after going behind, we created chances. David McMillan and Dane Massey both went close. We were level just after the half-hour mark – and deservedly so. Richie Towell's shot hit one of their defenders, Daryl Horgan pounced on the loose ball and teed up Davy to finish.

We knew we were doing well when we heard the jeers from the home support. But they got a lucky break shortly after the equaliser and were back in front when a long range shot took a nick off Chris Shields and bounced past Gary Rogers.

That's the way the game ended. A 2-1 defeat away from home, not a bad result. It meant we'd only need one goal at Oriel to progress. This crowd was a level up from Hajduk Split a year earlier. They had some really good players, such as Rodionov and Igor Stasevich. But we knew they wouldn't fancy the pitch at Oriel.

Unfortunately, because they were so good, when they decided that they wanted to play for a scoreless draw there was little we could do about it. The pitch ended up being shite for both sides. It was a sunny day and the surface was bone dry. The ball wouldn't move. It was the old pitch too, so we had to take an extra touch each time, because the ball bobbled all over the place.

It was so slow and sticky, and it didn't do us any favours.

Rodionov, who shouldn't have been playing, almost scored early on. We set out to attack from the start and his sharpness almost led to an away goal. It was one of those *Oh f**k* moments, where myself and Andy Boyle turned to each other and said, 'We need to liven up here'.

We quickly realised that we weren't playing League of Ireland, we were up a couple of notches from that. We got away with that scare and grew into the game. But for all our possession, we couldn't break them down. They were happy to sit and soak up all the pressure, and we couldn't find a way through.

That was when we realised that European football required more than just huff and puff. BATE wanted to stop us creating chances and they had the technical and tactical know-how to pull off their plan. They were able to change their shape at the drop of a hat. And they had a couple of players, such as Rodionov, who were sharper than anyone we'd ever met before.

It was another level, but at the same time we were only a goal away from going through. We always looked to take positives from games, no matter how good or bad the result. And while we were knocked out of Europe, the two games against BATE had us convinced that we were very close to making a big breakthrough. The confidence within the squad matched the mindset of Stephen Kenny. *Why couldn't we learn from this and beat them if we ever met them again?*

So, instead of coming away from that game with negative thoughts, we reminded ourselves how close we were to a big scalp. We couldn't wait for the next year. It was even more motivation to go on and win the league, to get back into the Champions League, and hopefully get a kinder first-round draw.

EVEN IF YOU don't know it at the time, you learn so much from these encounters. As for my own game, I picked up tips on positioning.

I learned how to react when coming up against wingers with greater technical ability… what to do when they'd come inside. The movement and passing of that BATE side simply didn't happen in the League of Ireland.

They created overloads that we struggled to deal with. We faced players who could see a situation developing on the pitch, who could find space out of nowhere and exploit it. Against Split a year earlier, we learned that you get punished in Europe if you are not fully switched on right from the first whistle. However, BATE were another step up. That was the start of a huge learning curve for this group.

And it also started a narrative for Stephen Kenny, one that he often preached in the wake of our European exit that season. *Why can't Dundalk be a BATE Borisov?* Why can't we get into the group stages, create a bigger buzz, build a bigger stadium? He was in Borisov in 2003 with Bohemians when they played in a run-down old ground. Just 12 years later they were the proud occupants of a state-of-the-art arena.

Stephen wanted to create a club in the image of BATE Borisov, he wanted to turn Dundalk into Ireland's version of the Belarus champions. That crept into our own mindsets. We started to ask why we couldn't replicate what BATE Borisov were doing. The biggest and most obvious reason was money. You don't get much help here in terms of funding.

On the pitch we had come up against players who had been in the Champions League group stages, who were seasoned internationals. They were good players, but seeing them up close and playing against them, we could see they had flaws too. We certainly didn't come away from that tie in awe of them. No, we came away thinking we were just one break away from progressing past them and into the second round.

We were convinced we could be as good as them.

That was the main takeaway from Europe in 2015; that on another night we could beat a BATE Borisov. We didn't leave Oriel Park that night ruing a missed opportunity, we left determined that next year we would be better.

It was all building up to 2016. What happened in Europe a year later was no accident. There were no limits to Stephen Kenny's goals. Looking back on it, I reckon he had a sense of what was to come with this group.

▪ CHAPTER 13 ▪

FROM DAY ONE of pre-season training, all eyes were on Europe.

Lessons had been learned against Hajduk Split and BATE Borisov. It was time to put them into practice. We knew we had the ability to do just that.

First, though, came our title defence. There were wins against Bray Wanderers, Finn Harps and Wexford. We were stopped in our tracks by Cork City.

That one hurt. But we bounced back a week later with a 4-0 win away to St Patrick's Athletic. After the Cork defeat we won nine of our next 10 league games. Then, on the eve of the mid-season break, we lost by a single goal once again to our main rivals, this time at Turner's Cross. To make matters worse, Chris Shields was sent off just before half-time.

That defeat was a real kick in the teeth. I was pissed off going into the break. The mood hadn't improved by the time we got back together. We were off to a training camp in Portugal. It was our first warm-weather camp at Dundalk. For many of us it was a first opportunity to live the life of a professional footballer. There was only one problem – we were sharing our hotel with Cork City!

WE WERE BOTH booked into the Colina Verde resort on the Algarve.

They had one side of the hotel – we had the other. We didn't really cross paths too much. Whenever we were training, they'd be at the pool, and vice versa.

Sure, players from both sides met a few times here and there, but we didn't socialise. Dinners were staggered. At this stage in our years-long rivalry, there was plenty of needle between both camps. If a couple of our lads saw some of them, we might quietly slag them off. I'm sure it was the same with them. Personally, I was never too bothered about stuff like that. My direct rival at that time was Mark O'Sullivan. We would spend 90 minutes battering the living daylights out of each other. But once the final whistle went we'd get on great.

We would have a bit of a laugh together as we walked off the pitch. We'd smash each other up, but we'd leave that all behind us after the game. Not everyone could leave it on the pitch, though. Particularly when we've just gone into the break having lost to them for a second time.

On our last night in Portugal, we were allowed out for a few drinks. The coaching staff came too. We all bundled onto a bus, which took us to nearby Vilamoura. At the end of the night, however, things kind of kicked off in the hotel lobby between players from both sides. Michael O'Connor was still only 17 at the time, so he was too young to come out. He was sitting in the lobby by himself when one of the Cork players passed and had too much to say for himself. It sparked a few handbags.

Nothing mad, but things had to be calmed and both sides had to be separated. It didn't amount to much, but it did add to the bite between the two sets of players for the remainder of the season. That incident pissed us off. There was a young lad sitting on his own in the lobby and they were out of order. I was in my room at the time, but I'd love to have been in the thick of it.

The same night, our bus had been scheduled to come back and collect us at a reasonable hour. We were in a nice spot in Vilamoura. After a few drinks, some of the lads suggested getting a bus into Albufeira, which was an hour away. Six or seven lads headed off.

The coaching staff were on the other side of the bar. They weren't aware of the split. Meanwhile, the rest of us stayed on and had great craic. Some of the new lads had to perform the initiation ritual of singing a song. Robbie Benson arrived early that year, but this was his first opportunity to perform in a social setting. He gave a great rendition of *Rock 'n' Roll Kids*.

Eventually, the curfew came and we walked up the lane to where the bus had dropped us off. We stood there waiting, but it was nowhere to be seen. Stephen Kenny noticed we were short a few and wondered where they were.

'Maybe they've gone back already?' someone suggested to him.

We waited a little while longer before someone shouted, 'We'll have to get a taxi'. But taxis seemed to be in short supply. Finally, one passed and we flagged it down. We offered it to Stephen and his staff. 'Gaffer, you get that one.'

As soon as they hopped in and closed the door, we turned around and legged it back down the lane to the pub. We still got back to the hotel at a reasonable hour. As for the lads who went into Albufeira? We were leaving for the airport at 6am the next morning and they arrived in with barely enough time to grab their bags.

That training camp was a huge success for us. I have no doubt that it contributed to our achievements that year at home and abroad. Everything about it; training in the heat, the rise in intensity levels… that week brought us to a new level. We got some really important work done in Portugal. We trained really hard, but we had plenty of time to recover too. There were already some strong foundations to what Stephen was building at Dundalk, but our week away added another layer.

There were no distractions. We were there for the football. It was a great bonding experience too, especially for the newcomers to the squad. Robbie Benson brought some strategy games, different to anything we'd ever played before. The lads really took to them.

During our downtime we played the games, went for a stroll, headed to the nearby shop, tried out the hotel's par-three golf course or just chilled with the lads. We were either training, working out in the gym, recovering or having a bit of craic. Back in Dundalk, when you weren't training you'd be at home living your regular life, along with all the stresses that come with it.

While we were away, there was nothing else to worry about. It was brilliant. It was football, football… *football*.

THE INTENSITY AND focus that week was all geared towards one thing – Europe. We worked really hard on the technical side of our game, on tactics and strategy.

When it comes to competing in Europe, League of Ireland clubs need that extra bit of work more than anyone. We have to punch above our weight if we want to do well.

We spent five days in each other's pockets in Portugal, we developed a mentality that ultimately brought us to the Europa League group stages. That trip gave Stephen Kenny an opportunity to give it one last big push before the European campaign began. He had time to instil a mindset within the group that we could make a big breakthrough this year. Stephen is fanatical about football and about how he wants things done. In that environment his attitude was contagious, his enthusiasm infectious.

ONCE WE GOT over the disappointment of our defeat to Cork, we viewed it as a blessing in disguise. There were a couple of kicks up the backside in the build-up to our European campaign. Before the Turner's Cross clash, we needed an injury-time penalty from Patrick McEleney to beat Wexford Youths 3-2. We were behind twice in that game. Then, after the break, in our last league match before the Champions League began, we needed an injury time winner to beat Longford Town 4-3 at home. We conceded three goals from set-pieces in that one. Unforgivable for a team such as ours. The day before the game, Andy Boyle's brother got married and Boyler was Best Man. He missed training. It was rare for Stephen Kenny to give such grace.

In hindsight, the Wexford and Cork games were just what we needed. It forced us to go into the training camp with a determined mindset. We knew we would have to double-down on our efforts. We put seven past Finn Harps up in Ballybofey. The pitch was like Wembley and we absolutely battered them. Ever since that game, the surface has been dire. Every time we've gone up since then, it's like they've driven five tractors over the pitch just before kick-off.

We were flying, we were scoring loads of goals and we weren't conceding.

Those two games, as well as the Longford match after the break, saw us press the reset button. They were reminders that we were not invincible. We came back from the training camp and beat Pat's 2-0, and won 5-0 away to Derry. The biggest danger when things are going so smoothly is that over-confidence kicks in, and the work-rate drops. Stephen Kenny's go-to word was 'relentless'.

That's how he wanted us to be at all times. We wanted it too. There was some serious competition within the squad. Each player was trying to outdo the other when it came to working hard on the training pitch. We were competing with each other as well as with the opposition. You didn't want to be the one dropping your standard in terms of work-rate or application. If anyone was found wanting in terms of effort, they'd be quickly found out at Dundalk. Especially with a big Champions League tie on the horizon.

· CHAPTER 14 ·

WHEN WE WERE drawn against Fimleikafélag Hafnarfjarðar, people had us down as bankers to get through. The bookies had us as favourites. Anyone I met around town felt the same way.

As a group, we were confident too. We wanted to get into the third qualifying round of the Champions League, because it was at that stage where the safety net of a Europa League play-off was on offer to the loser. But the first-leg at Oriel Park didn't exactly go to plan.

There's a photograph of me taken early in the game. We are attacking a corner kick. I'm in mid-air, about to connect with a scissors-kick, the ball just behind me at shoulder height. As I leap into the air I can see the headlines.

Gartland wonder goal seals win.

I did make good contact with the ball. Unfortunately it ricocheted off one of their defenders and was cleared. But that was the least of my concerns.

In the picture, their fella could be seen practically ripping my jersey off as I was horizontal, in mid-strike. Usually with a scissors-kick you'd land on your elbow or forearm to cushion the fall. But I was way off balance because of the way he pulled me. I put my hand down and landed on my wrist. It was agony.

We were only 30 or 35 minutes into the game at this stage and it was still scoreless. I was desperate to stay on the pitch. The doc and physio both came on and quickly examined it. The pain was excruciating.

The doc said it could be fractured.

I had no idea what a broken wrist felt like, as I'd never broken a bone before in my life. I'd usually be grand when it comes to pain threshold. I'd tell myself that it's all in my head, that I can run it off. I told the doctor to strap it up, so he did. I got back up and continued to play on.

For the next 10 minutes or so, I was running around but my hand was limp. I could feel an intense pain right across my wrist. I kept telling myself… *You'll be grand… you'll be grand.* There was a spell then when we were defending. Every so often I had to grab one of their players, give them a little nudge.

Each time, my wrist was in agony. It was killing me.

The pain was getting worse and worse, it wasn't easing off at all. So I went down at one stage, just to buy myself a bit of time. But it was no good. I had to go off. I signalled to the bench, told them to get someone ready to come on. Paddy Barrett started his warm – up and, moments before half-time, he came on in my place.

I was gutted. I watched on as David McMillan opened the scoring midway through the second-half. Relief. But then, 10 minutes later, Steven Lennon equalised and they saw out a 1-1 draw.

There was a real sense of disappointment in the dressing-room afterwards. We were looking to take a lead of a couple of goals over to Iceland. Instead, we were travelling with the disadvantage of drawing and conceding a crucial away goal. But we were still content that we'd score over there.

I decided against going to hospital straight after the game. I didn't fancy queuing for hours overnight. I went home, got a bit of sleep and headed to the VHI clinic in Dundrum. The x-ray confirmed a break, so I was booked in straightaway for a consultation with a surgeon. He said an operation would be required as soon as possible, that a pin would have to be inserted so the bone could set properly.

The operation was scheduled for the following week, the morning after the away leg. Grand. I was planning to travel to Iceland anyway. We were flying home straight after the game, so I'd be back in time for surgery.

We assembled at Dublin Airport on the morning of Tuesday July 19, the day before the game. Before we went through security, there was a whisper going around that the flight home would be delayed, that we'd have to wait a few hours overnight before taking off. I asked Martin Connolly, a former Dundalk goalkeeper who went on to become a key member of the club's staff, what the story was.

He said it was something to do with the pilots and the amount of time they were in the air. They had to take a break before they could fly again. We probably wouldn't get back into Dublin until nine or 10 the next morning. I'd miss my surgery slot in that case.

So, there I was at the airport, all ready to go with the lads, still nervous about the game even though I wasn't playing. At least I had the consolation, or so I thought, of being there. I had to turn around and go home. Ripping up my boarding pass, I tried to put on a brave face in front of the lads. But I was absolutely distraught.

THE NEXT DAY, match day, I sat alone in my living room, the blinds shut tight. Missing the trip had me more miserable than the knowledge that I wasn't going to play. For so long, the talk had been of Europe, Europe… *Europe*. But I was stuck at home. Alone.

Not even prepared to share my torment with the tiniest sliver of daylight. None of us wanted to miss a single moment. The pain of being away from the rest of the lads was worse than the moment I landed on my wrist. No exaggeration. I was close to tears for the entire day.

Poor Bronagh. She has been through a lot living with a footballer. She was at work while I sat at home, wallowing. She said she'd come home as quick as she could, that we could watch the game together. Some of her family were going to come around too.

I snapped at her, told her I wanted to be alone. I didn't even want Bronagh in the room. It was just as well no one else was around. The game was nuts.

We fell behind early on and struggled to get into our rhythm. It was 1-0 to FH at half-time. I could barely sit still. *Is this what it's like to have a nervous breakdown*, I wondered.

Robbie Benson came on at the break and he made a difference straightaway. He was five minutes on the pitch when he won a corner, which led to a penalty. Ronan Finn was outstanding in 2016, but he couldn't convert from the spot. I feared the worst. The big build-up to Europe all year and we were staring at an early exit. There was an almighty sigh of relief when, two minutes after the penalty miss, Davy McMillan equalised.

I remember his goal vividly. He was miles out.

I still don't know what he was thinking, shooting from that distance. The ball took forever to go in. It moved in slow motion. Ten minutes after Davy's first goal, he got on the end of a Daryl Horgan cross and put us ahead 2-1 on the day, 3-2 on aggregate. It wouldn't be the last time they'd link up so devastatingly in Europe.

That had to be enough, I thought. We were hardly going to concede twice. But with 12 minutes to go, FH were back in the tie. It was 3-3 on aggregate. We had the away goal advantage, but one more goal for them and it was curtains. Those last 12 minutes were horrible.

They had a few dangerous looking set-pieces and a penalty claim before the referee finally blew it up. We were through by the skin of our teeth.

What a great end to a horrible day.

This was the first time I truly got the old cliché that it's harder for a footballer to watch a match than to play in one. Never before had I to sit out such a big game through injury. Sure, I'd been suspended for matches, including the Rovers game in Tallaght when we won the league. But that was different. I was one hundred percent confident we'd get there, regardless of the outcome against the Hoops.

Anyway, I was sure that the lads would get the result they needed that night. You could take anyone out of our side and still beat every single team in the League of Ireland. But Europe was a journey into the unknown. This was different. I had never felt this miserable or this helpless before. And I wasn't even there to cheer them on.

Instead, I spent the entire day locked away on my own in a dark living room.

THAT GAME SHOWED a real toughness, a resilience about the team. People saw us as a team that played nice football, but this time we had to dig in for a result. FH were by no means a great outfit. They didn't have any real flair or a distinctive style. But they showed us another side to European football.

We were lacking experience at that level, while this was their 13th successive year in Europe. They were a unit, they were effective in their own way. Whatever we thought of ourselves in the League of Ireland, it meant nothing in Europe.

No game is easy at that level. Any team you face is going to be well organised and structured; set up in a way to get the best out of their players. That was a big takeaway from the trip to Iceland. Coming away from that match the lads were thinking… *They weren't any great shakes.* Yet we only got through on away goals. It was a serious lesson and it brought a new dimension to our dressing-room when it came to playing in Europe.

The win over FH was huge. Even if we lost in the next round, we'd still drop into the Europa League at the play-off stage. Win the next round and we'd be guaranteed group stage football in the Europa League – but only after competing in a play-off for the Champions League proper.

Anything could happen in either play-off.

It's all down to the luck of the draw.

What a rollercoaster that day was. From being close to tears, to jumping on the couch, to roaring at the top of my voice at the final whistle. The neighbours told me afterwards that they could hear me. I was banging on the walls, going ballistic… all on my own.

I was the ultimate fan. It felt like we'd won the World Cup.

The next morning, on my way in for surgery, I was buzzing.

Not for long, though. The surgeon told me I'd be six weeks in a cast. I just looked at him and said, 'Does it really need six weeks?'

He replied, 'We'll see how it sets'.

One thing was for certain, I'd miss our reunion with BATE Borisov.

▪ CHAPTER 15 ▪

THE FLIGHT TO Belarus took off without me. But on this occasion I wasn't racing to shut the living room blinds. For the away leg against BATE, I swapped a day in darkened isolation for the eir Sport studios.

I was asked to be a part of their live coverage, alongside regular analyst and former St Patrick's Athletic defender Damian Lynch. I played with Damian's brother Aidan at Monaghan United and met Damian himself a few times before. I'd always fancied myself as a TV pundit, but needed the green light from Stephen Kenny. 'No problem,' said the gaffer.

One of the benefits of working the night of the BATE tie – and I'm sure Stephen thought the same thing – was that it distracted me from the heartache of missing another huge game. There was no bouncing off the living room walls this time. I simply had to focus on the task at hand; making sure I was ready for my big break as a pundit.

Pre-match was grand, we chatted about the game, about Dundalk's prospects and our meeting with BATE the previous year. We were quite upbeat about the prospects of bringing home a decent result. That enthusiasm didn't last too long, however, as Borisov dominated from the very first minute. They bombarded us and fizzed some dangerous crosses into the area. Patrick McEleney started on the right wing, with Sean Gannon at right-full. They hit that flank with attack after attack.

Coming up to half-time I turned to Damian. The plan was to go back over all the key passages of play. The only problem for me was the lack of positives from a Dundalk perspective. It was all BATE.

Fats spent most of the half in the right-back position thanks to the quality and pace of their movement. Igor Stasevich kept coming inside and their left-back pushed right on, so Fats was constantly on the back-foot. At that time we tended to stay with our man, no matter where he went. I turned to Damian and said, 'I think you'll have to take a lot of this at half-time, I'll just come in with a few bits and pieces'. Damien addressed all the good BATE play and I interjected with a few thoughts on Dundalk's performance. The key one, of course, was that somehow we weren't being battered on the scoreboard!

The deadlock was finally broken on 70 minutes. After being under the cosh for so much of the game, I had one big worry. *Now they had broken us, were we going to cave mentally? Would the floodgates open up?* But the performance in those last 20 minutes was even more impressive than up to that point. To keep it at just a one-goal deficit was huge, because despite their dominance the tie was still alive.

The away leg against BATE remains the stuff of legend in Dundalk. We still talk about it as being the best 1-0 loss ever, because it could have been so much more. But in saying that, for all their possession and territorial advantage, they came up against a rock solid defence. Andy Boyle and Paddy Barrett were exceptional.

They threw their bodies in front of everything. Everyone did. All the lads in midfield put in some of the toughest shifts of their careers that night. All I could think about as I drove home from the TV studio was that it could have been a real hiding, that BATE missed a glorious opportunity to put the tie to bed. They were far better than us, but all the talk following that match – and not just from myself but from the whole team – was that we were still well and truly in the tie.

That sums up the confidence in the dressing-room and where our heads were at. It wasn't about how good they were – and they were much better than us – it was that we could turn them over at home. 'It's only 1-0,' we kept saying. 'Beat them at home and we're guaranteed group stage football.'

I COULDN'T DO any contact training that week, so I did some running and bike-work while the rest of the lads were out on the pitch. I wanted to be as much a part of the build-up as possible. That included watching the video analysis on how they moved us around in the first-leg. We had no league game in between the two BATE legs – a load of our matches were postponed during that period – so we could focus one hundred percent on the return in Tallaght.

MATCH DAY WAS an absolute cracker.

I was back on television duty, but I wanted to spend as much time as possible with the team. I spent the day with them and got plenty of stick for my wardrobe. They were all in their tracksuits, while I was wearing a blazer and jeans. When we arrived at the stadium, I went off and joined the eir Sport crew.

The plan was to be pitch-side for the pre-match, half-time and full-time analysis, and then to watch the action from the gantry in the stand opposite the dugouts. Again, it was a great way to take my mind off the injury.

Right from kick-off the crowd was amazing. I loved watching on from the gantry, looking down at the fans below. There were plenty of lads in the crowd giving me stick. A lot of it was coming at me in Dublin accents. I looked left and saw a St Pat's jersey, right and there was a Shelbourne jersey. Brilliant. We were all rivals, but this was a massive night for Irish football. Fans of all clubs were out because they wanted to see Irish football do well on the international stage.

As this was such a big day for Irish football, some of the biggest rivalries were set aside. I even saw some Shamrock Rovers lads there too. I wouldn't go as far as saying they were supporting Dundalk for the day, but they too wanted to see Irish football succeed in Europe. Rovers were there five years earlier, when they qualified for the Europa League group stages. I was delighted when they made that breakthrough. It was nice to see a few Hoops fans hoping – perhaps through gritted teeth – to see us follow in their footsteps.

As I headed towards pitch-side for a spot of half-time analysis, I went up to a few of them and said, 'Fair play'. I have always wanted to see Irish clubs doing well in Europe. If football in this country is to get any bit of respect from the large number of fans with little or no interest in the League of Ireland, we need to perform well in Europe on a regular basis. If we don't encourage or support each other to do well at this level – and that includes accommodating the rescheduling of league games – I think football here will stand still.

THIS WAS COMPLETELY different to the game in Borisov.

We played some great football and BATE were nowhere near the force they were a week earlier. Then, shortly before half-time, the place erupted. We got the breakthrough we deserved.

Daryl Horgan produced a trademark run down the wing. He had them on their heels. They didn't know which way he was going to go. He whipped over a brilliant cross with his right foot. There were two defenders around him at the time, he got hardly any back lift, but what a ball towards the back post.

David McMillan was so alert and sharp. He made one of those brilliant instinctive runs that became his speciality at Dundalk. Stretching, reaching, he got his head to the cross and planted it inside the upright.

As Davy wheeled away, I nearly leapt off the tiny gantry in celebration. The fans below us were going mad, the gantry was shaking from all the movement. It was wild. I thought... *Could it really happen?* I was trying to squeeze in between the commentator and co-commentator to see the replays. They were almost shoving me back out of the way.

We were all buzzing as we headed down onto the pitch for the half-time analysis. This was much easier than the week before, because it was pretty much all positive. The hardest part of our half-time spell in front of the cameras was trying to keep a lid on the excitement and enthusiasm. As the teams came out for the second-half the crowd was louder than I'd ever heard before at Tallaght. There were close to 5,000 people at the game, but I'd have believed you at that moment if you'd said it was at least double that figure. I know from speaking to the lads afterwards that the crowd was a huge driver for them, it gave them a real lift.

The players were really up for this one, but so too were the fans. It seemed like everyone in Dundalk had deserted the town that day. Countless buses made their way down the M1 and across the M50 to Tallaght. As a squad, we loved that stadium. Especially after our league win there the previous season. The pitch was always immaculate, but for the BATE game it was even better than ever. It was quite the change from playing them on a sticky artificial Oriel Park surface, as was the case a year earlier. And for most of the evening the weather was beautiful too. After that day, it's safe to say we loved Tallaght Stadium even more than ever.

AT HALF-TIME IN the first-leg, Patrick McEleney and Robbie Benson were taken off. Being whipped at the break is never a nice feeling for a footballer. But Stephen Kenny felt we needed a little more steel to cope with wave after wave of BATE attack, so he brought on Chris Shields and John Mountney. It was the right call at the time. They made us a lot more solid in midfield and on the right – two areas where we looked vulnerable during the first-half in Belarus.

Stephen loves Patrick and Robbie. They are two cracking players too. Patrick McEleney is one of the most gifted footballers I've played with, and he can see and do things that ninety percent of lads could never see or do! Robbie is a different midfielder again. He's so intelligent, covers so much ground and controls the tempo of the game brilliantly. As he got more experience and learned from Stevie O'Donnell, he got better and better. Both Patrick and Robbie are great fellas too.

For Stephen Kenny to take them off at half-time wasn't an easy call. It was a brave move. It was no reflection on either one of them as players, it was just that Fats was playing out of position. We were under so much pressure that we couldn't get the ball out to him often enough. Mounts away from home in Europe was phenomenal in terms of his work-rate. He would run up and down the line all night. No full-back could get the better of him. As for Shields, he was a more natural defensive-minded midfielder. Credit to the two lads at the time, there were no complaints from them when they were told they were coming off.

RONAN FINN PICKED up an injury around the half-hour mark in Tallaght. Stephen turned to Fats. Thirty-two minutes in and he had a chance for redemption. Another player might have had the hump with Stephen, but not Fats.

When he came on for Finner that night in Tallaght he was unbelievable.

Thirteen minutes into the second-half and Dane Massey came in from the left hand side, onto a deep, looping McEleney cross.

Don't f**king shoot! I thought. He does this a lot, racing inside and drilling the ball first-time at goal from a ridiculously tight angle. I could see him winding up. *DON'T F**KING SHOOT!*

He smashed the ball straight into the ground. He completely mis-kicked it, shanked it. Luckily it bounced right in front of Davy Mac on the six-yard line. All he had to do was nod his head and the ball was in the back of the net. Dane wheeled away, arms in the air as if he meant to pick out Davy! *Maybe he did?*

The stadium erupted. Everyone went mad. Scarves, hats, everything was thrown in the air. I was in dreamland. *We're going to the Champions League play-offs! The Europa League group stages at least!*

Then I remembered that there was still over half-an-hour to go. One goal for BATE and we were out. We hadn't the cushion of an away goal, so we were still vulnerable. One goal, one mistake, one bad refereeing decision and the dream would be dead.

The atmosphere was electric. Everyone was on the edge of their seats. My stomach was churning. I couldn't sit still. I felt sick watching on, unable to do anything to help the lads. Naturally, BATE came into the game a little more. They started to boss possession. But they didn't create too many chances. It wasn't as if we were clinging on and they were missing sitters. They were nothing like the attacking force we faced in the first-leg.

Stevie O'Donnell has this knack of controlling a game, no matter how strong the opposition is. His head is constantly turning, he is always aware of the space around him, of where his teammates are. He has his pass picked out long before the ball gets to his feet. And defensively he is such a rock.

That night, particularly after Davy's second goal, he led by example. It was a proper captain's performance. The whole team defended like I'd never seen before. They gave BATE very few opportunities to threaten our goal. If anything, as the game slowly crawled towards 90 minutes, we looked the stronger attacking side.

I couldn't hack being up in the gantry any longer.

I watched the last five or 10 minutes from pitch-side, running up and down the line on the concrete between the first row of seats and the wall separating the stand from the pitch. By now the skies had opened up. It was lashing rain.

There I was, blazer and jeans, chasing the ball and shouting at the lads…

'LEFT SHOULDER!'

'RIGHT SHOULDER!'

'MAN ON!' I honestly didn't know where I was at that stage.

I was completely lost in the moment. I remember thinking the next day… *I must have looked a right fool to everyone in the first few rows.* To everyone who had to crane their necks every time I ran past. I was leaning over the barrier, roaring at the lads. I was so desperate to do something, anything to help.

And then, 10 yards inside their own half, one of the BATE players passed in-field to a teammate who took a poor touch, tried to recover but only succeeded in playing the ball straight to Robbie Benson. All of a sudden, Robbie had a free run at goal.

He took off with this hunchback stride of his, went through a couple of gears and made a dart for the penalty area. He took a touch which put the ball onto his right foot. *No!* I thought to myself.

Not that he doesn't have a right foot, it's just that he's always more comfortable on his left. But he dinked the ball coolly over the goalkeeper, calm as you like.

Having been whipped at half-time the previous week, Robbie came on with 12 minutes to go for Davy in Tallaght. If he was sore about what happened in Borisov, it certainly didn't show in his cameo performance in the second-leg. As he wheeled away to the corner flag, I leaned over the wall roaring at the lads as they celebrated. 'YESSSSSSSSSSSS!'

I was about to jump over and join them when something stopped me at the last moment. I'd missed enough games through injury, I didn't want to pick up a stupid UEFA suspension with more big games to come.

The final whistle went and I said to the eir Sport lads that I'd be back in a bit.

I joined the players on the pitch, doing knee slides with them in my jeans. The feeling was unbelievable. The rain was lashing down, the crowd was going ballistic and we were ecstatic. We were going to the group stages – Europa League guaranteed, Champions League still a possibility.

ALONG WITH THE glory of qualifying for the group stages, the money was huge for us. I was earning €600 or €700-a-week at the time. The bonus for reaching the Europa League group stages was more than one-and-a-half times my annual pay. You have to remember that a lot of us couldn't get mortgages at the time. Banks weren't going to hand over a huge wedge of cash to someone on a short-term contract in a league with a sometimes dodgy past when it came to honouring those deals.

I make no bones about it – the money was a big factor for us.

A lot of us were at an age where we were hoping to get a house, to settle down. I was due to get married later that year. So this was a huge moment financially for every single player. It was the deposit for a house. Ultimately, playing football is a job. Yes, it's a dream job, but it's one that doesn't exactly pay well for the vast majority of us playing outside the big leagues. But on that night in Tallaght, our job delivered a massive one-off bonus.

We were competing against BATE with lads who were on €5,000 and

€10,000-a-week. We were competing against resources that were quite literally way out of our league. So to land a one-off pay-day that was the equivalent to just a few weeks' pay for some of our opponents was a real achievement.

Of course, at that stage we were still in line for the Champions League bonus, with the club set to get €12m if we qualified for that competition. With the player bonuses worked out as a percentage of the prize money, forget the deposit, that would have been the house paid for. Furnished and all.

And maybe a new car or two.

COMPLETELY FORGETTING MYSELF, I started to walk off the pitch and towards the dressing-rooms. Someone from eir Sport had to run over and grab me.

I headed back over to the far side. Stephen Kenny was being interviewed at the time. I was going to go up and grab him, give him a big bear hug. But I thought better of it. After all the knee slides, I figured I should try to act professionally in front of the cameras.

WHILE I WAS out on the pitch wrapping up the punditry work, I knew I was missing all the celebrations in the dressing-room. But I had a job to do and I wasn't going to bail on eir Sport after the opportunity they gave me to gain some experience in front of the camera. It's probably a good job that I did miss out on one part of the post-match revelry though. Martin O'Neill paid a visit to our dressing-room and said well done to the lads.

'I just want to say that was phenomenal… absolutely phenomenal,' he said. 'It is one of the best results in Irish history and you were phenomenal from start to finish… heart, soul… brilliant!'

Then he turned to Chris Shields and said, 'You're one of my favourites. You'll soon be able to pass the ball properly and you'll be brilliant. You've got a great heart… honestly!'

When I heard about it, I thought to myself… *That was no f**king place to say something like that to someone who was on cloud nine.* If it was me, I don't think I would have taken it so well. It definitely would have annoyed me.

But the mood that night was celebratory. Not in an 'everyone out on the town' kind of way, because we were away to Galway three days after the Borisov game. But a few of us skipped off for a quiet couple of drinks.

I was still injured and was booked in for another TV slot with eir Sport to cover the Galway game. So I headed out. As did Ronan Finn. He injured himself early that night, so he wasn't going to play at the weekend. Stevie O'Donnell had just put in an incredible shift, so he was going to be rested. He joined us.

And Davy Mac? Well, after scoring two in a game like that, how could you not come out for a sneaky couple of beers? I'm sure the lads had a few drinks too when they headed back to Dundalk. They were hardly expected go straight home to bed after such an adrenaline-packed night. We lost the game in Galway. But I think that was down more to the exertions on the pitch three nights earlier than anything else. We had just experienced the biggest high of our playing careers. It was hard to focus on anything in the days after Tallaght.

One thing I do remember from the Galway game was a picture taken in the home dressing-room after their win. President Michael D Higgins, a huge Galway United fan, popped in and was snapped in the middle of their celebrations. I remember thinking it was way over the top. It was just a league game after all. But when I had time to think about it, it brought home exactly what we'd achieved in beating BATE.

This is where we are now, a team beats us and they celebrate like it's a cup final.

We lost the next league game too, away to Bray Wanderers. Seven days later and we had a date with destiny at the Aviva Stadium.

▪ CHAPTER 16 ▪

WITH A CHAMPIONS League play-off against Legia Warsaw on the horizon, I literally ripped the cast off my wrist. I was desperate to be involved. The cast was meant to stay on for six weeks, but I removed it about halfway through.

I went for a check-up first and the surgeon was happy that my wrist was healing well. Not that he was in favour of me removing the cast. He did warn that a bad fall or knock might set back my recovery, as the bone hadn't yet fully set.

But I was happy to take that chance.

My wrist was now dressed in a much lighter support strap. There was a little piece of metal keeping things in place, which posed a potential problem. Obviously, you couldn't wear anything metal during a game, so the idea was to get a load of tape and wrap it around the strap. I was taped up like a boxer. But the strapping still had to pass a physical check by the match officials. That was a nervy experience, but luckily the tape did its job.

I WAS TRAINING like a madman.

Having not been able to run for the first few weeks, I really pushed myself once I was given the green light. The aim was to get as fit as possible for the Legia play-off. I wanted Stephen Kenny to be confident that he could turn to me if needed.

I'd hardly ever missed a game for Dundalk through injury prior to the start of our 2016 European run. I couldn't believe the timing. At the same time I was delighted for Paddy Barrett, who was brilliant when he came into the team. We were fortunate to have a player like Paddy in the squad. He was amazing in Borisov. He played a huge part in us escaping with just a one-goal deficit. We got on great off the pitch, Paddy and I. But I really wanted my place back.

I knew in my heart, though, that the first-leg at least would come too soon for me. I certainly wouldn't bounce straight back into the team in place of Paddy. But I was motivated to work as hard as possible, on the off-chance that one of the lads picked up an injury. I trained in altitude chambers, I did extra sessions and I ran until my legs and lungs were on fire. I knew I wouldn't make the team and that was crushing. It didn't affect my work-rate, however. Sometimes you just have to roll with the punches. My aim for that week was to be as positive an influence on the lads as I could be.

I said to Stephen, 'I'm not expecting to play, but just put me on the bench and if anything happens to any of the other lads, I'll be ready'. And he did.

I was back in the match-day squad for the first time since the home leg against FH just over a month earlier. It felt great to be involved once again, to run down the tunnel at the Aviva Stadium and step onto the pitch on such a massive occasion. By kick-off, there were 30,000-plus fans there, including a small number of Legia supporters in the corner. They might have been outnumbered, but we could still hear them. They were nuts.

THERE WAS SO much hype in the build-up to the game. Champions League, Aviva Stadium, the media interest, inching closer and closer to the dream of playing in the group stages. Everyone in Dundalk was buzzing.

The town emptied out the afternoon of the game in a way we had only ever seen before on cup final day. Literally, everyone I met on the street stopped me to wish us luck. Quite a few were already making requests for Liverpool or Real Madrid in the group stages!

Coming up to the big day, I spent some time thinking about Andy Connolly and Paul Brown, the two owners who saved the club from going out of business. Now they were on the brink of Champions League qualification and a possible €12m UEFA cheque. They were life-long fans and, despite their roles as owners, they were still going to games in their Dundalk jerseys, cheering us on like every other supporter.

After the BATE win in Tallaght, Martin Connolly stood outside the stadium talking to a UEFA executive. As they spoke, Paul left the stadium car park in his Fastfix van. He wound down the window, beeped his horn and let out a huge shout to Martin, 'Come on the Town!' The UEFA big-wig present asked who that was, to be informed it was one of the club's owners! That little moment spells out the beauty of Dundalk as a club, and *our story!*

Paul and his friends would later set up a supporters' group and call it 'The Tie Wrap Gang'. Why? Because they had to use a ton of tie wraps to make sure all the appropriate signage and advertising was securely in place in Tallaght. It was make-it-up-as-you-go-along sort of stuff. It just added to the fairytale feel of our adventure.

I'm sure Paul and Andy were wondering how we'd gotten to this stage, inches away from the Champions League. The club was guaranteed a windfall, but that money wouldn't arrive until much later. To finance everything that went with competing in the group stages, they had to go off and get bridging loans.

The truth is, a club our size shouldn't be there. The competitions are structured in a way that keeps clubs like ours out. That was another reason to be proud of our achievements that year. It was a little 'Up Yours' to the establishment.

ONCE THE WARM-UPS were finished and we had our last few minutes with Stephen Kenny and his staff in the dressing-room, it was time to line up in the tunnel next to the Legia players. This was when it really hit home – we were at a new level here.

There was a much bigger UEFA presence. We were using the Champions League ball, the Champions League anthem blared out over the loudspeakers. Everything was done with a greater intensity than in any other match we'd ever played.

We had prepared within an inch of our lives for this game. There was extensive video work in the week leading up to the first-leg. *They are good*, we thought, *but we could have gotten a much tougher side.* We had to believe they were beatable.

And we did. We were fearless.

There was a realism about us, don't get me wrong. We'd laugh and ask, 'Lads, how the hell are we here, playing for a place in the Champions League group stages?' But at the same time, we knew we had a real chance of beating Legia.

Gerry Spain, Vinny Perth and Stephen had done great work compiling all the videos. The way Stephen talks about the opposition, the way he constructs the video sessions, he shows you their strengths and where they can hurt you. By the end of each session, we come away with a respect for the opposition, knowing they will punish us if we aren't at the very top of our game. But ahead of the game against Legia we also came away going... *These guys are no Real Madrid or Barcelona... They aren't going to tear us apart!*

Stephen had us believing we could beat them. We knew ourselves that we had a great team packed with great players, and that we were going to be as fit as Legia.

As soon as the first whistle went, we looked confident. There was no panic, no booting the ball away. When we had possession, we tried to hold onto it. There was such courage about the way we played that night.

We didn't create a load of opportunities and Legia were dominant. But with the game scoreless at half-time, we felt we had a real chance.

Eleven minutes into the second-half, we went a goal down.

A penalty. It still annoys me to this day.

A couple of years later when UEFA and the FAI did presentations about the hand-ball rule, they used this as an example of what should NOT be given as hand-ball. A little too late for that, lads. I remember watching the presentation and we were all going mad. Andy Boyle went to block the ball, arms behind him.

The ball hit the underside of his leg, bounced up off the ground and came off his arm, which was still behind him, as he stretched to make the block.

I *still* can't believe it was given.

But at 1-0 down, we still had a chance. The game was deep into injury-time and I thought to myself... *We have a much better idea about them now, we know exactly what we are up against in the second-leg.* Videos will tell you a lot about the opposition, but playing against them fills in all the gaps. It gives you the complete picture. And one thing I thought we could exploit in Warsaw was the fact that their back line was not exactly the tallest.

Ciaran Kilduff came on for the final 15 minutes or so in the Aviva and he caused them a few problems.

But just as I was wondering how we would overturn a one-goal deficit the following week, they scored a second. Four minutes into injury-time and it looked like the tie was over. Another blow was the fact that Stevie O'Donnell was booked. It was enough to earn him a suspension for the Warsaw game.

A penalty that never was and a goal deep into stoppage time. These are the razor-edge moments on which dreams are either made or crushed.

DESPITE THE INJURY-TIME goal, we faced into the next six days with a real belief that the tie wasn't over. We told ourselves over and over that we would have a right go, that there were areas in which we could hurt them. A little more service into Killer and he could give their defenders a real headache.

Stephen Kenny took us down to Abbotstown for training ahead of the trip to Warsaw. The grass pitch next to Oriel Park could be hit or miss. Depending on the weather, it was often either too hard or too soft. It dries out too quickly in the summer and is rock hard, but as soon as a bit of rain falls, it's like a mud bath.

It's like a lot of issues in the League of Ireland – a bit of investment is needed. But the money never seems to be there.

The Abbotstown pitch was a cracking surface and everyone was in good spirits in training. At one stage we had a game between our likely first-XI and the rest of the squad. Kilduff was chopped down by a rash enough tackle, a pretty bad one if I'm being honest. Straightaway, it didn't look good, and sure enough he was out of the game.

There and then, we knew it could be costly for us.

When Killer came on in the Aviva, his presence was a real headache for their defence. His aerial ability – either from the start or off the bench – would have been a big help in the second-leg.

I WAS IN Warsaw once before, at the start of Euro 2012. I always fancied a return, but didn't think at the time that I'd be back for a Champions League play-off.

As usual, we had a bit of downtime, where most of us got out and had a wander around. Some people say that we're not there to be tourists and that we should be fully focused on the game one hundred percent of the time. But if you are sitting around the hotel for a couple of days, thinking about nothing other than the game, you are just piling needless pressure on yourself.

Any chance I get for a bit of a distraction, I always grab with both hands.

We do loads of work on each game and there is still plenty of sitting around hotel rooms or lobbies. So what harm in going out exploring or grabbing a coffee when you have a few free hours?

Myself and a few of the lads decided to get a taxi to a nearby shopping centre one afternoon. First thing we saw when we jumped in the back was a Legia Warsaw crest on the headrest. The driver was a big Legia fan, so we tried to wind him up and give him a bit of stick. He wasn't having any of it.

Seriously, he wasn't even up for a bit of banter.

He just said, 'Nah, you're shit'.

That was it, no more small talk for the rest of the journey. He had put us back in our box!

We quickly learned that the whole city was fanatical about their team. Michael O'Connor had arranged to meet his cousin, who was over as a fan. They decided to hook up in a shopping centre and grab a coffee together.

His cousin told him which shop she'd be waiting outside, so when Michael got into the centre he asked the first person he saw for directions. The Polish fella took one look at Michael, saw his tracksuit, said, 'Me Legia,' and walked off. After that, Michael decided he'd just walk around until he found the shop.

MATCH-NIGHT AND once again I was on the bench.

Paddy Barrett was picked to partner Andy Boyle. I had no complaints. We went out onto the pitch to warm-up and I was expecting maybe a few fans to be there that early. But as we stepped onto the pitch there were thousands in the ground. And already they were making loads of noise.

As each minute ticked by, the atmosphere grew louder and louder. The place was rocking. We were hoping to make history by reaching the Champions League group stages for the first time. But Legia had been gearing up for this moment for years… 21 years, in fact. They had spent big on trying to get back to the group stages for the first time since the 1995/96 season, when they made it all the way to the quarter-finals. Since then they'd lost out in the qualifying rounds to Barcelona, Shakhtar Donetsk, Steaua Bucharest and Celtic. So they saw this as their biggest chance yet to get back to the biggest stage in club football.

Usually when we are away in Europe, the home side has one stand packed with their ultras, all dressed in club colours. But all four sides of the Polish Army Stadium were blanketed in white that night. It seemed like their ultras had taken over all but the little corner that was reserved for Dundalk fans. Everyone in the stadium was on their feet and the noise was like nothing I'd ever heard before.

To the left of the dugout was the main ultras' group. There were four or five men standing on platforms at the front of the stand. Two had megaphones, while it was the job of the others to orchestrate the claps. None of them looked at the game. They had their backs to the action throughout.

All of a sudden, this giant banner was unfurled.

It was a quarter of a roulette wheel, with the ball landing on number 21… the 21 years since Legia last qualified for the Champions League group stages. Between the banner and the noise, it was spine-tingling stuff. Their supporters were going ballistic. We had an idea of how nuts they were from the game at the Aviva, but this was a completely different level of madness.

They must have let off one hundred flares in one go. It was insane.

Long after we played Legia, we saw how mad their fans really could be. When UEFA fined them €35,000 in 2016, they hit back with a huge banner depicting the UEFA logo, but with a pig in the middle of it. A couple of years later there was trouble at a game against Real Madrid, which led to more fines and bans. They had to play their home game against Madrid in an empty stadium. Thankfully, things didn't get that heated against us, but the atmosphere was still very intimidating.

The only time it dropped was when Robbie Benson scored one of the best goals I'd ever seen. Apart from the travelling supporters, the place went silent.

Robbie wasn't exactly screaming the house down either. For someone who'd just scored a massive goal in a Champions League play-off, a cracking volley with his weaker foot, he celebrated as if it was a last minute consolation. He just wheeled away with a cheeky little grin on his face.

I was thinking… *How on earth do you keep your cool like that?* Not once did he break stride… the run, the volley… the celebration. And when the rest of the lads caught up with him, he almost looked embarrassed by all the fuss.

As for us on the bench, we couldn't believe what had happened. We went crazy. A million thoughts ran through my head.

We travelled to Poland with practically nobody giving us a chance – because it was such a huge ask. But all of a sudden we were just one goal away from extra-time.

LEGIA WERE RATTLED.

We were playing much better than the first-leg. Then, with just over 20 minutes to go, they had a man sent off. I was itching to get on, but not as a centre-back. With Killer out injured, I was convinced that I could do a job up front. I'd scored a serious number of goals in my time at Dundalk up to that point and I was a handy enough striker whenever I played with my mates. As the game drifted towards the final 10 minutes, I put on my pads, took off my training top and pulled my jersey over my head.

Stephen Kenny was out on the edge of the technical area barking out the orders, so I kept making eye-contact with Vinny Perth, who was sitting at the end of the dugout. I was sure I'd dominate in the air against their defenders. I kept staring at Vinny, desperate to be sent on up top for the last few minutes.

But the outcome was the same as in the BATE game a year earlier, when Stephen ignored my pleas to go up for the final few minutes. I love the fact that he wanted to keep playing the Dundalk way. I'm really proud of how we played under Stephen.

But in that moment, I was desperate to help out the lads.

I wanted to get on, I wanted to be involved.

And I was one hundred percent sure I could bully the Legia defence. It's the old Irish way – throw the big centre-half up front and hope for the best. But that's not Stephen's way and he ended up bringing Michael O'Connor on for the last few minutes.

I was gutted.

As we pushed on for the goal we needed to take the game into extra-time, Legia equalised in injury time. We didn't really care that we were robbed of the win, all that mattered was the fact that we weren't going to the Champions League group stages.

We were so close.

We really believed that we could do it and when Robbie scored we had them on the ropes. It wasn't to be – but at least we still had the Europa League group stage draw to look forward to.

· CHAPTER 17 ·

THREE DAYS AFTER our Champions League play-off against Legia, and having played in front of 30,000-strong crowds for two games running, we were brought crashing back down to earth. We were away to Wexford and there can't have been any more than 700 fans at Ferrycarrig. But as far as I was concerned, it was the biggest game of the season.

A month and a half after I broke my wrist, I was back in the starting 11 and desperate to prove my fitness ahead of the Europa League group stages.

Up to that point in our European run, we had played just two league games – away to Galway United and Bray Wanderers – and lost both. This can happen in the middle of a European campaign. We were mentally exhausted.

And Europe was a big deal for us in 2016. We really believed we could do something special. Then there was the fact that Galway and Bray were so clearly up for the fight. This was highlighted by the picture of the Galway squad celebrating their win with President Higgins. But with a league title at stake, it was important that we got back to winning ways in Wexford.

Stephen Kenny placed huge importance on the game.

So much so that we stayed over in Wexford the night before. We were in our hotel when the draw for the group stages was made. It was an old-fashioned hotel; a bit dingy and dark. The rooms were small enough too. But 20 of us still managed to pile into one of the bedrooms to watch a live stream of the draw on one of the lads' laptops. There was huge excitement.

We all had our favourite teams that we wanted to draw... Manchester United, Roma, Ajax, Inter Milan, Fiorentina...

We all wanted ties that we could win. We weren't just happy to be there, we wanted to be competitive, to push for a spot in the knockout rounds after Christmas. But we knew we would get one big team, a top seed, so we wanted a glamour tie. Imagine selling out the Aviva Stadium for a game against Manchester United!

Or heading to Old Trafford or the San Siro! Southampton were in the draw too. That wouldn't have been a bad one either.

So there we were, all squashed into the room, watching the draw as it took forever to get through the formalities and then get all the way down to the fourth seeds. As the groups began to take shape, we could see the ones we wanted to avoid. We didn't want a load of long trips; nowhere that required a camel-back ride to get to an away game.

There was one group in particular that didn't look too appealing.

Group D... Zenit St Petersburg and Maccabi Tel Aviv.

Russia seemed a million miles away to me. I didn't realise at the time that St Petersburg was so far west that it was a handy flight away. Israel, though, was going to be a real slog to get to. So we all let out a huge roar when Hapoel Be'er Sheva were drawn in Group D.

Then the host intervened and said Hapoel had to be moved, as they couldn't have two Israeli teams in the same group. So we ended up in Group D, while Hapoel were placed in Group K with Southampton, Inter Milan and Sparta Prague.

The hotel room shook to a collective roar... AH FOR F**K SAKE!!!'

Straightaway we started to look up details about Zenit, AZ and Maccabi.

Zenit had signed Spain international Javi Garcia from Manchester City a couple of years earlier. Axel Witsel was a massive player with more than 70 caps for Belgium at that stage. One of those was against Ireland at Euro 2016, just a few months earlier. They had Portugal international Luis Neto and Italy full-back Domenico Criscito. They even had a Brazil international in Giuliano for good measure. And Aleksandr Kerzhakov had already become Russia's record goalscorer by the time we drew Zenit.

I remember thinking... *Wow, that's some team!*

After checking out the Zenit side, the excitement really started to build. Sure, there was still some disappointment that we didn't draw a Manchester United or a club of that prestige. But to think that we were going to face a team of Zenit's quality was the stuff of dreams. And nightmares too!

I think Stephen Kenny could see how excited we were, so he quickly reminded us that we had a job to do against Wexford. We had to park all thoughts of the group stages.

WEXFORD WAS THE first of six games in the Premier Division and FAI Cup before our Europa League opener away to AZ Alkmaar. Six games for me to prove my fitness and get back into Stephen's European plans.

Paddy Barrett had been so impressive against BATE and Legia, so I knew there was no margin for error. I was flying fit. I trained like mad once the cast came off and did everything I could to be in the best shape possible.

AZ on September 15 was circled in red on my calendar.

This was everything I'd ever dreamed of, to be playing at the top level of European competition. I was worried that Stephen would stick with Paddy. But I knew I'd get the chance to stake my claim. After a busy European qualification and play-off schedule, he would have to give some lads a rest and give others an opportunity.

You never know, though, with Stephen. He always kept you on your toes.

I wasn't going to corner him and ask if I featured in his plans. No one at Dundalk had a God-given right to be in the team. All I could do was leave everything on the pitch.

I started league games against Wexford, Bohs and Sligo – and chipped in with a goal against Bohs (one of my best goals, if not my *very* best). But coming up to the AZ game I was sweating. Stephen had opted for Andy Boyle and Paddy Barrett three days earlier against Finn Harps – and they kept a clean sheet in a 2-0 win.

Another reason to sweat was the heat when we arrived in Alkmaar.

I convinced Bronagh to come over for the game. The Russia and Israel trips were going to be much harder to get to, with issues such as visas and distance. I really wanted her at our first group stage game, so she agreed and spent a few days in Amsterdam with a friend before heading up on the day of the game.

I think half the town ended up in Amsterdam. I was in getting fuel a week or so before the game and a young lad came up to me.

'The boss won't give me time off work for the game,' he said.

He had been to all the other games and was going to get the sack if he took a couple of unsanctioned days off for this one.

'But I don't care,' he continued. 'If I lose my job… I lose my job.'

Sure enough I saw him over there. He rang in sick, his boss didn't believe him and he got the sack. He had no regrets.

Chris Shields' mate also pulled a sickie, as he couldn't get the time off work either, but he was caught on camera during the game, giving it loads in the middle of the Dundalk supporters! Nothing was going to stop people from getting to this one. It was history in the making.

A first for a club with a proud European history.

We did all the usual background on AZ before the game, studied their players and watched loads of video. I was going to be up against a striker called Freddy Friday, a 21-year-old with lightning pace. They had former Aston Villa man Ron Vlaar at centre-half. Just two years earlier he was a bronze medallist at the 2014 World Cup. Sure, he was 31 and had left Villa to return to his former club, but he was still a class act.

As far as I was concerned, he was one of the best defenders at the 2014 World Cup, so to have the opportunity to play against him was amazing. On the right wing they had Alireza Jahanbakhsh. Two years later he signed for Brighton for £20million.

Their stadium was beautiful. It was small, but tight and neat, and the stands hung over the immaculate pitch, trapping in the atmosphere. The weather was class too. Everything was shaping up nicely.

AZ started well. Jahanbakhsh was in top form down their right – Massey always seemed to get those lightning opponents! He cut inside after just two minutes and cracked a shot off the post. That was a real wake-up call for us. But we weren't rattled. Once again we showed great courage to get on the ball and keep it. For a team from the League of Ireland, unused to being on this stage, we didn't let anything faze us. We made the pitch big, held onto possession and slowed the game down.

And we found that we were able to cut through them.

Thinking back to that game, we were brilliant. I know when I'm shit and I know when I'm good, and this was one of my best performances. People say I'm slow. I read the comments online and in the media. But I can read the game really well. I beat Freddy Friday to the ball a couple of times and he was a real mover. *Not so slow now, eh?*

There was one moment early on, a foot-race down the wing for a ball played over the top. I read it, beat Friday to the ball, held him off and then checked back inside, leaving him for dead. I came away with the ball and then passed it on.

That moment still sticks in my head.

It gave me that extra bit of confidence that I could handle myself in a game like this. Maybe I surprised myself a little that I could pull off something like that at such a high level. I always felt I had the ability, but there was a mental block.

Early in my League of Ireland career, it was simply a case that defenders defended. No fancy stuff. I knew I could do flicks and tricks. I did them all the time with my mates. Ronaldinho was my hero! But as soon as I got into organised football, it was as if the shackles were locked on.

I was afraid to try something in case it went wrong. But then Stephen Kenny came along and said, within reason, not to be afraid to play.

That incident between me and Friday probably didn't look like much on television, but it meant a hell of a lot to me at the time. My confidence grew and *grew* from that moment.

The rest of the lads were flying too. Anytime I had the ball, there were always options. Players were moving into space, everyone was brave enough to look for the ball, even in tight situations. There were spells where we kept the ball and dominated possession. They had chances, but we did too.

At one stage Daryl Horgan got the ball and beat two or three of their players. *He's taking the piss,* I thought. We weren't afraid to attack. At another point the ball was sent down the channel towards Davy McMillan. He chopped World Cup star Vlaar and cut back inside. It was mad.

AZ came into the game a lot more after half-time. We were under more pressure and eventually they got the breakthrough. It was the infamous 'assault in Alkmaar'. It was a serious incident at the time, but since that night I don't think we've ever had more craic about anything that has happened on a football pitch. We could admit that, after we knew their lad was okay! *What am I talking about?*

The attempted punch by Gary Rogers that landed on Stijn Wuytens' jaw instead of the ball. Every so often a GIF or a picture of the incident appeared on the team WhatsApp group.

It was a ball over from the right, played high into the box.

Gary raced off his line.

Wuytens sprinted through the middle, with Ronan Finn chasing him; he ran between me and Sean Gannon, jumped into the air and, just as he made contact with the ball, he got a glove right in the mush. Gary absolutely 'Supermanned' him, knocked him unconscious.

Straightaway, there was concern on the pitch.

He was out cold.

We could see the referee signalling that the goal was given, but there were no celebrations on the pitch. Both sets of players were calling over to the benches, trying to alert the medical staff. Their players were freaking out. There was blood coming from Wuytens' mouth. No one knew what was going on.

The longer it went on, the more distressed their players became.

Jahanbakhsh was in tears. He didn't finish the game.

His head wasn't in it after that. I was standing close to the doctors and I remember asking if he was breathing. They replied that he was and that he had a pulse. It's not the kind of conversation you expect to have on a football pitch. Eventually the doctor said he was going to be alright.

As concerned as I was about Wuytens, I do remember thinking… *We've got a game to win. These lads, a few of their heads have gone here.*

Maybe it's a chance for us to get back into the game.

It sounds cold, I know, but I couldn't do anything to help him. Obviously I was concerned. But unless the referee said otherwise, we still had a game to play. He was going to be alright, he was breathing, he had a pulse. *Grand!*

Three important boxes ticked right there. But this was the biggest game of my life and we had just gone 1-0 down. We'd been playing so well, we didn't deserve to be behind.

And we didn't deserve to lose Stevie O'Donnell to a second yellow card shortly after the game restarted. When I talk about courage and composure on the ball, there was no better man in that Dundalk team that Stevie. It all came so naturally to him. He was so cool and calm in possession, no matter how strong the opposition. You weren't going to get defence-splitting 60-yard passes from him. But he was always the man to dictate the tempo – speed the game up, slow it down. And if you needed an option, he always seemed to be there. I have never played with another player like him. When he moved further up the pitch, he had this lovely little give-and-go, and he got involved in a few goals. He loved that side of the game too.

But his favourite role was deep, getting on the ball and setting up play. He constantly talked about Xavi and Iniesta. He loved them, he was obsessed with them. He was obsessed with football and had an amazing brain for the game. It's no wonder he went into management.

We had to play the final 20 or so minutes without our inspirational skipper. As far as we were concerned, the referee was conned. A goal down and a man down, we were really up against it.

Chris Shields came on for the final stretch. With just minutes remaining, he made a run towards the left wing and was picked out by Daryl Horgan. He bought a free-kick. *Lovely.* We were set-piece kings. Anytime we won a free-kick near the opposition area or a corner, we felt we could score.

Ciaran Kilduff, who was only on the pitch a few minutes, was just as hungry as me to get on the end of Horgs' delivery. The pair of us were wrestling in the area; Wout Weghorst had Killer, Vlaar was on Andy Boyle and Mattias Johansson was marking me.

Weghorst, a giant 6'4" forward, was on for Friday and he was a much bigger threat. He was very sharp and his movement off the shoulder was excellent. I remember thinking... *This fella is much better than Freddy Friday,* who we'd hyped up big time before the game. Weghorst ended up getting a move to Wolfsburg, and later he was sold to Burnley for €12m, but not before he was outfoxed by Killer.

I was convinced that I'd be the one on the end of Horgs' free-kick. Killer and Boyler had the two big men, clearing the way for me to grab the glory. Once again, I could see the headlines. All I had to do was get a yard of space so I could attack the ball. I said to Killer, 'Take the big man out of the area!' I wanted it, but Killer had a different idea.

The ball came in.

I held off my man and got ready to attack it.

Before I could, Killer muscled past Weghorst, got his head to the ball and sent it flying into the back of the net. Even thinking about it now, I can feel the hairs stand up on the back of my neck. I chased after Killer as he ran behind the goal. Suddenly, he realised that the fans were on the other side, so he took a sharp right turn and headed in their direction. I cut back and followed him.

We stood there below the Dundalk section.

It was a feeling of pure euphoria. They were going bonkers.

I recognised half the faces from walking around town. I tried to find Bronagh in the crowd. She was there with her friend Jenny and the other players' wives and partners. It was nuts. They were all jumping up and down, hugging each other, while we were absolutely ecstatic on the pitch.

Once the initial buzz died down, we knew we had to switch on again. The game was going into injury time and there was going to be plenty of it. With 10 men, we knew it would be backs-to-the-wall.

And that's how it played out. I hooked the ball clear from our six-yard box, Boyler got an important block in, everybody was back throwing their bodies in front of the ball. Finally, after an age, the referee blew it up.

I LET OUT a roar. Up to this point, it was all about getting to the group stages. But now that we were there, we weren't just happy to make up the numbers. We wanted to compete – and we had been brave enough to say so in interviews beforehand. Now we needed to back those words up.

It kind of felt like another 'F**k You' to the establishment, to people who didn't believe that an Irish team could compete at the very top by playing a traditionally un-Irish style of football. We showed that we could keep possession, we could defend when we needed to and we could attack by playing through teams, not just by lumping the ball forward.

We were so proud that night.

Stephen Kenny could hardly wipe the smile off his face. It was yet another vindication of his philosophy. We knew we could achieve success at home, but to do it at that level was massive for us.

Not that we were jumping around, popping champagne corks in the dressing-room. We were thrilled to get the point, but there was also a tinge of regret that we didn't get all three. Sure, we had to come from behind in the closing moments, but it was always about winning games for us. And as we'd scored once, why couldn't we have scored two?

We always took both positives and negatives from each game. We were never happy. It was never enough.

That's what kept the fire burning. That's how Stephen Kenny was with us – we could never reach our ceiling. It was constantly rising. No matter how good things got, we could always do better.

We got our draw, now we wanted a win.

That game was a huge deal for me on a personal level. I sat out the win against BATE Borisov, I was an unused sub in the play-off, so this was my moment, my time to show that I belonged on this stage. The other lads confirmed that they were comfortable at a high level against BATE and by being competitive until the death against Legia Warsaw.

As our bus drove out of Alkmaar that night and headed towards Brussels for our flight home, I sunk back into my seat.

Yeah, I belong here.

MY CONFIDENCE HAD never been higher than after the Alkmaar game. We had two league matches in the space of three days before the visit of Maccabi Tel Aviv and I could do no wrong.

My equaliser against Shamrock Rovers earned us a crucial Premier Division point and I scored again in the 3-1 win over Derry City. The Tel Aviv game was our eighth in the month of September, but no one was complaining of feeling tired.

I certainly wasn't, anyway. The form I was in, I would have played every single night if I had to. At this stage we weren't even training anymore. It was match, recovery, walk-through… match. We were getting through games on adrenaline.

September wasn't even our busiest month – we played 10 games in October… 18 games in two months? We played the equivalent of half-a-season in just over eight weeks! And there were no easy games either, with the title race heating up.

Reflecting now on that run of games, I don't know how we got through it. We had a much smaller group of players in 2016. But we just kept going. Stephen Kenny always told us, 'Tiredness is in your head'. That was our mentality.

'You can't be tired, you're grand,' he'd say.

And as players, we were happy to go along with that, because we all preferred playing games over training. And while we were in the Europa League, playing big games that were on TV right around Europe, there was a massive euphoria within the dressing-room that kept us going. Even within Ireland there were a load of new eyes on us.

People who never before gave a toss about football, about Irish football, were all eager to get a slice of us. We were getting the kind of attention that the international team, that rugby and GAA players were used to receiving. That was an extra buzz. This was what every single one of us wanted and dreamed of as kids. It helped carry us through games too.

Then there was the fact that we were extremely fit. We all lived our lives the right way. We ate the right way, trained, worked out and slept the right way. Everybody bought into it, everyone looked to get the best out of themselves and the team. No one wanted to be the person that let the dressing-room down.

No excuses, no hiding places.

If you were caught slacking, you'd hear about it from the rest of the lads.

There was no fear either of picking up injuries. There was no pulling out of challenges in league games or anything like that. We had to win the league, we wanted to make sure we'd be back in Europe the next year, maybe go one step further and qualify for the Champions League group stages. That was our mindset.

It was almost as if we felt indestructible. We went into each league game with one focus – get the three points and wrap up the title as soon as possible.

AHEAD OF THE Tel Aviv game we picked up four points from two tricky home games. We were never happy with anything less than one hundred percent, but these were exceptional circumstances. There was no time to beat ourselves up over two points dropped. We had too much on our plate, trying to digest Gerry Spain's analysis of our opponents.

We went through the team, how they set up, patterns of play, strengths and weaknesses, and so on… and then we moved onto the individual players.

The level of detail was incredible.

Gerry had a page on each player and beside each bio would be a comparison.

'Player X is like Makalele.'

'Player Y is an Henri-style player.'

Just a little something to scare the shite out of us!

Our previous game in Tallaght was against BATE Borisov, when we qualified for the group stages. We also won the league there a year earlier. We loved the place. The pitch was immaculate, even better than the surface at the Aviva Stadium. It was never in poor nick. And we knew we would fill that ground. It wouldn't be half-empty.

One thing about Maccabi was their wingers tended to go roaming around the pitch. We didn't often come up against that in the League of Ireland, but whenever we did we were strong enough to cope. If someone here tried a little overload, we often ended up exploiting it because they had key players out of position. But we were playing against a better standard in the Europa League.

If they produced an overload, they had the ability to make it count. Our full-backs were staying with their man and, as a result, were being dragged all over the pitch. There were times when Sean Gannon and Dane Massey ended up in midfield. At one stage, I remember Massey, our left-back, following his man all the way over to our right wing.

Maccabi had some really good players.

Tal Ben Haim spent years in England with clubs such as Chelsea, Manchester City and Bolton. And Yossi Benayoun was very good for them when he came on late in the game. He was 36 at this stage, but to see him coming on against us was a real thrill. I grew up supporting Liverpool and I remembered watching him play in big games at Anfield. Obviously, you are focused on the game itself, but it's hard to stop the football fan in you from coming out in moments like that.

That was another pinch-me moment.

So too was Ciaran Kilduff's winning goal. This was another superb performance by the whole team. We matched Maccabi and deserved the win. Of course, it was Killer again. The hero of Alkmaar with another big European goal.

What a feeling it was to win that game. Not that we were surprised. We had full confidence beforehand that we could get all three points. *Why not?* We had beaten BATE, who had plenty of Champions League group stage experience, while Legia Warsaw weren't exactly a million miles ahead of us. Then to draw in Alkmaar with 10 men, having bossed part of the game and proven we were able to hold our own at this level, we knew we had it within ourselves to get a win.

I looked at the crowd that night under the floodlights, tears rolling down the cheeks of so many jubilant fans. I could see old fellas from Dundalk, lads who would have been following the club for 60 or so years, jumping up and down and hugging each other, celebrating like teenagers. I looked out for my family and friends.

My brother was over from England for the game, my mam was there too. I was thinking also about my dad, wishing that he was one of the faces in the crowd. I knew exactly how he'd be at that moment.

He'd have this little chuckle and his eyes would mist up.

IT WAS A crazy feeling, winning a group stage game.

It was a huge moment for us because we talked all the time about the fact that we weren't just representing Dundalk FC, we were representing the League of Ireland and Irish football in general. It always killed us, the way the League of Ireland was – and still is – viewed in this country.

And it killed us how Irish football was viewed abroad. It was so rewarding after those European matches to hear opposition players and coaches say, 'Wow, we did not expect this from an Irish team'. There has long been a perception abroad that Irish teams are all about kick and run, route one; that we hadn't the ability to play a possession-based game.

Yet when they came up against us, they faced a team that played the ball out from the goalkeeper, that kept possession and attacked with purpose.

It was never just a case of keeping the ball for the sake of it. After tiki-taka exploded in popularity, thanks to Pep Guardiola's Barcelona, a lot of copycats adopted that style. But many teams went overboard. Players were passing the ball just to bring up their stats, but with no real attacking purpose. Stephen Kenny was never into possession for possession's sake. I remember one day he went mad at one of our players.

'What are you doing?' he roared.

'Keeping the ball!' came the reply.

'You had a chance to play it forward,' Stephen shouted back. 'Yes, we keep the ball, but when you have a chance to attack, you f**king attack!'

That's what I loved about him. He wanted to entertain, but he was focused on winning. And to win a match in the group stages, playing the way we play, that was a source of immense pride for everyone.

I once ended up in a fist-fight with a friend over his views on Irish football.

He was drunk, and said, 'I'm delighted for you Brian, but the League of Ireland is shite'. You get that everywhere you go, you read it online all the time. It really grinds my gears.

Even when you show that you can compete with teams on a bigger stage and win, it's hard to change opinions. So the Maccabi win in some respects was a 'F**k You' to anyone who ever called the League of Ireland shite.

COMING OFF THE pitch after the Maccabi game, I couldn't stop thinking about this phenomenal group of players.

We had a unique dressing-room, one I'd certainly never experienced before. The lads there were among the nicest I'd ever met in football. That boiled down to Stephen Kenny's recruitment.

He wasn't just after great players, he was after great characters too. We were all in it for each other, nobody put themselves first. There was a real intelligence there. Look at the number of lads who came from UCD, the percentage of players who had a third-level education behind them. And the ones that didn't were smart lads with plenty of cop-on.

A year earlier, it was 'The Richie Towell Show.' In another dressing-room, that might have put a few noses out of joint. But not in our dressing-room.

Richie was a nice fella, fair play to him.

He bangs in 30 goals and hogs all the headlines? Let him have it, as long as it wins us the league. From my experience, that sort of respect from every corner of the dressing-room was uncommon.

Most squads would have a couple of alpha males, which would lead to conflict. But not here. If someone did something wrong, you wouldn't turn around and slaughter him, you'd pick him up. There was never any finger-pointing.

We had too much respect for each other.

If you are looking at the contributing factors to our successes under Stephen Kenny, the unity within the dressing-room was one of the biggest.

PART **FIVE**

Dreams and Doubts

Dundalk grew and grew as a football force through our European adventures (above, before meeting Molde FK in the Europa League in 2020). We never stopped believing in one another and also celebrating as blood brothers (bottom right, I carry David McMillan after we clinched the FAI Cup title in 2020 against Shamrock Rovers).

*Dundalk was never just about us
as a group of footballers, and our
management team led by Stephen
Kenny... there were so many other people
who were a vital part of our 'family' like
owner Andy Connolly (whom I hug after
our group win over Tel Aviv, above left)
and our brilliant kitman Noelie Walsh (top
right). Then there was Harry Taaffe, a dear
friend who looked after everyone in the
club, and did nearly everything, until his
sad death... I meet Harry before a game in
Oriel Park (above) and celebrate with him
(right). Harry will be forever missed.*

■ CHAPTER 18 ■

BEFORE THE VISIT of Zenit St Petersburg, we had the small matter of five domestic games in just 15 days. Scratch that, SIX games in 15 days.

The first was an FAI Cup semi-final against Derry City.

We were 2-0 up with 25 minutes remaining, but they came back with Ronan Curtis, now an Ireland international, equalising five minutes from time. That meant a replay at the Brandywell just two days later. It was the last thing we needed. Curtis scored again early on, but we came back and won 2-1. We were heading for our second successive FAI Cup final meeting with Cork City.

Four days later we lost 3-0 to Sligo Rovers in the league, but we bounced back three days after that to beat Cork. Three quickly became the magic number.

Another three-day gap and we were away too Shamrock Rovers. We beat them 3-0. After another three days, another three-goal win, this time away to Longford Town.

That Longford result all but sealed our third league title in-a-row, but there was no time to dwell on that. In three more days we would face Zenit St Petersburg in Tallaght. Our seventh game in 18 days.

I'll always remember going into that match feeling like we kicked off against Derry City way back on October 2 and just we didn't stop playing. It felt like we were involved in one of those charity football marathons, but with league titles, FAI Cups and Europa League points at stake.

Heading into the Zenit game, we were on four points and they were on six. Not that we had much time to enjoy our lofty position in Group D, with all the games we had to squeeze in. When we finally got to those few days between Longford and Zenit, we had a chance to properly study their side.

Those analysis sessions weren't for the faint-hearted. Once again, Gerry Spain delivered a comprehensive analysis of each player. Even the lads we hadn't heard of before were full internationals with a wealth of Champions League and Europa League experience. There were senior caps for Italy, Brazil, Belgium, Spain and Russia. They had a giant up front in Artyom Dzyuba. He must have been nearly six-and-a-half feet tall. He ended up scoring three goals in the World Cup two years later, including one in the last 16 against Spain.

We were definitely going up yet another level here.

Zenit were in the Champions League group stages three out of the four seasons prior to 2016. And the one time during that spell that they didn't make the Champions League, they got as far as the quarter-finals of the Europa League, only to lose by a single goal over two legs to eventual winners Seville. *But were we scared?*

No!

I suppose deep in the back of our minds there was always the idea that they were capable of dishing out an absolute tanking. But we didn't think like that.

The lads were all in a positive frame of mind ahead of the game. Our momentum was so strong that we actually thought we could get a result against a team with a turnover roughly 60 times ours, with players worth tens of millions of euro. We hadn't really had any set-backs up to that point. Sure, there was Legia in the Champions League play-off, but even that kind of turned into a positive, thanks to our performance in the second-leg.

And the defeat to Sligo wasn't going to stop us winning the league. So we weren't burdened by a fear of failure. It was more the buzz of excitement, the contemplation of what could be achieved. We couldn't wait to face Zenit. On the home front, the league was pretty much wrapped up and we were in the final of the FAI Cup. All in all, we got a lot of business done between the Maccabi and Zenit games.

ZENIT STARTED WITH Dzyuba up front, but he wasn't getting much change off Andy and myself. We even bullied him off the ball a couple of times in the first-half. And as we walked off at half-time we said to each other, 'He's not up to much, is he?'

We were delighted with how things were going.

They hadn't created too many chances. Their biggest threats in the opening 45 minutes came from Axel Witsel and Giuliano. A few times when Witsel got the ball in midfield, he did this one-two where he would lay it off and explode away at a frightening speed. He would take players out of the game in one movement.

Fortunately, his trickery didn't lead to any scares in the opening half, because our shape in the back-four remained solid. Giuliano's movement in the number 10 role was unbelievable. It was as if the phrase, 'Turn on a sixpence', was coined for him. By the time we finished our group stage campaign, he was hands down the best player we came up against. Giuliano ended up being capped for Brazil in that 10 position. Their Italy international Domenico Criscito was another class act.

At one stage in the first-half, he nutmegged Patrick McEleney with a little stud-roll over by the bench. I remember thinking… *F**king hell, how's a left-back doing that going back towards his own goal?* Javi Garcia in midfield was a big, broad lad and Witsel was an athlete. The intensity of their team was so good.

But we were still comfortable enough. And we believed we had a chance against their centre-backs Luis Neto and Nicolas Lombaerts. It's a strange thing to say about a pair of international defenders for Portugal and Belgium, but that's how we felt on the night.

They certainly didn't do much to prevent Robbie Benson from getting his shot off seven minutes into the second-half. I don't know what their goalkeeper was thinking, but suddenly we were 1-0 ahead.

I was thinking… *How did that go in?*

Must have taken a deflection.

But it didn't. Robbie hit it straight at the 'keeper and he let it fly past him. Robbie scored a serious amount of big goals for us in Europe.

BATE Borisov, Legia Warsaw and now St Petersburg in the space of a few months? That was some collection for the highlights reel.

As the goal celebrations were wrapping up, I looked at Boyler and he looked back at me. The pair of us started laughing. One-up against Zenit St Petersburg, with their team packed with internationals… us top of the group at that stage?

We were living out our childhood dreams right there and then. But we had to quickly switch back on.

There was still plenty of work to get through. We knew they would get chances, that they'd have a lot of possession. But we were still dealing handily enough with their big target man Dzyuba.

Not long after Robbie's strike, we were centimetres from doubling our lead. Dane Massey's header, which smacked off the stub of the post, is still a topic of conversation in the dressing-room. It was a set-piece and we believed we could score from every dead-ball situation around the opposition's area. Of course it was harder to do so in Europe, because we were up against bigger, stronger players.

But we were still winning our fair share of aerial duels. And in that moment against Zenit, we couldn't believe the amount of space we had when the ball came across.

Whoever was marking me just stood still on the edge of the box. I was completely free at the back post, miles onside, when Massey got his head to the ball. I can still see it now. If his header had been a centimetre to the right, it would have gone in off the post or bounced to me and I would have had the easiest tap-in of my life.

Of course, going two-up wouldn't have meant it was game-over, but what a chance that was to put some extra daylight between ourselves and the mighty Zenit.

IMAGINE IF THAT had gone in and we'd held on?

Halfway through the group, unbeaten, the Premier Division all but wrapped up and through to the FAI Cup final; we could have really focused on getting through the group stages and into the knockouts.

But it wasn't to be. They started to pile on the pressure.

With about 20 minutes to go they got back on level terms. The ball was passed back to Gabriel Sava, but his clearance bounced off Chris Shields and spiralled into the air, and landed at the feet of Robert Mak, who equalised.

I know the decision to put Gabi in goal raised a few eyebrows. But Gabi had been brilliant for us over the years. He came in for Gary Rogers after the 3-0 defeat to Sligo and played against Cork, Shamrock Rovers and Longford. While it was disappointing for Gary to miss out, Gabi earned his place against Zenit.

Gabi had been so patient in waiting for his opportunity. His work-rate was phenomenal. A second-choice goalkeeper could easily do the bare minimum, but he was constantly doing extra work after training, sticking around to help the lads who wanted to do some additional shooting practice. He never once complained. He won trophies for us with his performances in cup games, while he filled in brilliantly for Gary in the league whenever he was needed.

The way we conceded against Zenit was cruel on him.

We were playing at a level where interest in our game was 20-fold to what it normally would be. There were more people watching, while there was more commentary on social media and in mainstream media.

It's tough being a goalkeeper. If you make a mistake as a forward or a midfielder, it generally doesn't lead to a goal. You'll have players behind you to bail you out. But as a centre-half or a goalkeeper, unfortunately it's an occupational hazard. Gabi came into a pressurised situation, having only played a handful of games. Goalkeepers need time on the pitch to get into their routine, to grow in confidence.

At the time, some said you can't change your goalkeeper at such a vital stage of the season. For Stephen Kenny, you're damned if you do and you're damned if you don't. As for Gabi, in that moment when his clearance led to Zenit's equaliser, you'd wonder who'd be a goalkeeper!

After they scored, Zenit held onto the ball for four or five minutes.

It was a period of sustained pressure, but we were holding our shape. Eventually, their dominance took its toll. They were making runs, shifting us from side to side, running us ragged.

It ended up with Ronan Finn and Chris Shields in between myself and Boyler in our own box. The ball landed at the feet of Witsel, just outside the area.

One touch inside and he was within shooting range so, being the closest to him, I moved to close him down. But he did another one of his explosive give-and-goes and was past me in the blink of an eye.

At the same time, we still had five or six players in the box. But our shape was all over the place and they got the ball to Giuliano, who slotted home from close range.

That was a real kick in the teeth.

We were so close to going two-up and suddenly we were 2-1 down. But when the dust settled, we realised that we were running on fumes in the final 20 minutes. After the sucker-punch of their equaliser, fatigue finally kicked in.

And it's little wonder, given the number of games we played in the build-up to the Zenit game. We had played three nights before to pretty much clinch the league title. We were on a run of six games in 15 days. How did we even compete up to the 70th minute?

They were always going to have the last 20 minutes, regardless of our schedule. The bigger team always dominates late on.

We were disappointed we didn't get more assistance from the league that we were representing, when it came to the fixture congestion. If you want Irish football to make these strides in Europe, try helping rather than hindering. We had a small enough squad at the time. We brought Alan Keane and Dean Shiels in for the extra games, but our pool of players was shallow compared to our Europa League rivals.

At the time, as players, we just got on with it. We didn't complain.

Of course, we didn't help ourselves by letting a two-goal lead slide against Derry, forcing a replay two days later. But rising to the level we were playing at, we needed everything to go in our favour. We needed everyone to be right at it one hundred percent of the time, we needed to be near perfect.

And we needed that bit of luck that deserted us against Zenit.

HAPPILY, WE HAD another game three days later to get the disappointment of our Europa League defeat out of our system. And what a way to banish the blues.

We beat Bohs 2-1 to win the league and I scored the winner, after Andy Boyle popped up with the opener. That was my second title-clinching goal in three years, after the second in the win against Cork City two years earlier.

It was a set-piece that we'd worked on for years, but that had never worked before. I bundled it in after Dane Massey flicked on a Ronan Finn free-kick. I'm not sure if Massey's header was going in, but I didn't care.

I was just happy to wrap up a third Premier Division title in-a-row. Now we could concentrate on the second half of our Europa League campaign and our double-double bid.

· CHAPTER 19 ·

OUR TRIP TO St Petersburg got off to the worst possible start.

Dundalk hired a charter flight to make things go as smoothly as possible, but we ended up stuck in the airport during a six-hour delay. Technical problems on the way over to Dublin had to be addressed before we could take off. We didn't arrive until midnight local time, which meant our team meeting, which had been scheduled for a reasonable hour, took place after one o'clock in the morning.

That wasn't the first problem we had with travel that year. And it wouldn't be the last. I couldn't travel with the team to Iceland because of a delay in our return journey. The lads had to wait for hours in the airport after the first-leg against BATE Borisov before boarding their flight home. Unfortunately, for them, Stephen Kenny took that opportunity to go absolutely ballistic at them after they had been so badly outplayed.

He had a right go at them, I was told, and scheduled a recovery session for the next morning. The poor lads were knackered. On another trip, the correct tow-bar for our airplane wasn't available and they had to fly one in.

And then Israel… well, we'll get to that one later.

SO, THERE WE were in our plush hotel in St Petersburg, everyone knackered after the delay and flight, sitting through a late-night (or early-morning) team meeting.

In fairness to the club, they didn't let us down once that year when it came to hotels. They made sure the standard of accommodation and food was top-class. Our St Petersburg hotel, much like the opposition, was another step up.

Most of us had never been to Russia before and had pre-conceived ideas about where we were headed. I expected a dull, drab place. But when we arrived there, we found a beautiful city, filled with the kind of architecture I'd only ever seen before on travel shows or in old James Bond films.

The heavy snowfall the next day added to the enchantment.

We all took the opportunity to have a walk around, to see as much of the city as we could during our down time. I did a bit with eir Sport. They asked me to do a video diary, a behind-the-scenes view of the build-up to the big game. Doing that sort of thing is fine when things are going well. If things aren't going your way, any extra work you take on can end up being a stick for people to beat you with.

We played in the old Petrovsky Stadium, located on an island in the Neva river. They were in the process of building a new stadium for the 2018 World Cup. I had hoped it would be finished in time for our game, but unfortunately work wasn't completed until five months after our visit.

It's fair to say though, that a lot of jaws dropped as we approached the Petrovsky for our training session the day before the game. It looked as if it was floating on the Neva. Its four floodlights reminded me of something you'd see in the American football drama *Friday Night Lights*. Except, these were massive. They towered into the sky, reached in and leaned in over the pitch.

As impressive and imposing as the stadium was, there was nothing fancy about the dressing-rooms. They were cramped and looked like they hadn't been given a lick of paint in decades. But we couldn't spend long in them, as we only had an hour on the pitch.

The ground staff were eager to ensure we didn't get a minute longer than we were entitled to. In the early qualifying rounds, home teams weren't so strict in enforcing the one-hour rule. But as we went on, there was a lot more clock-watching and wrist-tapping.

The UEFA delegate was there to make sure everything was done by the book. And I'm sure Zenit were eager that we had as little time as possible to prepare. Not that you do much anyway.

Training is meant to be behind closed doors after the first 15 minutes, but in a stadium that big I'm sure some of the stewards weren't exactly who they said they were. Who's to stop you from sticking a high-viz on a lesser-known member of the coaching staff? The late Harry Taaffe had a few great stories. Once he locked himself in a container and when the opposition arrived for training, he was able to record it and take some notes. I'm sure every team indulges in a spot of espionage.

We practiced a few set-pieces and did a little bit on our shape, trying not to give too much away. As the hour approached, the ground staff got agitated.

They came onto the pitch to try and usher us off.

It was like last orders in the pub. You're there with three drinks in front of you while the poor bouncer is shouting, 'Have you no homes to go to?'

They were really getting pissed off with us.

Suddenly, they were in amongst us, repairing the pitch while we were working on corners. We kept going. Our lads were there swinging the ball in and we were jostling together, trying to win headers, but also smashing into the ground staff at the same time. Stephen Kenny was going mad at them too.

WHILE WE WERE in St Petersburg, Andy Boyle and Daryl Horgan were called up by Martin O'Neill to the senior Ireland squad. I was delighted for them – and quite envious too. As far as I'm concerned, playing for your country has to be the goal for every single footballer. It's the pinnacle. I remember the debates years earlier – would you rather win the Champions League with your club or the World Cup with your country? Hands down, it was always the World Cup for me.

I was jealous. *So jealous.*

But at the same time I was so happy for them. They deserved it.

The way I saw it was that the call-up was also recognition of what we were doing as a team. You couldn't deny their individual qualities, but they were part of a much bigger movement in Irish football.

Whenever there is a League of Ireland link to the international squad, it fills me with pride about our game. Jack Byrne is the most recent success story. Our own Michael Duffy has been close to a call. I'm sure it will come for him.

Then you have the lads like James McClean, Seamus Coleman, Kevin Doyle, Wes Hoolahan, Shane Long and many more who started off in this league.

Long ago, I dreamed of joining that list, but I never even made it as far as the underage teams.

WE WERE ITCHING for the game to start. The pitch had been cleared but there was still plenty of snow lying around. The stadium was packed.

It was proper old-school. Even the noise from the fans sounded old-school. You could almost feel the crowd; their chants reverberating through you. When Zenit pushed forward, their supporters seemed to rise up with them. The roar from the stands seemed to act as a tail-wind. We started off alright, but they had a much stronger intensity about them compared to the Tallaght game.

Despite their improved performance, we were doing well until three minutes before the break, when they opened the scoring. It's a moment seared into my memory for all the wrong reasons.

WE WON A free-kick about 15 yards inside our own half.

We never lumped the ball down the pitch. It wasn't in our make-up.

With it so close to half-time, I thought we could hold onto the ball.

They were such a good team. I didn't want to hand possession straight back to them with a 50/50 punt. So, I played into Chris Shields. I suppose it was my fault for not anticipating it, but I was caught cold when the ball fizzed straight back at me.

Giuliano was standing right in front of me.

In that situation, I'd usually play it to the right-full, but Sean Gannon was too far up the pitch, and I had no ball to him. I should have booted it, but the thought didn't even enter my head.

Instinct kicked in. I was full of confidence at the time.

So I tried to check back... with a f**king Cruyff turn. In the circumstances – the ice, the snow – it wasn't the wisest thing to do.

I slipped and Giuliano pounced.

We were miles out, so I should have grabbed him.

But he was that nippy that I didn't even have a chance to do that. As he raced towards goal, I could hear this roar go up around the ground.

It acted as his tail-wind, while I felt like I was running into a head-wind. I tried to get back, Boyler tried to get back, but they had a two-on-one.

Giuliano slotted it home.

Right there and then I knew I had messed up badly. I felt sick.

It was a horrible feeling.

Such a big occasion, millions tuning in across Russia, Ireland, the UK… all over the world. That wasn't my first thought, though. That swept over me like a second wave of misery after the final whistle. There and then, all I could think about was how badly I'd messed up. It was a brutal feeling. But we still had another half and a bit to play, so I had to roll up my sleeves and put it behind me.

Looking back at the incident, my biggest mistake was trying to turn back like that. I don't regret trying to play the ball out, because that was how we were programmed to play. The Cruyff turn though; it was the wrong time and wrong place for such extravagant play.

I should have asked the full-backs to drop back, so that I'd have an out-ball.

Daryl Horgan equalised seven minutes after the break. It was a great goal, demonstrating his lightning pace, anticipation and finishing. Giuliano scored again with 12 minutes left, but we almost snatched a point when Patrick McEleney hit the crossbar late on.

They put us under a lot of pressure throughout. There were waves of attacks coming at us. Aleksandr Kerzhakov played up front and, although he was just a few weeks off his 34th birthday, he was sensational. He was a much bigger threat than Artem Dzyuba.

Kerzhakov loved to play off the shoulder. He was so sharp and unpredictable. One moment he'd come in and show for the ball, and the next he'd make a ghosting run past you.

Giuliano was so good once again. His technique was amazing and his positioning as a number 10 between the lines made him so hard to pick up.

It's easy to talk about, but for a player to be able to drift in and out, just off the number six but not far enough onto the centre-half, is such a tricky thing to pull off.

I was constantly asking myself… *Should I move out and attack Giuliano?* If I did push up, Kerzhakov was ready to go the other way. The dynamic between the two players was like nothing I'd ever faced before.

As physically tough as it was playing against Zenit, we were so fit that we felt we could keep running forever. But mentally it was so draining. We had to be so alert and on our toes throughout the 90 minutes.

Yet we still believed we could get a result against them. Despite having a lot of games in the run-up to Zenit, we finished the game well enough, which showed the fitness, desire and mentality behind our team. It was no consolation though. We came away from two games against Zenit without a point and that was really disappointing. We never took any comfort out of *nearly* doing something.

I'M SURE A few of the lads came away from that game cursing me. I was devastated and distraught with the outcome, and that my mistake was so costly. I was always so serious about football. If I lost a game, it would really hurt me.

It would stick with me for a while. If I didn't play well, I'd be a disaster at home. No one would come near me. And if I made a big mistake, I'd be like a ticking time-bomb.

When you get to that level, when you have lived the highs of the games beforehand – the performance in Alkmaar, scoring the title-clinching goal against Bohs – what a way to come crashing back down to earth.

It was the lowest I'd felt coming off a football pitch.

I couldn't sleep that night. I didn't *want* to sleep.

So I went for a walk with Davy McMillan. We wandered around central St Petersburg at two in the morning. We must have walked for two hours, looking at the landmarks in the snow. My head was in the bin at that stage.

I needed the company.

Davy is a good mate. He's level-headed and a great fella. He helped me out big-time that night. We didn't talk about football, we just spoke about life and any old shite that popped into our heads.

WE'D USUALLY FLY home straight after a Euro away game, but with the FAI Cup final on Sunday – less than three days away – we stayed on for another night.

We were straight down to the hotel gym the next morning for a recovery session. It was a big day for me – my 30th birthday. But after what had happened the night before I didn't feel like celebrating. I was doing a bit of stretching with the rest of the lads when Stephen Kenny and Vinny Perth walked into the gym.

They wanted to go through the goal – and they wanted to go *through* me too.

I don't remember any other occasion when they went through a game or an incident the next morning. A few days later, maybe. But not the next morning.

Out came the laptop.

All I could think of in my head was... *Is there any need for this?*

It was clear as day that I messed up. I didn't need to be told – especially in front of the rest of the squad. I apologised in the dressing-room straightaway after the game.

But when Stephen and Vinny appeared the next day, I had to keep my mouth shut. I made a mistake. It was indefensible. Sometimes you just have to sit there and face the music.

They started the video. Stephen laid into me.

'A f**king Cruyff turn in the f**king snow?'

'Why were you going short to Shieldsy in the first place?'

'If you are going to go short, you need him here, him there... the two full-backs were too high.'

Fair enough. I couldn't say anything.

But I still didn't see the point in them humiliating me in front of the boys. I was miserable. *Some way to celebrate your 30th,* I thought.

ONE OF MY best friends was getting married later that day.

The plan was to head straight to the hotel when we landed, hopefully make the meal and have a bit of craic. But I just wanted to get home, to see Bronagh, to lock myself in a room; anything to get away from people.

I had to go to the wedding though. He was one of my best mates and we were a close group. I couldn't skip it just because I'd had a disaster the night before.

Bronagh picked me up from the airport and drove me to the wedding. We arrived just in time for the main course. I was glad I went. It was far better than heading home and wallowing in self-pity. Another group of mates might have slagged me repeatedly over the night before, but this was a good bunch. It was a great evening, it was a welcome distraction.

It was a dry one too, because we were training the next morning – a quick session on the Saturday ahead of Sunday's cup final.

I met up with the rest of the squad at the Portmarnock Hotel on Saturday morning, ahead of training. While the wedding was a welcome distraction, Thursday night in St Petersburg was still swirling around in my head.

I was still hurting.

Actually, I was dying inside.

Living in Dundalk as well, I knew I wasn't going to get away from it.

To this day, I think about the next morning, about Stephen Kenny going through me for a shortcut. *Could he not have done it away from everybody else?* That wasn't a thing we did at Dundalk. We didn't do public humiliations.

Why did this have to be the exception?

I had one or two theories.

ONE INVOLVED MY stag, which had been pencilled in for November 25 long before we qualified for the group stages. *Season over*, I thought, it wouldn't be a problem.

Then, when we made it to the Europa League, I looked at the dates for the games. We were at home to Alkmaar on the 24th. Our last game, away to Maccabi Tel Aviv, was another two weeks away. I hadn't approached Stephen about it by the time word got out.

He found out and was pretty pissed off.

It ended up causing a bit of a rift between the two of us.

Whether the stag was a factor or not, I couldn't shake the hurt I felt over the mistake against Zenit and the fallout the next morning. I asked myself over and over again… *Was there any need?* It was that obvious, it wasn't as if it was something we needed to fix as a team.

Anyone could tell I was crushed, that it was killing me.

Stephen could easily have taken me to one side. *Hammer me in private all you want, but not in front of the lads.* But at the same time, I had to accept it. That's football. Whatever a manager chooses to do, you just have to take it on the chin. And having played for Dermot Keely for a year at a young age, I was experienced enough when it came to taking a bollocking.

ON MY WAY to training on Saturday morning I was fairly sure I was going to be left out of the side. But when we went through the shape for the cup final, I realised I was in the team. I always say actions speak louder than words and Stephen's actions showed he still had confidence in me.

That gave me a much-needed boost. After making a mistake like that, you are always going to give it everything in the next game. If anyone was going to mess up in the cup final, it wasn't going to be me.

What an opportunity for redemption. Be the big player in the big game; concentrate, do my job; lift the trophy. That was my mindset going into the final.

Of course the mistake was still in the back of my mind. We had more media on us than ever before, so the reminders were everywhere. For the first time in our careers, we were being subjected to almost forensic-style coverage. But being on €600 or €700-a-week, I wasn't being paid enough to cope with that level of criticism. I wasn't getting the big bucks to take the shite that Premier League players get.

I couldn't go home and console myself by counting my fortune.

I couldn't hide away in a big mansion. But I had to get on with it. This was what I always wanted, this level of exposure, playing in all these big games. The increased scrutiny was always going to come with the territory.

I still wonder how we managed to get through the cup final. We had eight games in September, 10 in October and already this was our second game in November – with a good 3,000km distance between the two match venues.

Ronan Finn was struggling with an injury and was rated 50/50 ahead of the game. He got a pain-killer and ended up winning the Man of the Match award. He was phenomenal that day. We were all excellent, I felt.

We were the better team. It was a typical Dundalk-Cork City game; we had a lot of the ball and they defended and went route one.

Seáni Maguire did very well for them. I'd played against him a few times and he was brilliant.

You never had a second against him.

He was always so sharp. And he was a great finisher too. But we defended very well and Seáni didn't get much of a sniff against Andy Boyle and myself.

Attacking-wise we just weren't at it. We didn't click.

It was partly down to fatigue – Daryl Horgan, Davy McMillan and Patrick McEleney had put up a lot of miles on the clock at that stage. But at the same time, Cork had a lot of players behind the ball. That was their style and they were really good at it. Space was so tight in the final third.

They were looking for counter-attacking opportunities, firing long balls into our half. But we were mopping that up handily enough.

The game dragged towards extra-time, which we needed about as much as we needed a replay in the semi-finals. Yet we still looked the livelier side.

Then, as penalties loomed, a real sickener.

A Cork throw-in. They went long.

Seáni dropped off a bit, but we were well set-up at the back. As the ball came to Seáni, he gave Finner a little nudge.

He hit it… scuffed it.

I made my body as big as possible to block his shot. It was probably going near-post, straight at Gary Rogers. But it hit the inside of my left heel.

The rest happened in slow motion.

I even had time to turn around and see the ball spinning towards the far corner. With Gary wrong-footed, it rolled into the net. The Cork fans behind the goal went crazy. I looked up at the clock on the giant scoreboard behind me… 120 minutes.

As a player, you know when you've had a good game or a poor one, and I had a really strong performance in the cup final. But now this? After St Petersburg I did everything I could to pick myself up and go again. *And for what?*

So that 120 minutes of hard work could be undone by a jammy last-minute deflection?

Everything we'd done over the previous month or so, the amount of games we'd played, the travelling we did, and we were the better side in extra-time; we deserved better. We went to new levels in terms of football in Ireland. We were playing against our nearest rivals, who had a week or so off.

Heads dropped. I was so deflated that I didn't even shout at the referee for the foul on Finner.

Imagine doing the double while competing in the group stages in Europe, while playing games every couple of days.

It would have been an unbelievable achievement. But that's cup football, isn't it?

Cup finals can be devastatingly cruel occasions. That game really knocked the wind out of me. I knew that this time I wasn't to blame.

It was a deflection. Bad luck.

Nothing more than that. But the accumulation of events had gotten to me. Before the final, we were determined to empty the tank, because we knew we had 18 days to our next match in the Europa League, at home to AZ Alkmaar.

And then another two weeks to Maccabi.

So we were ready to push the boat out one more time, then reset and go again for the next one. And we did. We just didn't get the result we deserved.

We were telling ourselves that we weren't tired. And because the results and performances were so good, we were fuelled by the buzz they generated.

Your head can tell your body that it can do more, and somehow you find the energy to keep going. The feel-good factor definitely helps.

But I think that cup final took its toll mentally. The manner of it, the last-minute deflection. I believe it knocked the wind out of our sails. Between that and having lots of time to dwell on it – given the gap between that and the AZ match – fatigue finally set in. We probably would have been better off having another game two or three days later.

LOOKING BACK AT 2016, we reached unbelievable levels of endurance and fitness to go so far. The mentality in the dressing-room was unrivalled. The character, motivation and drive was like nothing I'd ever witnessed before.

But we were starting to feel it. Players were picking up knocks in every game; ankles, knees, little strains, a sore neck, back or shoulder. We had a small squad and there wasn't a lot of rotation. We had players who could come in here and there, and we added some quality to the squad ahead of the group stages, but it was tough going.

We didn't feel those knocks while we were winning – and if we did, we certainly didn't dwell on them. It was easy to convince yourself to just get on with it.

But once that switch flicks in your head, once you allow yourself to feel the pain, it's hard to turn it off again. That FAI Cup final and the manner in which we lost, without us realising at the time, probably played a big factor in our final two Europa League games.

· CHAPTER 20 ·

MY HEAD WAS upside down after the cup final.

I couldn't shake the feeling of utter desolation. It changed me as a person for the next few months. I spent a long time trying to reason why these things were suddenly happening to me.

There had been a quick accumulation of incidents, while I felt things had changed between Stephen Kenny and myself. Looking back now, the breakdown in the relationship between me and the gaffer had a lot to do with my own perception of things. Our relationship was definitely frostier – and there were more clashes to come – but the way my head was certainly didn't help.

A WEEK BEFORE the Alkmaar game, we went over to England to play Brentford in a friendly. The idea was to keep up the intensity. It was an early flight over and a coach journey to the training ground for the match. We were fairly wrecked by the time we got there.

I played centre-half alongside Paddy Barrett, while John Mountney was in midfield. With different people having knocks and niggles, and it all being about getting lads' decent minutes, we were a bit disjointed with players in unfamiliar positions.

Brentford used it as a training exercise.

They were mad into their stats and analysis, and supposedly they had done video on us two or three times before the game. Whatever research they did on us, it worked. We couldn't string three passes together. They had us blocked off every which way.

Shortly before half-time, they scored. It was a ball down the other side... Gabriel Sava came out and took their man down. They slotted home the penalty. We got into the dressing-room and, out of nowhere, Stephen Kenny went mad at me.

HE HAD A pop at me.

I sat there thinking... *Is this for real?* The goal had nothing to do with me.

'Why am I a coward?' I asked.

He replied that I didn't have a go at the referee over the penalty decision. Sure, I was captain, but it was a training ground friendly – and it was a blatant penalty. Their striker took a touch past Gabi and was brought down. There was no disputing the call.

Ah f**k this, I said to myself. *Any excuse to have a pop at me.* I was shattered.

Nobody is ever going to hit me harder than myself. Ever since Zenit, I had crucified myself over and over in my head. The cup final? I knew there was nothing I could do about it. My luck was out. It still hurt.

But then this? It was mid-November, my body and mind were both exhausted. This was my longest season ever and the most intense too. I suppose I didn't realise how much of a toll it had taken.

I'd be tough enough on myself.

I'd just get on with things, put the pain and the fatigue right to the back of my mind. *Just suck it up and get on with it.* But the aches – both physical and mental – were getting harder and harder to ignore.

WE LOST AT home to Alkmaar. As a team we didn't play very well, but I had a decent performance. Collectively we looked tired. They were quick out of the traps, they scored after 10 minutes and we never looked like getting back into the game.

Hindsight is a great thing, but maybe we did too much in between the cup final and the Alkmaar game. Our performance was leggy.

Mentally and physically, we were drained.

I'm not having a go at anyone. It was unchartered territory for us. If we turned down the intensity in training, we could well have struggled to pick it up again for the game. We gave it our all against Alkmaar. We left everything on the pitch. But that alone doesn't get you results at this level.

Despite the result, I walked away from Tallaght Stadium that night feeling a little relieved. It was relief that I got through the game without making a costly mistake. I've played hundreds of games and I've been responsible for conceding on a few occasions. That's happens to every centre-half. Yet I never had this mindset before.

I suppose it was a sign of where my head was at. Mentally, I was in a place I'd never been before. I never came away from a defeat thinking… *Ah well, at least I wasn't responsible for the goal.* But there was one moment against Alkmaar that had me sweating.

I passed the ball into Ronan Finn's feet, but their midfielder read it, jumped in front of Finner and made the interception. That played on my mind over the next while. I kept thinking… *If that went the other way and they scored… Here we go again!* My way of thinking had flipped 180 degrees from a few weeks earlier. Instead of enjoying the game and the occasion, I was just relieved to get through 90 minutes without making a costly f**k-up.

There was also the pressure of the whole country watching on.

Supporters across Europe was tuning in too. After our blistering start, the story kept getting bigger and bigger. Random people from all over the world were popping up on social media, sending messages of support. They loved the underdog story.

I loved that attention and pressure at the start. But in the end it was just another reason to fear making a mistake.

MY STAG WAS pencilled in for the day after the Alkmaar game. I have already referenced the friction it caused. I felt the flak I got over it was unwarranted. It was booked long before we made the group stages.

And even then, it was almost two weeks before our trip to Tel Aviv.

Stephen Kenny was adamant that I couldn't go. I pleaded. I said I would have a few drinks on the first night and take it handy after that. Again, the answer was no. Then, a training session was organised for that Saturday afternoon.

We never trained on Saturday afternoons!

To make matters worse, we ended up being invited as guests of honour to a civic reception in Dundalk that Saturday evening.

One thing that really pissed me off was that on another weekend, a teammate jetted off to Leeds with his pals for a session. He had badgered Vinny to get training moved to earlier in the day, in order to make the flight. In that context, it was hard not to feel aggrieved.

In the end, I went for one night and flew home on the Saturday. I was told that I had to be at the civic reception. As it happens, the first night was so heavy that some of the lads on the stag bought a seat on my flight back and gave the second night a miss. *Lightweights!* But, my stag continued… without me!

I was still raging, though. It was another thing that got into my head and stayed there for months.

Have I not shown my dedication to the cause by now?

The stag was a good day and night, though, a good distraction. I was still gutted that we lost against Alkmaar. But we had almost two weeks to put things right before our final group game away to Maccabi.

ONCE AGAIN, THE training in between games was intense.

I found my body hurting more and more that week. When we were over in Israel I popped into our athletic therapist's room for a rub down. Sam Rice was phenomenal in terms of his work-rate. If you needed anything, no matter what time of the day or night, he was available. He was a great fella too, someone you could chat to for hours.

My body was aching at this stage – tendinitis in the knee, other niggles popping up. The nerve pain in my leg that had arrived pre-season had got steadily worse, and was agony between games. Even climbing a flight of stairs to get to Sam's room was an effort. I don't think I would have felt the knocks had it been business as usual. I certainly wouldn't have dwelled on them. However, my mindset had switched and for the first time in my life I was thinking negatively. I questioned myself and wondered… *Should I really be playing?*

Am I up to this?

Even the process of visualising all the positive things that could happen went out the window. Instead of forcing myself to visualise scoring a goal or winning a big challenge, I allowed myself to think... *Don't let this happen... don't let that happen.* For the first time in my career, I was haunted by a fear of failure, by the dread of making a mistake.

I was thinking about all the negative things that could happen, rather than the positives.

I have to admit that I didn't help myself. I don't place the blame on anyone else, because regardless of outside factors, it's up to me to control my own mind. I was always the sort of character who could take a bollocking, while others needed the arm around the shoulder treatment. I usually responded well to bollockings. But everyone needs some praise and support, at times too.

I seemed to get that sort of treatment a lot. I just let it slide and got on with business. However, my mindset had changed. It was a different me, a different mentality. I was more vulnerable. I let doubt creep in.

Twenty minutes into the Maccabi game, Andy Boyle passed the ball across to me. I took a touch. As I turned to play it, Tal Ben Chaim sprinted towards me.

Because I didn't have a clear train of thought in my head, I made a hurried and indecisive action. He blocked my attempted pass and sent Vidar Orn Kjartansson racing into the penalty area.

As the ball fell to Kjartansson, I was thinking... *Gary, just save it... please just save it.* Gary Rogers took him down and they scored from the penalty spot.

After that, mentally I was no longer one hundred percent there. At one stage, as I went to challenge for the ball, I could hear Stephen Kenny shouting from the touchline. I'm pretty sure now that it was encouragement. But at that moment everything was blurred. It was all taking place at a million miles an hour.

I heard Stephen shouting and all I could think was... *What the f**k have I done wrong now?*

AS WE WENT in at half-time, I saw Paddy Barrett head out to warm-up.

I knew what that meant. I sat in the dressing-room in a daze as Stephen spoke. I was devastated, head down. I can't even remember if I apologised to the lads this time. Stephen went through a few things and then said, 'Brian, you're coming off'.

Any other time, if I was being whipped at half-time, I would have put up a fight. But I couldn't argue with the decision. I wasn't fully at it.

Paddy deserved his chance.

We lost 2-1 and it was a really disappointing end to a campaign that had promised so much after two games. Leaving the ground, a few journalists tried to stop me for a chat. I just said, 'Would you mind if I don't do it today!' That wasn't like me.

Whether good times or bad, I'd always step up. But I didn't want the story to be any more about me than it already was.

To make matters worse, when we were sitting on the runway, waiting to head home, all the lights went out at the airport. Apparently, once it went past a certain time, no flights could leave. No exception.

Not even if the engines were revving and the airplane was ready to take off. So we had to go back to the terminal, get our bags and find a hotel in Tel Aviv for the night. Some of the squad had a few drinks at the hotel, while I hopped into a taxi with five or six others and headed to a club. Ronan Finn got the name of a place that was open late.

We got to the entrance. The club was a dingy old place… dark, smoke machines, the lot. We walked in and there was a fella there in a pair of shorts and no top, with a backpack. He was about 50 and wasn't in great shape. He was dancing by himself.

We looked at each other. *What the HELL is this place?*

We had a few drinks there, went back to the hotel and flew home the next day. I was in the doldrums, more than ever before. Bronagh picked me up from the airport. We were meant to go to a gig, but I said I didn't want to go. I didn't want to be seen.

I didn't want to be anywhere.

I was so disappointed with myself. All I could think of was that I let people down. I was kicking myself. I was in a horrible way.

THERE WERE A couple of weeks left until Christmas and to our wedding on the 27th. We had loads to do and Bronagh was determined that we'd get out and enjoy ourselves. We hadn't been out in months.

We loved going out in Dublin… dinner, a few drinks, catching up with friends we hadn't seen in months because football took over.

It wasn't just 2016, every season at Dundalk was the same. Our success was built on the kind of dedication that meant I didn't see my mates for most of the year. I couldn't do pints or late nights. We would train Sunday mornings, so that would rule out Saturday night. And we played on Friday nights, when most of my mates would head out after work. I spent the whole time consumed by football.

It dictated everything. Even if Bronagh wanted to do something that required a bit of activity – walking up a mountain or going for a cycle – I had to say no. I had to save my legs, I had to be fresh for the next training session.

I'd barely see my family in Galway during the season, because there was rarely such a thing as a weekend off. On the odd occasion when we did get a free Saturday and Sunday, we usually didn't find out until the day before. So I couldn't plan anything.

I don't think people realise the lengths you have to go to. I have missed nearly ninety percent of my mates' stags and probably eighty percent of their weddings, birthdays, the lot. As my brother and his family live in England, I only get to see them once or twice a year because of the football. If they come over, they have to schedule their visit for when it might suit me the best.

But with the season over, I could finally let my hair down, head out and catch up with everyone. With all that went on, however, it was a struggle at the start to get going. Bronagh was determined to get my mind off what had happened. She wanted the build-up to the wedding to be enjoyable. I put on a face and headed out.

It was Christmas time; the craic in the pubs, the vibe around town, meeting old pals, it was a great distraction. I ended up arranging a couple of extra nights out in Dublin just to get out and avoid sitting at home, thinking about the football and what happened in St Petersburg and Tel Aviv.

BETWEEN THE LAST Europa League game and Christmas, I was asked to participate in an eir Sport documentary on our European run. I agreed. I told myself I'd face the music, own up to my mistakes. That's the way my head was. I was so wrapped up in my own misery that I forgot I wasn't the only one to make a mistake.

When it came to anyone else making a mistake, I just thought, shit happens. But when it came to me, I was killing myself.

After I came out of the studio, I met a few mates for pints. I thought to myself... *I'm not helping myself here*. I was brutally honest about the f**k-ups, but ultimately they were just two mistakes.

Big mistakes, granted. But out of the six games, I didn't even mention all the great moments I had, all the great performances, the amount of times I bailed out other lads when they made mistakes that could have cost us a goal. Because I was so hard on myself, I never watched the documentary. I don't think I ever want to see it.

All these negative thoughts kept swirling around my head right up to our wedding, despite the fact that I enjoyed the build-up and the distraction from football. So, before Christmas I asked Stephen Kenny for a meeting.

I NEEDED TO thrash things out.

I told him how I felt. I brought up the video incident in St Petersburg, but acknowledged that he was the manager and was entitled to deal with us as he pleased. He was surprised that those feelings still lingered.

It was all in the past as far as he was concerned. In my mind, I created a conflict where none existed. I was angry with myself.

I was angry with Stephen.

It felt like the walls were closing in around me.

But this was news to Stephen. He had so much else going on. He had a whole squad of players to think about. But to me it was the worst feeling in the world.

I'm not exaggerating when I say I felt as bad as when my parents separated and when my dad died.

THE WEDDING ITSELF was great.

Bronagh looked beautiful and getting married to her was the best thing I ever did. But even that day took a turn! Neil was Best Man and his speech stayed away from any football talk. The same couldn't be said when Bronagh's dad stood up and grabbed the microphone. When I first stayed with Bronagh, she lived at home with her folks. I slept on the couch and was woken the next morning by someone shouting… 'Georgie, Georgie!'

I was hungover and disoriented. I popped my head up and asked, 'What are you shouting 'Georgie' for?

'Georgie Best… *it's Georgie Best!*' came the reply. Bronagh's family is GAA through and through. So when she said she was seeing this fella who plays soccer for Dundalk, I don't think they were too impressed!

As I got to know the family, I quickly realised that her dad Pat was mad. He has a real Dundalk sense of humour and is great craic. Before we bought a house together, I spent a lot of time in Bronagh's parents' house.

You have to be able to slag back to survive with her dad.

Pat took the microphone from Neil and went into his speech. It was all about how he and Bronagh's mam Margaret had to go into hiding after I gifted Zenit their goal. There were 280 people in the room and most of them were in stitches.

As it was our wedding day, I just laughed.

It was great craic for most people in the room, but I sat there getting redder and redder. This thing had been eating away inside of me for weeks. I thought I'd be able to forget about it for one day. *How wrong was I?*

Bronagh knew I was still struggling, so before we left for our honeymoon she told me to let it go, to enjoy the break. She was right. We were heading to Thailand and Dubai, two of my favourite places. We got engaged in Dubai a year earlier. Any chance I'd get, I'd arrange a stopover there.

We went travelling around the islands off Thailand and the weather was poor for much of it. I got food poisoning for a few days too. Other than that, it was great craic. We get on so well together, Bronagh and I. Whenever we go out for drinks, we always have a great laugh together. I am lucky to have found someone like her. She is kind, laid-back, great fun and stunningly beautiful – and the best mother our kids could ask for. I'm so lucky to have her as my wife.

When we got home from our honeymoon, however, all I could think about was getting back onto the pitch so that I could put things right.

PART **SIX**

Legacy

Our Europa League campaign in 2020 saw Dundalk play some of the best football the team ever produced, and we also got to meet teams like the mighty Arsenal (above, against The Gunners in the Aviva Stadium and their own amazing Emirates Stadium). Of course, Covid 19 (left) was tough on all of us, especially for those who were nearing the end of our careers and were in danger of not getting the final season of our dreams.

Walking onto the pitch at the Emirates was a dream come true... it's a game that will live with me forever. However, another game I can never forget was in April of 2021 against Shamrock Rovers in the Premier League when I received the toughest injury of my whole career (below). Recovering in 'Recovery Room' (right) at Junction 6, Blanchardstown.

■ CHAPTER 21 ■

ONE YEAR AFTER we put the League of Ireland on the map, after we showed not only the country, but Europe, that an Irish team could compete by playing an attractive brand of football, Cork City long-balled their way to the league and FAI Cup double. Ouch. As far as I was concerned, the shine was taken off our double a couple of years earlier. *If a team like this could do the double,* I thought, *is it really that big an achievement?*

That wasn't me being a sore loser. It just didn't make sense to me at the time.

They completed the double when they beat us in the FAI Cup final on penalties. It was another awful game and they did little to win it inside 120 minutes. We had our way of playing and it was pleasing to the eye.

Cork had their own way and it was effective, but it wasn't pretty. But, that's football, and there are many ways to win a game.

It wasn't worthy of a double-winning team, in our eyes. But that is the competitiveness in us! It did open my eyes to football and all of its different styles. We had to understand how they got the better of us, and think about how we would have to adapt against them in our future meetings.

We were better than Cork.

We were *above* them and their approach to the game. But that year they got the better of us in our head-to-heads.

And it killed us.

THE CUP FINAL defeat was a horrible end to a year that started with my head still firmly in the toilet. Despite thrashing out things with Stephen Kenny, marrying Bronagh and hitting some great honeymoon hotspots, I was still struggling in my own head. So much so that I would have considered leaving Dundalk if I was out of contract, but I still had another season left on my deal. On May 1, I was offered the chance to leave Oriel Park. I'll admit I was tempted to go.

It was exactly six months to the end of my contract when Jonathan Roche, the Shamrock Rovers chairman, sent me a text. It was the first day that other clubs could contact me. He asked for an opportunity to chat before I agreed anything with Dundalk, or anyone else for that matter. I knew Jonathan well. I coached his kids at basketball. So I agreed to meet with him and Stephen McPhail.

The season wasn't going well for Dundalk. We were way behind Cork City in the league at the time. There was nothing on the table at Oriel Park either, despite assurances every so often that a new contract would be sorted. I drove down to Roadstone and met Jonathan, Stephen and Stephen Bradley.

They showed me their plans for Roadstone and gave me a tour of the training ground. It all looked so impressive. They made me an offer. I turned it down.

I was wise and experienced enough by now to reject any first offer, no matter how attractive. Sure enough, they came back with an improved deal.

MEANWHILE, THINGS WERE happening slowly at Dundalk. I hadn't heard a peep about a new contract for weeks. On the other hand, there was Rovers, making me feel wanted. There was something else to consider – was this the end of the road for Dundalk's dominance? A lot of pundits felt it was.

Key players had left over the previous few years – among them Richie Towell, Daryl Horgan and Andy Boyle. Suggestions that we were on a downward spiral grew louder and louder. And when a new contract finally materialised, it wasn't as good as the one offered by Rovers, who took a more long-term view of me.

They wanted me to sign, play for a few years and then move upstairs, in a coaching capacity or in some other form. They were aware of my work coaching kids and they knew I was from the area. Their plans looked great.

But for some reason, I just couldn't leave Dundalk. I felt I couldn't jump ship just because things weren't going well. By now I considered Dundalk to be my town, my club. Sure, I was born and reared in Dublin, but I married a Dundalk girl and we bought a house together in the town. Before I signed for Dundalk, Rovers had been my local team and obviously a team I'd like to have signed for. But after I signed for Dundalk, that changed. I saw how big the club was, how fanatical the town is for football. I was hooked.

I'd love to have signed the contract that Rovers put on the table – both from a financial and a long-term point of view. But I wasn't finished with Dundalk.

This team wasn't finished, regardless of how that season would pan out. I was confident of that. So I said thanks, but no thanks to Rovers.

I'LL BE HONEST, it was touch and go for a while.

There were lots of things swirling around my head that year. This was when it clicked with me why the top Premier League footballers get paid so much money. I know it's worlds apart, but I certainly wasn't earning enough for some of the shit I got. The same goes for the rest of the lads on the team.

At the end of 2016, I was afraid to show my face around town. Living in the centre of Dundalk, the chances of meeting someone dying to give an opinion on the Zenit or Maccabi games were high. I realise the big Premier League stars are under the microscope every single day – and not just during one European campaign – but I could see why footballers would lose their heads.

It wasn't something I was prepared for. I don't think any of us were.

We never had so many eyes on us. Or maybe I just made it worse in my head. *Who knows?*

We started 2017 poorly by our standards, losing heavily to Cork in the President's Cup. We went up to Maginn Park in Buncrana early in the season and took the lead against Derry City, only to lose 3-1. Ryan McBride scored their third. Tragically, he passed away suddenly six days later. His death really affected our Derry lads in particular – Michael Duffy and Patrick McEleney. Ryan was a fierce competitor; fearsome on the pitch and a real leader for Derry. Our lads told us that, off the pitch, he was a gentleman. It hit the league hard. A second player from Derry who had passed away during our football careers! Moments like that make us cherish life, and what we have!

We lost to Cork in the league, to Bray Wanderers, Galway United and Shamrock Rovers. Then Cork came to Oriel Park before the break and thumped us 3-0. Seáni Maguire's hat-trick saw them open up an 18-point lead.

The atmosphere around town, at the games, it all added to the pressure that we were putting on ourselves. There was an expectancy like never before. Only months earlier we hit a historic high for Irish football. But we struggled to build on that – particularly after losing Andy Boyle, Daryl Horgan and Ronan Finn.

Criticism started to appear online.

I remember reading a few things about myself. 'Boyle carried him for years'… 'He's 30 now, finished' – stuff like that. Everything was flung at us. It was impossible to get away from it. I was being tagged in people's conversations on social media, where lads were arguing over just how shite me or my teammates were. I didn't need that. Certainly not while I was trying desperately to rebuild my confidence.

I GET LOADS of random messages on Twitter and Instagram. Plenty of abuse, and then some nice stuff too. Recently, someone sent me my latest ratings on the FIFA game. He said, 'This is a crime, you should get onto someone about this'.

They were all really low, apart from my strength which was 85 out of 100.

As for speed… that was 20. And that's a perception people have always had about me. *He's a big lad, so he must be slow.*

But I rarely get done for pace.

I'll be honest, it does annoy me occasionally. As a footballer, you want compliments. You crave positive feedback. Even at this late stage in my career, the right words from the right person can make me feel 10-feet tall.

My old Knocklyon coach Alan McGovern gave me a few drills when I was a teenager, to improve my speed. I spent hours in the field around the corner from our house working out, thinking it was normal. On reflection, it probably wasn't at that age. It was obsessive.

WHEN WE GOT back after the mid-season break, it was time once again to turn our attention to the Champions League. The Premier Division had pretty much slipped away from us. Europe was an opportunity to press the reset button.

A change of scenery helped us change our mindsets. Part of that was down to Stephen Kenny. I'm not sure if he ever studied psychology, but he had a great knack of getting into our heads.

We were straight into the second qualifying round, where we were drawn against Rosenborg. It wasn't the easiest of ties. But Stephen had us firmly believing we could take them and set up a meeting in the next round with Celtic.

We battered Rosenborg in the first-half at Oriel Park and were 1-0 up through Davy McMillan. But they equalised just before half-time when my man, Tore Ruginiussen, scored from a scrappy set-piece that trickled in. They were a different team in the second-half.

They sat in tight, compact, and were happy to escape with the draw. They were shell-shocked. Rosenborg didn't expect an Irish club to be so dominant against them. Michael Duffy signed for us that year and he was phenomenal against them.

I remember the first time I saw Mickey play. We were on a pre-season training camp in Spain and he arrived along with Stephen Kinsella, who was only 17. I never saw anyone with the feet that Stephen has in a possession box. He was unbelievable. But he was desperately unlucky with injuries.

Mickey was amazing too. We did a drill and someone played a diagonal, from one side to the other; Mickey came in, hit it first time on the volley and, BOOM… far top corner. We wondered how we'd replace Daryl Horgan and then Mickey came in and did that on his first day!

THAT TRAINING CAMP was a nightmare for me personally. I ended up getting sick. My throat closed up, I couldn't get out of bed.

I had to get a taxi to visit a nearby doctor. Whatever he prescribed, it didn't work. I felt even worse the next day – and we were flying home 24 hours later. So I phoned for an emergency doctor to come out to our hotel. He took one look at my throat and said he never saw one so closed in. The doctor gave me an injection so that I could fly home in some degree of comfort. It would have been agony otherwise. A great trip for Mickey Duffy, a brutal one for me.

DESPITE MICKEY'S PERFORMANCE against Rosenborg and Davy's goal, we had to settle for a 1-1 draw. We were disappointed, but still felt we could finish the job in Norway.

The morning after the first-leg, I was in good form, despite the result.

In football it's always useful to have an 'enemy'. It's good motivation to want to prove some people, or those who are doubting you, wrong. There is a downside to this, though. I'm rarely happy with where I'm at or how I played. I'm always looking at how I could have done this or that better. *I had a cracking game? Well, what about that one pass that didn't hit its target. Could I have done this a little quicker?* Bronagh reckons I'm negative, but I disagree. I say I'm realistic. It's part of my make-up as a footballer, it's what keeps me on my toes. And if I can prove a few people wrong along the way, all the better.

I talk a lot about visualisation, and it was never as strong as the night before the second-leg. There was the usual stuff, trying to keep a clean-sheet.

But the biggest thing I pictured was scoring… and getting that goal back.

IT TOOK JUST 11 minutes for me to find the Rosenborg net. But I didn't want to settle for just one goal. I actually said to one of my mates beforehand that I was gunning for two. I'm not sure why, but I was convinced I'd get two goals in the Lerkendal Stadion. We got another set-piece five minutes later.

Davy McMillan came flying in and launched himself at the cross, and forced a brilliant save from their keeper. Davy had a clean header and he hit it sweetly. He was just unlucky. We conceded just before half-time. Mike Jensen got a run inside Ganno and teed up Yann-Erik de Lanlay to score. It's not often that anyone gets a run on Ganno, but the pace of players in Europe is on another level to the League of Ireland. The game went to extra-time and they went in front midway through the first period. Matthias Vilhjalmsson, who replaced de Lanlay late in normal time, scored. His fresh legs were the difference.

We had a great chance late on to get the goal we needed to go through. I cushioned a header down to Ciaran Kilduff, but he cracked his shot off the crossbar and over. One thing that was notable to me in that game was that a load of our lads cramped up. Maybe it was the effort we put in week after week. Or maybe it was going to extra-time. But it surprised me.

I spent most of the match looking after Nicklas Bendtner. He was brilliant, but I thought we both had good games. It was a really enjoyable duel with a big-name player. Afterwards, I got a load of messages on Facebook and Twitter from people all over the world asking me about him. He's obviously a cult hero to thousands of fans.

'Oh my god, you got to mark Nicklas Bendtner', stuff like that. It was mad… 'Lord Bendtner' as he is known!

We were gutted with the result. We were convinced we'd have a good chance in the next round against Celtic. *Imagine.* The reaction here to Celtic getting knocked out of the Champions League by an Irish club? The amount of people in Ireland who follow Celtic and Scottish football, and turn their noses up at the league here really pisses me off. If we'd played Celtic and beaten them, it would have been two fingers up to people who stick their two fingers up at the League of Ireland. It also would have been huge for the club. A sold-out Aviva, an unbelievable atmosphere; we relished those types of occasions.

I don't have anything against people here following clubs in other countries – I grew up a Liverpool fan, remember! It's the dismissiveness and speed at which some people put our league down, that annoys me. I'm used to that now, but the League of Ireland might never get the level of recognition it deserves with a large proportion of the country having that attitude.

There's no reason why we can't follow football abroad, and have our favourite teams and players... and also support football here!

Rosenborg drew in Glasgow, but Celtic edged through by a single goal in the return game. We were so close to beating Rosenborg. I often wonder what could have been had we faced Celtic. But that's football. It would have been one hell of a tie – and with a genuine chance that we'd progress too.

OUT OF EUROPE and seemingly out of contention for the league, we soon found ourselves eating into Cork City's lead at the top of the table. Seáni Maguire left Turner's Cross for Preston in July and, suddenly, they were a shadow of the side that couldn't stop winning in the first-half of the season.

Seáni was amazing. He was so sharp, so quick, and his finishing was outstanding. If anyone made a mistake, he was there to pounce. He was never lazy, he was always on his toes waiting for an opportunity. We saw that when he was in with us for a brief spell. In training he was deadly, I thought.

But he couldn't force his way past Davy McMillan and Ciaran Kilduff, so he wanted to move on. After only a handful of appearances, we couldn't blame him for wanting to leave. He was after more game-time and it was clearly the right decision, given how things went once he left us. Not many, however, anticipated the way Cork would fall off in his absence.

Well, a few people did. Stephen Bradley was one.

I remember the Shamrock Rovers manager got lots of stick when he said something earlier that year about Maguire and Cork City.

'If you stop him, then you do stop a lot of their game.'

But he was right. Maguire was the difference in games between Rovers and Cork in the first-half of 2017. Bradley was talking about the way they played football. They sat in, played the ball long. There was no better player to have in that system than Seáni.

He was always first to the ball. The way he pushed forward left space down either flank. Of course, Cork had some excellent players that year. Stephen Dooley and Steven Beattie had good seasons, as did Karl Sheppard. But ultimately, they needed someone of Maguire's calibre up front for their game to be successful. And when he went, so did their form.

We got close, but not close enough.

They won the league by seven points. We were 18 points behind after Seáni's Oriel Park hat-trick. We would have been even closer had we not lost at home to Bohs on the second last day of the campaign, with things already wrapped up. Our motto in the second-half of the season was boring, but effective… 'one game at a time'.

Keep chipping away and see how things turn out. We kept believing we could do it until eventually it became a mathematical impossibility.

I'M NOT A big reader – and when I do pick up a book it's usually an autobiography. I have never been one for motivational quotes. I hate seeing people repeatedly posting them online, and not changing anything about themselves… whether it is their work-rate, fitness or general healthiness. Actions speak loudest!

In saying all that, one quote has stuck with me. It comes from the late Jim Stynes' autobiography, *My Journey*. It's one of the best books I've ever read. Stynes was the only foreign player to win the Brownlow Medal, awarded to the best player in a Australian Rules season. He set up the Reach Foundation to help children from poor social backgrounds reach their full potential.

He became a sporting and social icon in Australia.

After his diagnosis with cancer, he documented his journey through the process, which sadly ended with his passing in March 2012. Jim grew up down the road from me. We attended the same primary school. I would have been familiar with his brother Brian, who was a huge player for my local GAA club and for Dublin. When I was a kid, the Stynes' brothers were our heroes. So I couldn't wait to get my hands on Jim's book.

There is a line in it, where Jim says the difference between good and great players is how they respond in adversity. Like I said, I'm not one for motivational quotes, but that one has stuck with me. I always believed I was a good player, but I wanted to be a great player. When the chips are down or when things are going against your team, it's the players who aren't fazed by it, who remain mentally strong and who don't go missing… they are remembered as the greats.

I guess I lost sight of that for a while after the mistakes in St Petersburg and Tel Aviv. I went against Jim's code.

How did I respond in adversity?

I felt sorry for myself, put up barriers, felt the world was against me. But I didn't need to do any of that. I just needed to carry on playing my own game. I just needed to be realistic and address my weaknesses. See what the problem is, instead of ignoring it… and *right* it! But also remember my strengths and take confidence from them too! When I did, eventually things clicked once again.

You don't have to do something amazing to announce your return to form. You don't have to beat three players or pull off a load of 60-yard passes. You don't have to be the match-winner.

Just keep doing everything that you'd do if you were having a good game. Don't try too hard. And off the pitch, strip everything back to the basics… sleep, diet, training, lifestyle. Just build yourself back up, slowly but surely.

Do the things that got you to the top in the first place.

In the end, my head got there. It took a while, but I got there. And by the end of 2017, despite the disappointment of Cork winning the double, I was in a much better place than 12 months earlier.

As a team we knew going into 2018 that we were back to our best. We knew we'd get our trophies back.

· CHAPTER 22 ·

WE DID WHAT we set out to achieve in 2018 by regaining the Premier Division and FAI Cup, but it was the one that got away that really annoyed me. After beating St Pat's and Bohs in the first two rounds of the League Cup, we were drawn against Cobh Ramblers in the semi-finals.

The match was on a Monday, just four days after we were bounced out of Europe by AEK Larnaca. After beating Levadia Tallinn in the first round, we drew 0-0 against Larnaca at home. They were a decent side, but we still fancied our chances in Cyprus. We certainly didn't see the 4-0 tonking coming.

The heat we experienced over there was sapping. As soon as we stepped out of our hotel, it was like a fan-heater whacking us directly in the face. We made some changes… Sean Hoare at right back, Dan Cleary at centre-back with me, and Dean Jarvis at left-back. Robbie Benson was in the middle with Chris Shields and Jamie McGrath… Dylan Connolly right, Mickey Duffy left… and Pat Hoban up front. Hindsight is a great thing, but when you look at that side, the level of European experience was not as high as in previous years. Larnaca had pumped millions into their team; they had a Spanish manager and some Spanish players. Ivan Trickovski up front was a good player and he scored twice that day.

We set out to attack, as we always did, but we probably should have tempered our aggression to suit the climate.

They upped their performance from the first-leg. They dragged some of our lads exactly where they wanted them and played through the gaps that were left in their wake. Whatever weaknesses we had, they exploited them.

Personally, it wasn't a good night. I suffered a shoulder injury in the second-half and, although I played on to the end, I knew I was in trouble.

CHRONIC PAIN IS part and parcel of being a footballer.

Unfortunately, I'm no exception. The pain I felt in Cyprus brought me back to 2015, playing away to Bray Wanderers. I was convinced I pulled a hamstring in my right leg, but it wasn't testing like a pulled hamstring. It turned out to be a nerve problem. It was killing me, but I decided to play through the pain.

Mentality has always been one of my strengths. I knew if I wasn't doing any damage to the muscle, I could get through games. It was treated with an injection of Botox into my right glute. This relaxed the muscle and took the tension off the nerve. Then, in pre-season training ahead of the 2016 season, I felt the same pain again, but this time down the left hand side. I'd get through a game but, for the next day or two, it would be agony. Walking around town, I'd swear I was being stabbed in the hamstring.

It would take the warm-up and maybe 20 minutes into the game for the pain to ease, but even at that, it was hard to reach one hundred percent. In 2016 and '17 it was agony at times.

I decided to get epidurals and cortisone into my back. Former rugby international Paul O'Connell described Stephen Eustace as the best in the business, so I put my faith in him. I would get some relief, but usually the pain would come back, and warming-up for a game I would feel it. The pain would come and go after that. The epidurals were offering me temporary relief but, after a while, I realised I had to address the problem another way. I had to learn how to manage it. I didn't squat the same kind of weight that I once did. The same went for any other lifts that put pressure on my spine. I figured that less pressure on my spine might help stop the nerve from pinching. I strengthened up my core and my glutes, and that helped, though the pain never fully went away for the next few years.

Then, in 2017 I did some serious damage to one of my shoulders against Shamrock Rovers. I went up for a header, crashed to the ground and landed badly.

So, going into the Larnaca game, I had hamstring pain and a bad shoulder

– to the extent that I couldn't do a single bench-press. And then I did the other shoulder in Cyprus! I was battered and bruised coming off the pitch against Larnaca; drenched in sweat and gutted. It was a real set-back.

WE GOT HOME from Cyprus in the early hours. My head wasn't in a good place. 'F**k this,' I said to Dane Massey and we headed into Temple Bar and got hammered. I hadn't had a drink in months. I knew I wasn't going to be involved in Cobh the following Monday and Dane was told the same thing – although he ended up having to play!

Late that Friday, I got a phone call from a mate of mine from Monaghan United, Paul Whelan. He was on a stag at the Galway Races. He asked me to come down. I'd always wanted to go to the Galway Races, so with a load of jars on me I said I'd be down. I texted Bronagh, who was at home in Dundalk, and told her we were heading west the following morning.

I woke up to a phone call. It was Bronagh. 'I'll be there in half an hour, make sure you're showered and ready to go, I don't want to be late,' she said.

'Ready to go? Where?'

'We're going to the Galway Races!' I didn't have a breeze. I checked my texts. *No recollection.* I told Bronagh she'd have to drive.

I couldn't drink that day in Galway – and it was nothing to do with the day before. I wouldn't play in Cobh, but I still had to train on Sunday.

Whelo is known for being generous – and he made it very hard for me to be sober. He turned to Bronagh and said, 'Come on, let's go to the champagne bar'. So there I was, sitting with a glass of orange juice while the two of them were living it up. Bronagh had a belter of a day. I had great craic myself, but was stone cold sober. Imagine, then, how pissed off I was when I arrived into training on the Sunday and saw that lads who were certain starters in Cobh were clearly out on the gargle the day before. I'm talking about lads who hadn't been playing, who should have been hungry for this chance to impress. No wonder we lost 1-0. It was a brutal performance in what should have been a free ticket to the final, to an historic treble.

The Cobh game was a watershed moment in our season. We hadn't been playing well for a while. We were winning games, but standards were slipping. So Stevie O'Donnell and I – as we had done a few times before – decided we needed to have a word with the squad.

We let a few of the other senior players know this was coming and then called a meeting in the gym. Just players. The coaching staff knew nothing about it.

We told them it wasn't good enough. Even though we'd won three or four games in-a-row in the league, standards had dropped below what was expected.

You always saw it with Stephen Kenny's Dundalk; a group of players who might not play that much and would move on at the end of the year. That wasn't necessarily down to their talent; mentality was huge when it came to surviving at such a demanding club. Lads with more talent than me came and went.

So too did our chance to win the treble that year. No disrespect to Cobh, but we should have beaten them easily. But that's football; nobody has a divine right to win every game!

THE POST-COBH SUMMIT seemed to do the trick. We went on to win the league by 10 points, and the FAI Cup against Cork City *without* the need for extra-time or penalties. I lived out a lifelong dream by wearing the armband for those two successes. The circumstances, however, weren't ideal.

Stevie O'Donnell was our captain, our leader. He was the player we all looked up to. But he broke his leg in Waterford at the start of May, right before half-time in a 2-1 defeat. Incredibly, all three goals were scored in the nine minutes' injury-time awarded for the delay while Stevie received treatment on the pitch.

For the rest of that season, anytime anyone referred to me as captain, I corrected them and told them that regardless of whether he was playing or not, Stevie was still our skipper. I had – and still have – such admiration and respect for Stevie. So when it came to lifting the league trophy, I begged him to do the honours. 'No Garts, I'm not going up!' he replied.

'At least we could do it together?' It was still a… 'NO'.

And then the cup final. It was great to win it in normal time for once. The 2018 decider was more open than previous finals against Cork City.

Cork shipped a lot of criticism for their style of play. It wasn't very attractive, but it worked for them. I was surprised that they came out with a more expansive style, but I knew some of their players wanted to change things up. Ultimately it led to their downfall. Maybe they grew frustrated that we managed to counter their direct play. It was predictable, but effective. They'd go back-to-front early, their wingers would come inside and suddenly the pitch would get very narrow. Even if we won the first header, the ball would drop into an area where they might have five against our three.

They were good players, and they were good at what they did. But they got under our skin. This was illustrated a year earlier when things weren't going so well for us. We were about to kick-off against Cork and one of our lads shouted… 'GET INTO THESE C**TS… COME ON!'

I remember thinking… *This isn't a good sign… this isn't us!*

We were better than that. We work hard – that's a given. But the c**ts thing? We looked after ourselves, and didn't concern ourselves with other teams. If we applied ourselves, we believed that should be enough to win the league. And if we didn't win, that was not down to anyone else… it was our fault!

It reminded me of when we played St Pat's in 2014, the year after they beat us to the Premier Division title. There were a few tell-tale signs from them – some shouts, teammates arguing – that led me to believe their heads were gone. Turning on one another showed to us that they were soft mentally. That sort of display doesn't add to a team's confidence. It's only papering over cracks, in my opinion.

We never concerned ourselves about other players or other clubs, we only cared about Dundalk and about the next game. That was crucial.

Fast-forward to the start of the 2021 season and some players were doing media. We had started poorly, but journalists were being told that if we went on a run we could be in the title mix. I felt… *We haven't won a match and lads are talking about league titles?* This is no slight on anyone; it's just my opinion.

Think about winning the next game, and then the game after that. All of a sudden you are on a run. But you don't talk about it before it happens. Stephen Kenny was brilliant at getting us to look no further than the next game. *Don't look too far ahead and don't let external noise influence what goes on inside your dressing-room or on the pitch.* As we were about to kick-off in that 2017 game against Cork, I realised they had gotten into our heads. It worked for them. They took our trophies away that year.

But the psychological battle had swung in our direction by the 2018 cup final, a game that effectively marked the end of that great rivalry. Our mental strength and their weakness had shown up long before then.

For the second time in a few weeks, I wore the armband for a trophy lift. But

I wasn't going to take no for an answer from Stevie this time. A few of us pushed him up the steps. We honestly didn't know if it was going to be his last chance to lift some silverware with Dundalk. He had been such a leader to the entire squad. Even when he was injured, he was always there with us. He had a presence that was impossible to describe, but unique in my experience in football.

We climbed up to the presentation area and I said, 'Right lads, make some room!' But as we turned to lift the cup, two of the boys stood right in front of us. So you couldn't see us lifting the trophy! The local photographer Ciaran Culligan shouted up to us. 'Garts, lift it up again, I couldn't get you the first time'. So I threw the cup up in the air again, but at this stage the rest of the lads were brushing foil and confetti off themselves.

SOMETHING SIMILAR HAPPENED when I lifted the league trophy.

My hair was thinning at the time and I was very conscious of it. I used to put a product into it, a dust, which sticks to your hair and fills it out a bit. Whenever we played on TV, I made sure I used it. That's admitting to the vanity within me.

I was last onto the podium and was about to receive the trophy when Patrick McEleney, Georgie Poynton and Mickey Duffy poured a bottle of champagne on top of my head. My hair went flat and all you could see was this black stuff dripping down the sides of my face. The lads burst themselves laughing, while I did my best to balance on the podium and lift the trophy.

Suddenly, Georgie jumped in front of me and sprayed me with a bottle. Right into my face. I couldn't see a thing. You dream of these moments as a child… captaining a team to league and cup glory, lifting trophies in front of a full house. You watch it on TV – Champions Leagues, World Cups – and it's perfect, it goes without a hitch. But there I was… blind, one foot slipping off the podium… black stuff running down my face. All I could do was laugh. They got me good.

I had the armband for most of 2018 and I was immensely proud to lift the trophies. But to me, Stevie was the captain. When he retired in early 2019, however, suddenly it was a different story. I was named captain of Dundalk FC and it was an enormously proud moment for myself and my family!

■ CHAPTER 23 ■

I'LL NEVER FORGET Stevie O'Donnell's wedding. It's where we learned that the Stephen Kenny era was over. Spanish Point in Clare, the day after the ceremony… most of the lads were still there, huddled together.

'What happens now?' I heard a whisper before the news broke in the media, so I phoned our chairman Mike Treacy. I had a great relationship with him. When it came to the Peak6 takeover a year earlier, I had no interest in boardroom affairs. But we instantly hit it off, Mike and I. A lot of people within the League of Ireland are sceptical of outsiders, but Mike loved the club. He had a different way of doing things. It wasn't always popular with everyone. He was stats-driven. He was all about numbers and risk analysis. He had a lot of experience in the game from his time with Bournemouth in the Premier League.

When he came to Dundalk, I asked him for one favour. *Keep us informed.*

Everybody has an interest in our job. And everyone has an opinion too. It's the nature of the game, I understand that. Mike understood this too from his time in the Premier League. And he knew there was nothing worse than finding things out on Twitter. Or even worse, from a neighbour.

'Would you keep us up to date with anything that might affect us as players?' I asked Mike. He did. The dressing-room appreciated that.

Stephen was gone. *Confirmed.* Despite the rumours, the initial rejection of the under-21 job, his exit came as a surprise. *So what next?*

I remember saying to Mike that, because the American owners weren't long in the door, and that this was their first big decision, they should take their time.

I was worried. *What effect would Stephen's departure have on Dundalk?* Key players had left at the end of every season, but Stephen? Replacing him wouldn't be as easy as signing a new midfielder or striker. He started it all, he put the structures in place. Stephen Kenny methodically built everything at Dundalk. Of course, as players, we assumed a degree of authority on the pitch. We made some decisions because we felt we were better placed than those on the bench to see how a game was unfolding. But that too, in my mind, was part of Stephen's plan – to construct a team of leaders, players who could think for themselves.

It's only when I look back now that I truly see what a great manager he was; how he carefully assembled all the pieces of the Dundalk jigsaw.

I said on the phone to Mike, 'Don't do anything rash, we don't need anyone to reinvent the wheel. No matter who comes in, this dressing-room will win you the league'. Once the owners didn't bring in somebody who wanted to change everything and put their own stamp on things, the players would do the rest. Continuity would be key.

Vinny Perth was already there, as were Ruaidhri Higgins and Stevie O'Donnell. We didn't know at that stage whether Stevie would play on or go into coaching. Either way, he should have a massive role to play at the club. The same went for Higgy. We all knew he had a great footballing head. We all valued his in-put. I could see straight away that he was destined to be a manager rather than a coach.

If we had that continuity, I said to Mike… a manager that knew the players and who wouldn't look to make sweeping changes, we'd keep delivering on the pitch.

Another potential complication, meanwhile, was the arrival of Andy Burton as Technical Director. Andy was best known for his work as a Sky Sports reporter, but he had worked with Mike Treacy at Bournemouth, where Andy was a senior recruitment consultant. Andy had a different way of doing things. He was brash and to the point. He ruffled a few feathers, as people don't like change, and can be uncertain about someone coming in from outside with new ideas or ways. But, in the end, I found him grand, and even though we had our few work-related arguments, we both understood we were both doing our jobs. I said to him that he thought that he could get a better centre-half, a younger one, but… 'Until you do, you need me here!'

But at the start I was wary, probably, like everyone else when Andy arrived. But I need not have been, as with Mike, Andy and Martin running the club we were in good hands, and we were only a penalty shootout from making it a clean sweep of trophies. On a personal and professional level, I found Andy great to work with!

Vinny's appointment hadn't been sealed at this stage and there were rumours that the club would try to hire a high-profile manager. Vinny rang me one day. I was driving on the M1 and his name flashed up. It was unusual to get a call from him, but with the Andy Burton arrival, and talk of different people for the job, he asked me to stay in the owners' ears for him.

I told him I was backing him anyway. I felt Vinny, Higgs and Stevie would be a good combination for us. Ultimately the club went in that direction. And John Gill came in, and I found him a great character. Giller was a good man to have around, and especially so when things weren't so good, he could lighten the mood with his quick wit and humour.

Later in the off-season, we found out Stevie was retiring. The squad desperately wanted him to remain involved in a coaching capacity. I rang Vinny and told him how the players felt about Stevie. It was my job as captain to make him aware! In the end, Stevie was appointed as senior opposition analyst and scout. Even in that role I felt he was under-used. It was frustrating for the players, so I can only imagine it was difficult for Stevie.

As for Stephen Kenny, as a squad we never had a farewell bash with the man who led us to so much glory at home and in Europe. We all wanted it to happen, including Stephen. But various commitments kept getting in the way.

WE MADE A slow start in 2019. Our only win in the first four games was at home to UCD. At one stage Shamrock Rovers were 13 points ahead, although we had a couple of games in hand.

The dynamic in the dressing-room had changed. I remember the St Pat's game in Inchicore. We lost 1-0… a Dan Cleary own goal just before half-time.

Vinny took me off with about 15 minutes to go. Apart from the own goal, Pat's didn't really create too much against us. It was a *nothing* game really. We didn't attack very well and they didn't have many chances.

We were awful in our next game, away to Sligo. Sean Gannon made a mistake for their first goal after two minutes. Romeo Parkes stuck his toe in front of mine and tapped it in. At the time, I felt I didn't attack the cross urgently enough. But the whole team was playing poorly.

This time, I got whipped at half-time and I wasn't happy with it.

I'd shown enough during my career that I could bounce back after a poor first-half. But I didn't say anything, because I knew I hadn't performed at my best. The whole team was off; we were out of sync.

A football manager has to choose his words very carefully. Top bosses such as Alex Ferguson and Roy Hodgson always talk about the importance of communication with their players. We lost 2-1 to Sligo and Vinny stormed into the dressing-room afterwards. This was rubbish… that was rubbish… that kind of thing. I sat there saying nothing. I'd been hooked at half-time, so even though I was skipper, I kept my mouth shut. But then Vinny said something that pushed me over the edge.

'You downed tools on me!' he yelled.

Regardless of what he meant to say, it sounded to me like he was accusing the players of not caring about the performance… of just giving up.

Everyone was silent. A few seconds passed. I piped up…

'HOLD ON A F**KING MINUTE!' Everyone looked around at me.

'Are you f**king kidding me? Accusing players of chucking it? Not one player here goes out to perform badly… I'm not having that!'

He said he wasn't accusing anyone. Then Ruaidhri Higgins stepped in. He told us we were 'spoilt'… and he was right. We had new training facilities, dressing-rooms, food laid on after training… the club had invested big-time in us. *We had everything.* The essence of his message was that we had no excuses. What he said hit home straightaway with the players. Just look at our record in the league after that Sligo match – 22 wins and two draws before our next defeat away to Bohs at Dalymount Park. And by that stage we had already won the league title against Shamrock Rovers.

I DIDN'T THINK too much about the row with Vinny. After all, I had heated exchanges with Stephen Kenny… although not too many. Then there was the bust-up with Mick Cooke. And I had my fair share of arguments with Ronnie McFaul up north. In such a competitive environment, tempers will fray.

But the majority of the time, both parties leave those rows behind them. It's part of the game. You say what you believe, and once you've said it, you leave it behind you. Not for one moment did I feel I over-stepped the mark. After all, I had backed Vinny for the job just a few months earlier.

But as the season went on, I wondered if I was being punished for my words in the Showgrounds dressing-room. A few months later Vinny went all out to sign Andy Boyle – at a time when we had three of the best centre-halves in the league.

We had clawed back a 13-point deficit with Shamrock Rovers, and after a 21-point swing over a couple of months we were now eight points clear. We were flying. Higgy's speech, calling us 'spoilt', hit the nail on the head. Egos – not that there were many – were left at the door. We played Rovers just after the mid-season break in Tallaght and we won 1-0. Ganno scored the winner. I had a very good game. I felt I was solid and composed. Vinny had a different view.

SO MUCH OF football management is how you communicate with your players. We can be delicate! It's easy to mess with our heads.

Vinny used to comment frequently on my distribution. I rarely tried an extravagant pass at Dundalk, because I had players such as Stevie O'Donnell, Sean Gannon, Patrick McEleney or Richie Towell around me. A 10 or 15-yard pass always did the trick. I played the percentages. But Vinny would talk about the other centre-halves and how their distribution was better than mine.

On the other hand, I had Ruaidhri Higgins complimenting me on the fact that so many of my passes, even if they were short, were to the free side of a player.

Higgy gave me confidence. And so did Filippo Giovagnoli. I was hitting 60-yard diagonals left and right under him! It's all about communication.

WE PLAYED IN Europe shortly after Andy Boyle's return. I was playing regularly, playing well… I was flying fit. I didn't feature against Derry City, five days before the first-leg against Riga. I figured I was being rested for Europe.

I was surprised when the team was named and I was on the bench. I asked Vinny why, and he said we were going to have a lot of the ball. Then that word again… *Distribution.* He told me the other lads' passing was more suited to the game. He told me there would be times where we'd need a lot of organisation, and that was my strength. I was on the bench alongside Andy, who was effectively in his off-season. He had only been training with us for about 10 days.

I was given a new contract the day before the Riga game. So, within 24 hours, I went from a high to a deep low.

During the first-half Chris Shields got injured – a clash of heads with Dan Cleary – and had to come off at half-time. Andy was told to warm-up. I sat there in shock. Nothing against Andy, he's a great player, but he was still building his fitness.

We went over to Riga, having drawn 0-0 at Oriel. I was sure I'd get the nod. We'd need strong organisation for sure. But I was on the bench again. Andy started with Sean Hoare. Another 0-0. Penalties. Fortunately we got through, thanks to Gary Rogers, who set a record for European appearances by a League of Ireland footballer and was the hero of the evening in the penalty shootout.

Qarabag were next. *They'll definitely need organisation here*, I thought. But I wasn't even on the bench this time. No communication whatsoever.

I'd asked beforehand for a heads-up. 'If I'm not involved, just let me know… because I need to do some extra training so I don't fall behind.'

I went up early to Oriel Park before the Qarabag game and did a bit of running on the pitch. Journalists were coming in at this stage, so I was asked to stop. But I was flying fit and I wanted everyone to know, so I raced around the pitch at full speed. We drew 1-1 in the home leg. We would *definitely* need organisation to get through in Azerbaijan. *Nope*, I was back on the bench.

I started five of the 12 remaining league games after our European run kicked off in early July. It started to weigh on me. But I wasn't going to let my standards slip. I wanted to keep myself right so that, if called upon, I'd do myself justice. Another thing that drove me was the fact that I was still the captain.

THERE HAD BEEN no communication for several weeks, so sometime in August I approached Vinny for a talk. We closed the video room door and got down to it. I kept calm and didn't raise my voice. I referenced games that I missed where distribution and organisation were poor.

Vinny threw out a few excuses for dropping me and in the end I said to him, 'You're entitled to your opinion, just don't give me any bullshit excuses'.

That's when he raised his voice to me. I was waiting for that moment. Suddenly, it all poured out. I stood up and I hammered him.

I told him that a lot of people weren't happy – and not just people who, like me, weren't playing. He looked for names. I didn't give him any.

'I'm just telling you what the feeling is inside the dressing-room… it's not a good environment!' I said. I asked him why contracts hadn't been sorted for a number of key players… Gary Rogers, Robbie Benson, Pat Hoban and Jamie McGrath. I told him that if he wasn't going to sign Gary back, he'd better have someone special lined up. There weren't many better than Gary in the country.

The Hoban deal was dragging on. He was at loggerheads with the club. I felt Robbie was on the verge of wanting to leave. The same went for Jamie.

I walked out of the video room no closer to the starting 11 than beforehand. At least I got a lot off my chest, but I felt Vinny was in denial. He didn't seem to understand that I was trying to help, and had the future of the team at heart.

EARLY IN THE season we played Derry at the Brandywell and won 2-0. I played alongside Dan Cleary and, as a team, we controlled the game. I didn't make the starting 11 for the next couple of league games against Derry. We drew 2-2 both times.

We were back at the Brandywell in late-August for the second round of the FAI Cup, and I wasn't playing again. I asked Vinny why I was overlooked again, having played in our only clean sheet against them.

His reply? 'I think the pitch is too big for you up there.' I just looked and laughed. I said, 'Are you for real? You're just running out of excuses at this stage!'

We conceded two goals again. Luckily, we scored three and progressed.

We played Waterford in the cup quarter-final a few weeks later. I was back in the side. Steve Williams, our goalkeeping coach, knows the dimensions of every single pitch in the league. Willow is the nicest guy in the world, and he would do anything for the team and the club. Nobody ever found him in bad form, and he always brought energy and positive noise to the training pitch. Not enough people appreciated him, in my opinion. So when we got to the RSC I asked him to walk the pitch with me. There was a yard or two in the difference between the Waterford and Derry surfaces. *Yet I was able to play against Waterford?*

We cruised to a 3-1 win, scoring our three goals inside the first 33 minutes.

NOT PLAYING REALLY got me down. We were away to Sligo Rovers in the FAI Cup semi-final. I was told that I wasn't in the squad, but that Vinny wanted me to travel down and stay overnight with the lads. Before the game, I went out onto the pitch to do a bit of fitness work. The fans at the Showgrounds were never shy in throwing abuse at me – and I usually laughed it off. But this time I nearly lost the rag. It was an hour before the game and the two teams weren't out to warm-up yet, so I went out and worked with the fitness coach.

One young fella really got under my skin. I said, 'You're a big man when you're standing behind a wall… why don't you step this side of the wall?'

He did, so I walked towards him and he legged it. *My head was gone.*

But I kept in shape and played at home to St Pat's in the last league game of the season. I had a cracking game and lifted the trophy at the end. Even so, I'd convinced myself that I wouldn't even make the bench for the FAI Cup final.

To my surprise, I started at the Aviva against Shamrock Rovers, but only because the club messed up with Chris Shields, who was suspended for the final. He picked up his eighth yellow card of the season in our penultimate league game, away to Cork City. The league was already won, he should never have played.

When the suspensions came out, the club argued that you couldn't miss an FAI Cup final anymore over yellow cards. Sure, that was the case with five bookings, but not eight.

We were all gutted for Chris, he was a massive player for us, but his misfortune put me straight into the team. Sean Hoare went into midfield, and I took Sean's spot in defence.

Rovers won on penalties and it hurt. Another chance to win a treble dashed. I was awarded our Man of the Match, so there was a bit of personal pride there. I'd been thrown to one side that year yet I bounced back and proved my worth.

As an emotion, that's right up there with winning stuff, because it's personal.

WE STILL HAD two more games against Linfield in the Unite the Union Cup. We drew 1-1 at Windsor, but we knew we were on a different level to them. I remember the huddle at Oriel Park. I did the talking and said something along the lines of… *Go out and enjoy this, put on a show, let everyone know the gulf in class.*

We were magic. Mickey Duffy was on fire. We won 6-0, and I got our second goal. *What a brilliant feeling after a few shitty months.* You question yourself. *Is my distribution really that bad? Am I still cut out for this level?*

I wasn't going to hang around to be a bit-part player. By the latter part of the 2019 season – prior to the cup final and the Linfield games – I was convinced I was done at Dundalk. They were a horrible few months. I thought I'd been there long enough to have earned a bit of respect. I was captain, but I went from playing every week to suddenly being dropped. I was hurting and I couldn't hide it. It was torture. The hardest part was that not a word was being said to me.

This isn't for me, I thought. Stevie O'Donnell had left Dundalk that August to take up his first managerial role. He was in charge at St Pat's and I was pretty sure that's where I was heading. We talked. I was in contract, so there was no approach. But Stevie knew I wasn't happy. And then the cup final happened. People were singing my praises again. Afterwards, Stevie said to me, 'I was delighted for you, performing like that, but I knew straightaway that you weren't going to leave them'.

I thought I'd proved myself to Vinny, that I'd be back in for pre-season with a clean slate. I just wanted a level playing field. But a couple of things happened off the pitch that winter. Firstly, there was a change in the boardroom. Mike Treacy left and was replaced by Bill Hulsizer. I can still remember my first encounter with Bill. It was near the end of the summer and I boarded the coach at the Spa Hotel in Lucan ahead of an away trip, and there was an older man sitting in the manager's seat.

Who was he? One of the lads that got on the bus at Dundalk said it was the owner's father. He stayed for a week or so and was very inquisitive. I remember him asking me who I was... and where I played? I didn't realise it at the time, but he was sussing everything and everyone out.

SEPARATE TO EVENTS at the club, I went to set up a business – Recovery Room – and planned it so that I'd have the premises for the off-season, that we'd get the building work done before Christmas and have it up and running by pre-season.

Vinny actually encouraged me to look to my future post-football, which I appreciated, and this was the first step on that road.

Of course, everything got delayed. The building work really only started in January. So I had to keep going down to Junction 6 in Blanchardstown where Recovery Room is based to check on things.

A few months earlier, on October 1, Bronagh gave birth to our first child Bobbie. Bobbie was tongue-tied and for a while we didn't realise it. He was breast-fed and wasn't feeding well. He'd sleep for 40 minutes, feed for 40 minutes... sleep for 20 minutes, feed again for half-an-hour... sleep for half-an-hour... it was during that time that I realised why sleep deprivation was used in Guantanamo. You just can't function.

There was one more complication. My hair.

I had thought for years about getting a transplant. When the 2019 season ended, I decided... *To hell with it, I'll go and get it done.*

I flew out to Turkey for the procedure, but not before running it past Vinny. I told him that it meant I couldn't do any exercise for four-to-six weeks. This was the start of November. I'd be able to run again by Christmas.

The lads were starting a fitness programme on December 12, but I was told it wouldn't be a problem. In the end, I was back running on December 22.

I knew I wasn't in the best shape going into pre-season, that I'd have to work extra hard to get to where I wanted to be. Yet when we were in Spain on a training camp I was still near the top of the squad when it came to running.

NEW SEASON, SAME old story. I was out of the team again. We got to our first midweek game, Cork on a Monday night, and I wasn't in the side. I had to say *something*. Nothing was being said to me. I had to speak up, again!

We were training the day before the game, working on shape. All the lads who hadn't played the first two games were rotated in. All, it seemed, except me.

I said to Vinny, 'What's the story? How am I not playing?' He said we'd have a chat, so I followed him into his office. He said, 'I suppose this has been coming.'

'What do you mean?' I replied.

Nothing had been said to me over pre-season. I'll admit my focus hadn't been one hundred percent on football, with Bobbie struggling to feed and sleep, and with the business. Even with those issues, football always came first.

Vinny went on. 'You missed the start of the running with the lads.'

I was 10 days behind them! Plus, the older I got, the more rest I had in the off-season. So hair procedure or not, I probably wasn't going to start at the same time as the younger lads anyway.

He told me that getting my hair done had set me back. I said it hadn't! He told me I was six or seven kilos heavier than the other centre-halves. I replied that I'd always been bigger than the others. Here are the figures...

I was around 94kg going into pre-season. I try to play at around 90 to 92 kg. By the 2019 FAI Cup final, though, I was around 92.5kg. Honestly, I could have a piss first thing in the morning and lose a kilo! I could wake up at 90kg and go to bed that night at 92 or 93. It's one of the things I love about fitness – seeing the effects that your day has on your body. By the way, I was 92.5kg around the time of the Cork game, the same weight as cup final day a few months earlier.

Vinny felt that my head was elsewhere for two or three months. His opinion on whether I was distracted from football was not something that disappointed me. In football, we are all entitled to our opinions. What really disappointed me was that if he or any of the staff thought this, why hadn't they said anything to me during those two or three months? It disappointed me that they had this presumption that I had been prioritising my new business. If they thought I was that far off, why hadn't they spoken up? Or tried to give me a dig-out? It didn't add up that I would be left there, with nothing said to me for months.

When I explained about my sleep problem, or lack of sleep, I felt this was simply dismissed. I realised then, fully, that I was on my own.

I was getting close to breaking-point. For two months I had gone to training, then to Junction 6, just off the M50, where Recovery Room is based… and home again. All this, on very little sleep. I hardly saw Bronagh or Bobbie. The stress of not knowing where I stood at Dundalk only compounded things. I felt like I was going to snap.

And then came lockdown.

GLOBAL PANDEMICS ARE never a good thing, but the arrival of Covid-19 was actually something of a relief for me. It gave me a break from what had become a difficult environment.

As for my new business, it was only open a few days when the nation went into lockdown. I hadn't planned on using my own money.

But between time constraints, developing a business plan and getting to the bank to apply for a loan, I decided to pump some savings into it.

The plan was to get a few weeks' takings to repay my investment, then get a loan to really get things going. I learned my lesson there, because with the business closed there was no money coming in.

For the first two weeks I was stuck in my office in the spare bedroom, working remotely with the local enterprise office. They provided a mentor to help draw up a new business plan, so that I could get some loans to cover me during lockdown.

Honestly, there were days when I was in tears because of the stress of it.

Once I got the business plan written up and all the application forms filled out, I felt like I was back to my old self. I got busy; painted the house inside and out, built a patio… I was flat out. On top of that, I kept up with the training programme that we were given by the club S and C coach Graham Norton.

After a few weeks of seeing me buzz around the house, Bronagh turned to me and said, 'Would you just spend an hour a day with us?' I'd completely neglected Bronagh and Bobbie. I was busy painting, fixing skirting boards, doing things I felt would save money in the long run, just in case the business flopped.

We got into a nice routine; early to bed and up early in the morning.

The weather during the first lockdown was beautiful, so we went for walks in the morning before my training. Then I did my work, before spending the afternoons with Bronagh and Bobbie. I still got stuff done, just not at 100 miles an hour. It was the best thing ever. Without lockdown, I would never have had all that time with my wife and son. My lockdown experience was like a big reset button. The stresses in my life had disappeared. I was in unbelievable shape again.

I'm not saying it was all bad at Oriel Park. My teammates were brilliant. And the kitman Noel Walsh… he had this sixth sense when it came to players feeling down. It might be something simple like laying out a brand new pair of socks, when everyone else had to wear the old washed ones! New socks, and a little wink… he knew how to lift our spirits. Noelie was great… a good friend, and always happy to chat.

And I had Dane Massey and Gary Rogers either side of me in the dressing-room… two of my best mates in football.

OUTSIDE OF MY football career, I now have three businesses to look after… basketball coaching, Recovery Room and Nude Foods. That entrepreneurial streak isn't a recent phenomenon.

In First and Second Year in school, I entered the Young Entrepreneur Scheme with a few friends. The year that wheelie bins came out, we hit the jackpot. We saw how loads of people got their bins mixed up with their neighbours, so we came up with a plan. Some people painted their house numbers on the side of their bins, but we spent a few pounds buying some number stencils, a roll of masking tape and a bucket of paint.

We went door-to-door, offering to neatly paint numbers on bins for £1.50-a-number. But it always worked out at £3 per bin, because if someone lived in house number three, we'd paint 03 on theirs! People were happy to hand over £3 to a few young lads, so the money quickly rolled in.

How can we speed things up? we thought. *How can we make even more money?*

So we bought some spray paint and got through thousands of houses.

We did well enough in the Young Entrepreneurs competition, but we didn't really care about that. We were making a fortune! The next year, a group of us got together and called our business… 'Bits and Pieces'.

We all brought something different to the table. One of the lads, his mam had an account with Musgraves, so he got stuff at wholesale and sold them on at mark-up. Another lad's dad had moulds for garden ornaments, so he got some cement and went around selling his wares. My thing was Christmas logs. My uncle was a forest ranger and my family in Galway had loads of trees on their farm. My uncle had the machinery to cut up timber, so he sent bags of logs down to us.

I went into Smithfield first thing on Saturday mornings, when the markets opened up, and bought candles, ornamental robins and plastic berries.

We set up a conveyor belt on the kitchen floor… mam and I.

I drilled the holes for the candles and robins, and mam placed them on each log. Then we decorated them with the plastic berries, before I sprayed them with fake snow. I sold them for £5 and off-loaded hundreds at Christmas fairs. They actually looked really well and loads of people told me that they had them on their dinner table. A year or so later, however, one fella came back to me and said he was having Christmas dinner with his family when the candle melted into the log and it went up in flames! Health and safety wasn't what it is these days.

I WAS SO interested in business that I did a degree in Sports Management in UCD while playing part-time football with Bray Wanderers and then Shelbourne. Before that, I tried out for a scholarship at UCD but didn't make it. The degree covered all areas of sports science and all business subjects in relation to sport.

It was a strong foundation for what was to come later in my career, particularly with Recovery Room and Nude Foods.

Recovery Room opened up just before Covid. Nude Foods has only taken off in the second half of 2021. Business is booming. We are selling locally in

Dundalk to everyone and anyone. My little lad Bobbie loves it! He loves our MacSagne... a healthy hybrid of mac and cheese, and lasagne.

The idea behind Nude Foods came from years earlier, when I had loads of time to meal-prep for several days ahead. With two children now, I don't have as much time to cook food, and there are loads of people out there in the same boat.

I was approached by a company last year from the north and asked to bring it down south. It was a good product, but I thought I could do it better myself. Lots of ready-made meal companies outsource to big factories, and use frozen chicken from outside the EU. I wanted to produce something with high quality traceable meats – top grade fillets from within the EU – with locally supplied and fresh ingredients.

I got onto one of Bronagh's cousins. He owns a wholesale meat factory that supplies some of the top restaurants. We looked into setting up our own production and things quickly gathered pace.

We shoot videos in the kitchen, and show where the meals are cooked and how they are cooked. Transparency is important for us. While it might cost more to bring in local ingredients, we have crunched the numbers and can still make money. Others might make more, but I'd rather produce a top-quality product.

At the time of writing, we are still in the development phase. We had 50 orders in the first week. They sold out in no time. Then 80 the next week and they sold out too. Then 100... and then 1,000.

We've already had retail onto us looking for 2,000 to 3,000 meals a week. To keep the quality as high as possible, however, we want to increase the numbers gradually. The business has taken off quicker than we ever expected. We got a great chef because of Covid, and the fact that the restaurants were closed. And we've brought in some excellent staff.

We've looked at ways of being as sustainable as possible too. We started out with recyclable trays, but then found compostable trays. It costs a few extra cent per meal, but again we want the product to be as good as possible.

There are vegetarian meals and a few vegan options too.

I've dived head-first into this because the football industry here is so unpredictable. At Dundalk, the players certainly aren't being offered any long-term security anymore. With a family to look after, thinking about the next chapter is more important than ever.

I'M NOT SURE what I would have done without the break of lockdown. The first few months of the year were a fog of stress, non-stop work, a lack of sleep, tears… lockdown gave me a chance to take stock.

Bronagh helped me relax again, take a step back, appreciate what really mattered. I honestly loved the first lockdown. I was in great shape when training resumed in the summer. I was running sub-18-minute 5ks. People didn't believe me. They were looking for screenshots for proof. I even got a text from America asking for evidence, from one of Mike Treacy's mates.

But just when it seemed like my luck had turned…

I started wearing a Whoop strap, my favourite piece of health and fitness technology. It tells you if you are in the red, yellow or green zone; whether your body is under too much stress.

We were playing an 11 vs 11 match one day in training and my Whoop was in the red zone. *Maybe I hadn't slept well or hydrated sufficiently?* But I couldn't exactly go to Vinny and say, 'I can't train today… this thing on my wrist is telling me to chill out!' I chased a ball over the top with Mickey Duffy. We were both at full sprint and then… SNAP… my hamstring went.

I thought to myself… *I've done all this work, I'm in great shape… And now I'm facing three weeks on the sidelines.* There was more turmoil in the dugout too, as Ruaidhri Higgins left to join Stephen Kenny's senior Ireland coaching staff. It was a massive blow, particularly after losing Stevie O'Donnell a year earlier. Ruaidhri knew the club, he knew the players and he knew how to win.

Alan Reynolds came in and I think he was surprised at how messed up things were at the club. From the outside, it looked like the same old Dundalk; a well-oiled machine. Rennie was taken aback by the mood in the dressing-room.

All of a sudden another coach, Mark Burton, came in. He had been a coach at Manchester City and had worked one-on-one with some big names in England. It turns out he did some video work with Pat Hoban prior to our 2019 European games. He was a nice fella and a good coach, but he mainly did individual work with a few of the lads.

He looked frustrated with his limited role. It was just another bit of stress that we, as a group, didn't need – and that's not a dig at Mark, who soon left the club.

FOOTBALL HAS BEEN simple for the previous six or seven years, but everything seemed so complicated now. People were trying to reinvent the wheel, change the fundamentals that had us sweeping up trophy after trophy.

Players were brought in who were thrown into the deep end ahead of lads who were tried and tested. Lads who were fresh in the door were earning more than players who had been there and done it. The mood was horrible. Problems were brought into the dressing-room, whereas Stephen Kenny always shielded us from anything that didn't directly relate to our next game.

Deep down, many parts of football make it a horrible industry. The majority of people are in it for themselves, there is no loyalty from clubs to players… or from players to clubs. Dundalk hadn't been like that for years, but suddenly it crept in.

In the weeks after lockdown we picked up just two points from three league games, and we were beaten comfortably by Slovenian side NK Celje in the Champions League.

Meanwhile, players arrived all the time from America. They were told this would be a chance to get to Europe, to be seen by big teams. Some of the lads weren't good enough. They brought down the standard of training.

I felt bad for them, but at the same time a lot of us were getting pissed off. We were trying to win a league, to progress in Europe. Yet we had to work with a bunch of players who had little or no chance of making the grade.

Some had poor attitudes, others weren't technically up to it. If you were landed with one of them in five-a-side at training, you were effectively down a man. This had a big effect on performances.

It culminated in our 3-0 defeat to Celje on August 19. Less than 24 hours later, Vinny was gone.

▪ CHAPTER 24 ▪

VINNY WAS GONE. The atmosphere in the dressing-room was poor. It wasn't much better around the club.

With Mike Treacy also gone, the players hadn't a clue what was going on. There were rumours, plenty of rumours. But we were in the dark about who would replace Vinny. Then the news broke. *But who the hell were Filippo Giovagnoli and Giuseppe Rossi?*

Dundalk is a huge job. Neither man had a Pro Licence. They also lacked experience in professional football management. It was easy enough to mock their appointments. A little *too* easy.

I didn't like some of the reaction. People ignored the fact that Filippo played to a decent standard in Italy. I'm not saying I was fully convinced of their merits for the job. But once they were in the door, they were going to get my full support. It didn't take them long to earn it. I got on great with the two of them and I still do. I enjoyed playing under them.

When they arrived, one of the first things they did was to split up training; defenders in the morning, attackers in later. They had a project, a plan, an objective. They knew exactly what they wanted to do and how they were going to achieve it.

Filippo told the Board, 'I'll get this team to the group stages'.

He came across as a confident man, charismatic, with an intense likability and serious drive too. They arrived mid-season so were limited in what they could do… so they had us in every day. They worked us hard.

And they wanted to work us even *harder*.

But being a pro athlete is a 24/7 life, and a crucial part of that life is recovery. Rest and recovery!

When the schedule was produced, and we were told to be in from 9am to 4pm, it came as a shock to everyone. Thankfully, after talks with the staff, common sense prevailed and the hours were reduced.

As for the work on the pitch, some of it was basic. It wasn't as enjoyable as under previous managers. There were no five-a-side or short-sided games. Everything was so organised. Sometimes you need more intensity, less structure.

On the other hand, I loved the fact that they brought in one-vs-one defending drills, that they got to work on the finer details of the game. We were struggling in the league. We needed to be reminded of the basics… movement, footwork… *The works.*

FILIPPO AND GIUSEPPE also brought in new tactics. We were going three at the back. Some felt I could only play in the centre of a three, that I was too old and slow to play on the right. But that's where I ended up.

I loved it. It was something new. I might have been one of the oldest members in the squad, but I relished a fresh challenge.

If there was one flaw to Filippo's managerial style, it was that he was too nice. I played under Dermot Keely and he had no problem f**king his players out of it. It's a fine line these days, players are delicate and they can't take much of a bollocking. But there's a balance to be struck.

I spoke with Filippo towards the end of the season. I said I could sense an aggressive, tougher side to him. I said, 'I hope we see a bit of that!' Without an element of fear within the dressing-room, players will get away with murder.

Filippo had an opportunity to let rip at the start of the 2021 season. We were playing poorly… a couple of the big players were off-form. I thought to myself… *Just hammer them. Pick one or two senior lads and tear into them.*

Filippo didn't. I thought afterwards, *That was your chance, you needed to nail them in front of everyone!* When I spoke to him about it, his reply was something like… *That would be like shooting a wounded dog.*

It was a missed opportunity.

OF COURSE, ONE big undermining factor to Filippo's authority was the fiasco that unfolded ahead of the 2021 season.

It was early March. Dundalk held a media day ahead of the President's Cup against Shamrock Rovers, where it was announced that Shane Keegan – a Pro Licence holder – would front the coaching set-up. Filippo was going to be the first team coach.

I had lost the captaincy to Chris Shields a good while back and it hurt. But on that day I was happy I didn't have the armband. No one in the dressing-room had a clue about this new coaching structure until that day.

Meanwhile, poor Chris had to face the media.

This goes back to my conversation with Mike Treacy after Stephen Kenny's departure. *Just let us know what's going on and the senior players will feed it back into the rest of the squad... So that we'll know what's going on before finding out in the media.* With Mike gone, we lost a valuable line of communication with the owners.

Chris had to sit there while journalists quizzed him about the bizarre set-up. It was pure nonsense from day one. It couldn't work. And it summed up the course the club was on.

Shane wasn't happy with it. It wasn't what he signed up for. To his credit, Shane had already been acting in Martin Connolly's role, sorting out visa issues and club licensing. He stepped up for the good of the club, even though it wasn't what he was hired to do.

Filippo wasn't happy either. He couldn't do interviews after matches, he couldn't protect his players. *Sorry... Shane's players!* He felt he should be facing the media, especially after a poor performance, but he was gagged.

While so many things in the background were a mess, the results on the pitch were poor. Everywhere you looked, it was negative headline after negative headline.

That put additional pressure on the squad. The players were getting more and more frustrated with what was going on behind the scenes and it showed whenever we played.

It was easy to forget that just months earlier we were competing, for the second time in just five years, in the Europa League group stages.

LOSING THE CAPTAINCY at Dundalk crushed me. Not being told why for another six months made the situation worse. When the conversation eventually happened in July 2020, I almost wished it didn't.

I was working in Recovery Room one evening, just as the league was returning from Covid cold storage. Vinny Perth called and asked if I had 10 minutes for a chat?

'Yeah, sure,' I said.

He popped in and told me he was taking the captaincy off me. He went on about how he wanted me to concentrate on myself, which I felt was bulls**t.

We went back and forth, me disagreeing obviously, and Vinny digging his heels in. Then he said something I'll never forget.

'Listen, you were sluggish. You were carrying weight in pre-season against Cluj.' He told me that at the time he thought I was finished.

Those were his words to me.

But, by July, he realised he would have to play me again, and that the captaincy issue would come up. So it had to be confronted.

It wasn't a problem for him before the country went into lockdown, because I played all of five minutes of our opening five matches.

Pat Hoban had been our vice-captain. When I didn't start the first game, I thought he would get the armband. Instead, it went to Chris Shields. Pat asked me what was going on. I didn't have a clue and presumed the change was at vice-captaincy level.

After all, no one had said a word to me about my role.

That conversation about my future role as captain came six months later! I was devastated.

THE DISARRAY WAS magnified by the fact that the club had let so many key players leave... *And leave to join our rivals!*

Incredibly, Sean Hoare was offered a one-year deal. He rejected that, not surprisingly, and accepted a four-year contract with Shamrock Rovers that brought the stability he wished for in his career. Sean Gannon was also treated poorly for someone who is one of the most decorated footballers in the game.

Ganno also left for Rovers, after he was offered the same one-year deal, with a second year to kick in if he did the business on the field for the club.

Dane Massey moved to Drogheda United. He was also treated badly, after giving *everything* and winning everything with the club for seven seasons.

Simply put, not enough was done to keep Gary Rogers at the club.

And after winning five league titles, three FAI Cups, three EA Sports Cup and being an integral part of two brilliant Europa League group stage campaigns, John Mountney couldn't watch the drop in standards any longer. He joined Stevie O'Donnell at St Pat's.

All of these players were the foundation on which a winning team had been built for almost a decade. They turned up every day and gave one hundred percent... Every day!

More than that, they created the culture within the winning dressing-room.

Seánie and Ganno both called me before their departures were announced.

Neither wanted to leave Dundalk.

But what choice did they have?

Rovers showed that they wanted them!

Dundalk didn't.

■ CHAPTER 25 ■

SHORTLY AFTER FILIPPO'S arrival, all eyes were once again on Europe and a Europa League second qualifying round clash with Inter d'Escaldes. Because of Covid, all ties were played over one-leg, so we headed to Andorra for the straight knockout clash. I won't say too much about the referee, other than we were very careful whenever the ball came into our area. Best not give him an excuse to award them a penalty!

We had a load of chances in the first-half and played well enough, scoring early on through Davy McMillan. But they were dirty as hell. At one stage Andy Boyle went to head the ball. One of their fellas jumped straight into Andy... no attempt to win the ball. Boyler won the header, their lad headed Boyler in the elbow... and the referee gave a free in. Yellow card.

The same thing happened again in the second-half. Boyler won another header, and their player hit the deck like a ton of bricks... and the ref gave a free.

It felt like a good 30 seconds had passed before the ref saw a trickle of blood run down the Andorran lad's face. He showed Andy a second yellow and sent him off. On neither occasion did he lead with the elbow.

Then the icing on the cake. Davy McMillan made a run to the front post and looked certain to get his head to the ball. One of their players delivered a clothesline... WWE-style... laid Davy flat out on the ground. The referee was right in front of me... perfect view. He gave a goal-kick! It was nuts. I'd never seen refereeing that bad before. We escaped with a 1-0 win and were relieved to do so.

Meanwhile, another row was brewing within the club…

THERE WAS A disconnect between players and club officials. It came to a head soon after we lost our Champions League qualifier against Celje.

Whenever we won the league in the past, part of our bonus was a percentage of the prize money from the first round in Europe. But because we didn't progress in the Champions League, we were told we weren't getting the money. Of course, the pot increases massively if you progress. And to a lesser extent if you are parachuted into the Europa League.

So, as we the players saw it, we never got our 2019 league-winning bonus. Did we have it in writing? Unfortunately, we didn't. Prior to this, we never had a reason to have a written agreement with the club. There was always a trust between the two parties. Unfortunately, the row over bonuses didn't end there.

THE TIME TO negotiate European payments is in pre-season, but it always seems to drag into the campaign because the club never rushes back to us… and 2020 was no different. Many calls between some of the senior players, myself included, and the club chairman Bill Hulsizer on the subject lasted well over an hour.

The deal had always been that the squad would receive a percentage of the group stage prize money. Win a game and it's an extra €500,000 from UEFA. Qualify from the group and another €500,000 goes into the club kitty.

Previously, the squad shared fifty percent of any prize money. In 2016 we secured a win and a draw. At the time those results were worth €360,000 and €180,000 respectively. Half of that split between the squad was huge for lads on League of Ireland wages. The club now offered us twenty percent instead of fifty. I couldn't believe it. I mean, we were playing the likes of Arsenal and Rapid Vienna. How much did they expect to have to hand over?

The biggest bonus row, with potentially the most serious consequences, was still to come…

AFTER ANDORRA, WE travelled to Moldova to face Sheriff. People are really seeing the value of that win now that they have won away to Real Madrid in the Champions League group stages. But we knew at the time that they were a top outfit. Their facilities were ridiculous. Sheriff have three stadiums side-by-side – the one we played in, another with a running track, and then a smaller one. There are also loads of floodlit training pitches. Clearly they have money to burn.

Sheriff brought in players from all over the world, so they expected to beat us handily. But we took them all the way to penalties… and won.

I wanted to take one of the penalties. I always fancied myself but never got the chance, whether it was a Malone Cup or an FAI Cup final. Stephen Kenny always picked attacking players. Filippo was new to the job, so I approached him after the final whistle and asked to be one of the five. I was too late. He said to me in his thick Italian accent, 'Everyone can't take a penalty!' I was down for the first sudden-death kick. We were 4-3 up and Chris Shields had the chance to win it. Miss and they score… and I'm next. I really wanted to take one, but I wanted to get through even more.

Chris scored. We were one game away from the group stages and our opponents were from the Faroe Islands. I could hardly believe it. We weren't playing well in the league, but all I could think of was… Do the basics *right* and we're through!

First of all, though, we had to get out of Sheriff's stadium. As we attempted to leave, they wouldn't open the gates.

Lads on the bus were shouting up to the driver, asking what's the hold-up?

In European games, home sides tend to supply towels to the away team, so that you're not carrying a ton of wet towels in your luggage for the flight home.

Sheriff provided us with 60 or 70 flimsy white towels, and as we tried to leave they said two were missing. We were stuck there for at least 20 minutes before they finally let us go. By the time we got to the airport, we were led upstairs to a small VIP area. The whole place was kitted out with food… bread with salmon, pastries, fruit, pizza slices. There was one fridge packed with minerals and another beside it with beer. One of the lads asked, is this for us?

'Yes.'

'Do I have to pay for a drink?'

'No.' I approached Filippo.

'Is there any chance the lads can have a beer?'

'Yeah… three beers max!' he replied. Everyone let out a cheer. All you could hear was clink, clink from the bags as we boarded the airplane! We were buzzing with our wins – both on the pitch and in the VIP area. But something was missing…

WHENEVER I THINK of European 'aways', one of the first people to pop into my head is Harry Taaffe. If he wasn't helping lobby for the lads to have a few drinks, he'd be making sure we got back to the team hotel safely and at a reasonable time… or onto the team bus before it left for the airport.

He passed away in July 2020 and it hit us hard. Harry was a fixture at the club.

Regardless of who was in charge, he was the boss. You could have great craic with him, but you'd never want to get on the wrong side of Harry.

He bailed boys out of bad situations over the years, whether it was a row with people in town or if they needed an emergency taxi service. If you were out on the town and couldn't get home, Harry would be there. Even if it meant driving from Dundalk to Dublin and back in the early hours.

He was our IT guy when I first joined the club. In the early days, Vinny worked the video while Stephen spoke over it. But rarely would a video session go by without some issue with the internet or with cables or the projector. Harry to the rescue! Harry would fix this, he'd fix that… he'd have DVDs of games for every player. He tended to the grass… and then to the astro. If anything at the club needed mending, Harry was on the case. He did so much for Stephen Kenny in the background, stuff that never came to light. We didn't have many resources early in my Dundalk career, but Harry always had a way to get things done.

He was on every away trip. Our last with Harry was in pre-season ahead of the 2020 season. Myself, Dane Massey and Gary Rogers spent a lot of time in Noel the kitman's room, playing games, drinking tea. Harry was there too, having a laugh and being a good friend. He was the backbone of the club for so long.

There are layers to the devastation I felt when he passed away.

Firstly, Harry wasn't the only Taaffe to give so much to the club. Maria, his wife, was always in the club shop. Anything that needed doing that Harry couldn't get to, his daughter Orla was there to help out. And his son Shane was with Harry every second of the day, working on videos or on the pitch.

Secondly, Harry always appeared to be so strong and fearless. I know it's wrong, but you don't expect people like him to die by suicide. His brother Paul spoke out critically after his passing about the mental health services in Ireland.

Harry had a loving family and so many friends. People did all they could, but it's so hard without the help of professional support and services.

Harry's passing certainly opened my eyes to how powerful the mind can be.

OVER THE PAST year or two I have experienced stresses and pressures like never before, through football and business. I was one of the main men at Dundalk for years and then, suddenly, I was binned and hardly spoken to. Throw in sleep deprivation and things can spiral quickly out of control.

I am not for one minute comparing my situation with Harry's, but it made me realise just how easily your own mind can work against you. That is why I always try to put things into perspective. Things could always be worse... and be thankful for what you have!

But Harry... he always seemed so strong, so busy, so focused. The club tractors, they were all his. He owned the machinery that kept the pitches – grass and astro – in good nick. I'm talking tens of thousands of euro worth of kit.

I remember once he needed a replacement piece for a tractor and it was going to cost a fortune. But Harry saw an advert on Done Deal for a bigger piece, one that contained the item Harry needed. Whoever was selling the bigger piece didn't realise its value. So Harry jumped into his van with Shane and drove straight to Kerry to pick it up. Those were the lengths to which he went for the club.

Harry was missed around the club and also on trips such as the one to Moldova. He would always have a laugh and a joke.

As we knocked back beers in the VIP room that night, after beating Sheriff on penalties to qualify for the Europa League play-offs, I'm pretty sure we all paused at one point or another to remember Harry.

WE STAYED AT the Radisson St Helen's in Dublin ahead of the play-off against KI. Having watched hours of video, we knew we had a great chance to win. We were playing at the Aviva on a big pitch. They weren't a footballing team.

All we had to do was make the surface as big as possible.

We started poorly. I think the boys were panicking. They were there for the taking in the first 20 or 30 minutes. We were creating chances, but a few of the lads seemed hesitant. I remember saying we needed to relax, to get the ball and knock it around. The stadium was empty, aside from a handful of Dundalk fans and club volunteers working as ball-people.

I knew at the time that we were in danger of screwing it up. We weren't playing well, we were struggling in the league, and we were up against a team we should be beating comfortably in an empty stadium. Fortunately, we settled soon after that and kept the ball… side to side, side to side. As soon as we did that and produced our first piece of good possession, we scored… Sean Murray after the half-hour. We were well on top for the remainder of the first-half and moments after the interval we went two-up through Dan Cleary. And then, for some reason, we stopped playing.

I thought to myself… *These are bang-average at best, the game should be wrapped up… We should be enjoying the moment.* But the ball was getting kicked long, we were being pushed back, we weren't picking up second balls. Things were getting nervy. They pulled one back through a deflected Ole Midtskogen effort on 65 minutes.

Suddenly, we were inviting pressure onto us. There were a couple of scares.

I cleared one off the line. Then relief… 11 minutes from time we got a breakaway goal through Daniel Kelly. We were through. But it should have been far more comfortable. We were rubbish in the second-half. I was raging walking off the pitch. All eyes were on us again, we were playing against a team that wasn't good enough for that stage and we could easily have thrown it away.

OF COURSE, WE had some luck getting to the group stages.

We probably wouldn't have made it if Covid hadn't happened. KI got a walkover against Slovan Bratislava – thanks to Covid – and then scored a freak 6-1 win against a Georgian team. Would we have beaten Sheriff over two-legs?

Who knows, but it is certainly easier as an underdog to win a one-off tie.

Yet there we were. Group stages for the second time in five years. On a personal level, it was a huge triumph. A few months earlier I was practically being retired, but there I was wearing the armband as we qualified for the group stages.

I was sure my time had gone. A year earlier, I thought my days of European football were definitely over. I was bombed out at a time when we were poor in Europe. I spoke to Stephen O'Donnell at the end of 2019 and he knew what I was going through… and he knew what to say.

'Garts, you've been told that because of your age you are slowing down, you are not up to it. But you have another two or three seasons at the top… no bother.

You're cruising.' He was there before and he added, 'If people keep telling you you're finished, you'll end up believing it. But you're not'.

Stevie was right. Along with everyone else, I was delighted with my role in getting us back to the group stages. The same went for Cameron Dummigan and

Sean Murray. They were both in a similar boat to me at one stage. But Sean's goals got us into the groups and Cameron was probably our best player once we got there.

WE WERE BUZZING ahead of the Molde game, but once again there was plenty of noise in the background. We ended up playing in Tallaght, which was fine for the players; we've had some great nights there. But the build-up was dominated by a huge row over access to the Aviva Stadium. The Irish rugby team needed it for kicking practice before their Six Nations game with Italy. There was also something about the advertising hoardings already being in place for the rugby.

This was another example, however, of the club not helping itself. We were at loggerheads with the IRFU at the time. There was a headline in one paper that read… *IRFU slams disappointing and misleading comments from Dundalk chairman Hulsizer.* Bill had said there was 'bad blood between the two institutions (Dundalk and the IRFU)'.

Remember, Peak6 wanted to take over the FAI's stake in the Aviva Stadium. They felt the stadium could be put to 'better use'. We ended up having to pay extra – €50,000 was the figure widely reported at the time – to stage one game in Tallaght, to satisfy all the UEFA regulations. But again, as players, we were delighted. The pitch in Tallaght was often better than at the Aviva, especially around that time of year.

WE FELT WE were capable of beating Molde. We had a great first-half, Sean Murray scored with a header. Once again, though, at half-time it was like a switch flicked. We didn't play in the second-half.

Molde upped the tempo and intensity; they made a few changes and they had some clever players. Magnus Eikrem was excellent at finding space to pick up the ball, and his through-balls were so dangerous. The goals we conceded were both avoidable, but they were also inevitable because we invited them on.

At 2-1 down with about 18 minutes to go, we started to play again. Towards the end of the game I made a run up the pitch. Dan Cleary had the ball on the left and he found me with a big cross-field pass. I played a one-two and got to the end-line, pulled the ball across and there was Dan, charging in at the back post.

He didn't make contact – and that was really disappointing, but we got a kick out of the fact that it was the two centre-halves linking up deep in enemy territory.

NEXT UP WAS Arsenal away. A 3-0 defeat, but the scoreline makes it look worse than it was. We frustrated them until just before half-time, but as a team, and a group, we would like to have created more going forward. Hindsight is a great thing – maybe, if we had been more adventurous, we'd have got a hammering. They were so sharp, so fast in everything they did. We made it hard for the Gunners and I got plenty of praise for my performance. I'll be honest, a backs-to-the-wall display like that suits defenders. Things are compact, you get a few blocks in, the odd tackle… and you look really good.

But I didn't expect the reaction I got afterwards. When I came off the pitch my phone was hopping. Ian Darke, the BT commentator, tweeted that I was outstanding and literally everyone I knew sent that tweet onto me.

Then there were thousands of social media posts from random people from all over the world. I had Arsenal fans saying… 'Sign for us!'

It was some laugh scrolling through the messages.

When you get to this level, messages flood in from all around the world. But playing against a team with the profile of Arsenal, it goes ballistic. 'We should pay £1m for Gartland'… stuff like that. Just give me the million!

THE EMIRATES WAS a great experience, but once again, there were off-field distractions in the run-up to the game.

Looking at other teams in the group stages, they all travelled to away games wearing face masks decorated with their club crests. Now, I had a load of masks made for my new business, Recovery Room. The fella that made them also manufactured masks with the Dundalk crest for sale around the town.

I offered to buy 100 of them… two for each player and staff members. I paid up front and got some of the money back. I was a couple of hundred euro short, but didn't think anything of it. *At least we'll look well walking through the airport and going to the games*, I thought.

When I returned for more masks, he did them with the crest on one side and the Recovery Room logo on the other. *Why not*, I thought… *After all, I am paying for them*. I had a feeling this might put one or two noses out of joint. But on the other hand, if it wasn't for me we'd be one of the only sides in the group stages wearing random masks to games. Heading to the airport for our flight to London, I handed the masks with the Recovery Room logo out to some of the lads.

Sportsfile, the photography agency, always had a snapper at the check-in desks. One photo ended up in the papers. It was Sean Murray and me, and all you could see was the Recovery Room logo. *Happy days*, I thought!

But someone sent the photo to the U.S. and I was told they were not happy. *Who would bother doing that?* I wondered. *Is there someone out there looking to hurt us? Hurt me?* I'm also told a complaint was made about an interview I did in the week leading up to the Arsenal game. The interviewer asked, 'Could you have seen this a few months ago, a Europa League game at the Emirates?'

I laughed and replied, 'A few months ago I thought I'd be lucky to play in the Leinster Senior Cup! It's surreal.'

It was obviously a joke, but I genuinely thought my European days were over. A group stage game against Arsenal at the Emirates? No chance.

Another complaint was lodged after I actually paid the club to advertise Recovery Room on the pitchside boards during one of our games. Did I piss someone off? At this stage I had the feeling someone was definitely out to get me.

Someone then moaned that Gary Rogers and I were doing loads of media – but media that the *club* had organised!

After the play-off game, I did a few things with Virgin. They were going to cover our group stages games, so they were keen to build up the matches. Ahead of one interview I went up to the club and said, 'Let's do this right, get the 4k camera and a board with the club sponsors in the background'.

It didn't happen, so I decided to do the interview at home, upstairs in my office. I have pictures of Dundalk and some of my medals hanging on the wall behind my desk, but I also have a Recovery Room logo.

That upset the club.

And when CNBC Sport got onto the club for an interview, I was sent the links and told to organise it myself. I don't think they were impressed when that aired in the U.S., with my company website in the background.

But I'd given them the chance to do it at the club, with our main sponsors in the background and it was thrown back at me.

All I could think about was the lost opportunities to showcase our club and our sponsors, and to boost our brand on prime time television. It made no sense to me. So I zipped it for a while. I didn't put much up on social media. I just wanted to play football.

DESPITE BEING ONE of our best players against Arsenal, I was dropped for the game away to Rapid Vienna. We could have won that game. How often does a League of Ireland side go away in Europe, score three times and come home with nothing? I was annoyed over being dropped, but decided there was no point in fighting it. But when we played Vienna at home and I was out of the team again, I turned to Filippo and asked, 'What's the story, what's actually going on?'

It couldn't just be football. My form was good and we'd just conceded four goals in our previous game. Filippo mentioned to me that the masks had caused some hassle. He laughed about it, but it was something he still had to deal with, he informed me. I felt bad for him, and I told a few of the lads to bin their masks. The stress of it! Over *nothing*!

Getting on the bus to the Emirates, Filippo had said to me, 'Brian, you don't know the stress that this shit causes me!' He was half-joking again, but it was obviously a matter that had been on-going. I sat there, on the team bus to play Arsenal, with this unnerving feeling in my stomach. *What now?* I thought.

I had also been told that someone wanted me pulled from the game. There was a war going on, involving silly shit and egos.

When I had asked Filippo about what was going on, he had replied, 'We need to protect you'.

I didn't need protection at this stage of my career. I needed to play as many big games as I could.

I was told that Dan had been coming out with the ball on the left, so Rapid would probably try to lock him up. In that case, Sean Hoare would be the perfect man to bring the ball out on the right. Unfortunately for Sean, he made a mistake in that exact scenario and we went one-down.

Once again, I was sure my time at Dundalk was coming to an end. So I spoke with Filippo.

He told me that he wanted me next season. He said that when he came in, he was told by somebody at the club that this player is 'Dead'… that player is 'Dead'.

Filippo named a few… Cameron Dummigan, Sean Murray and me.

But he said to me, 'I want you here next season!'

That was nice to hear, but I wasn't convinced I would be!

Our next game was away to Molde, but all eyes at that stage were on the FAI Cup final three days later. I was in the side to face Molde, so straightaway I wondered if I was out of the cup final. Those fears intensified when I played the 90 minutes in Norway.

Filippo kept me in for the Aviva Stadium clash against Shamrock Rovers, which we won after extra-time, but I was out again for the visit of Arsenal the following Thursday. Again, I pulled Filippo to one side.

'What the hell?'

I'd missed two European games already. I knew Sean Hoare was in contract talks and in the back of my head I wondered if that had anything to do with the selection. This isn't a slight on anyone else… you have to fight your own corner.

Particularly when I still hadn't signed a new deal myself.

I knew I could get another club. I thought at that stage that I'd end up at St Pat's. But they dragged their heels.

I came on at half-time against Arsenal and played well enough. The game was far more open than the others, real end-to-end stuff. We lost 4-2… the end of another group stage campaign.

SIGNING MY NEW deal was harder work than it should have been. I was told that I'd be staying in November, but we were well into December now. Filippo asked, 'Has the club not been onto you?' I hadn't heard from anyone. Jim Magilton had arrived as our Sporting Director, so I got in touch with him.

'We need to sort this out,' I said.

He replied that he was under the impression that everything had been agreed.

Pat's was still a potential option, but in my heart I wanted to finish my career at Dundalk. *I'll sign, ignore the crap in the background, and let my football do the talking*, I resolved. I live here, a short goal-kick from the stadium. And I enjoyed working under Filippo. But there was no movement regarding a new contract.

Eventually, I received a letter of intent to offer me a deal. What's the point in that? Why sign a letter of intent and then have to sign a contract? 'Just send me the contract,' I said.

Then Filippo rang me. He said, 'I'm after getting this, but I didn't want to send it onto you because it's wrong. It's twenty percent down on what you were on'.

I had agreed with the club to continue on the same contract that I had been on. I wasn't looking for a pay rise. Later on, Filippo rang me back.

He was laughing.

'Brian, you wouldn't believe it,' he said. 'The club made a mistake.'

Relief. Then more frustration. I didn't hear from the club again for another week. It was eight o'clock on New Year's Eve and I was on the phone trying to find out what was going on. Once the clock struck midnight, I was out of contract. St Pat's was still a possibility, but there was no firm offer on the table. I knew a couple of lads took pay cuts to go there, but Stevie knew I couldn't, not with the commute from Dundalk.

Finally, a contract landed at Oriel Park. I was happy to sign. Time to block out everything else and get back to doing the business on the pitch. Or so I thought.

Martin Connolly, our general manager and a good friend of mine, who ran the club for years, was suddenly considered surplus to requirements. Gone was another link to the town, another local who knew how the club was run. No one knew better than Martin how the club needed the town and the town needed the club.

NOTHING IS EASY in life, is it? I had a tendon injury on my heel from the end of the 2020 season, but thought some rest would do the job. But when I started running on it in January, it got sorer and sorer. I was back off my feet again for a few weeks.

We were away to Shamrock Rovers on April 2 and I was determined to make that one. I probably rushed back too quickly, but we had started poorly in the league, drawing away to Sligo Rovers and losing at home to Finn Harps.

We played with three at the back and the plan was that if their No 10 advanced, Dan Cleary and I would press. I got my quads rubbed for the previous three days. They were tight from ball striking after so long on the sidelines. But I was buzzing, full of adrenaline and couldn't wait to get into the action.

Suddenly, the ball came down my side. I turned to give chase and crumpled in a heap after a challenge from Danny Mandroiu. I knew straightaway that it wasn't right. I heard a click or a crack, not the pop that others who've done their ACL often talk about.

It was sore, but the pain soon went away.

Maybe the tight quads played a part; they couldn't take the force and it all went on the knee. Just minutes into my first appearance of 2021... and I knew my season was all but over.

I'VE OFTEN BEEN stopped in the street and asked what went wrong? Why did we go from the highs of winning leagues and cups, and playing in the European group stages, to where the club was at now?

The basics were neglected and forgotten on and off the pitch. The more money that came into Oriel Park, the more people seemed to look out for themselves, rather than the club. This was the case *on and off* the pitch.

In football, money often brings attention, much of it unwanted and unhelpful.

The environment changed in a negative way. Previously, it was conducive to development and progress, but it quickly became toxic. It makes me sad and angry that it has happened in my time at the club. Is there more that I could have done? I know I'm only a player, but I have often involved myself in background issues.

Maybe I have overstepped the mark on occasion, but my intentions were always good. I know how much this club means to the town.
I am a Dub, but Dundalk is now my home.

WE MOVED INTO our house, Bronagh and I, in May 2016. By the start of that year, I was spending half the week in Bronagh's parents' house. I guess I moved in by stealth – one night the first week, two nights the next…

Bronagh is so easy-going. Before I met her I thought, *I'm in my mid-twenties, I won't settle down for a while.* But we clicked straightaway. I was blown away by how natural we were together.

She comes from a great family. Her dad is great craic and her mam is just as relaxed as Bronagh. Her brothers were quick to welcome me into the family too.

Their house, which is just eight doors down from where we bought, is a great place to be. So too is the town itself. Dundalk is football mad.

It's raw. What you see is what you get.

The history of the town is different to anywhere else in the country, because it's a border town. It's been on the front line for decades. You only get a true appreciation for that when you spend some time here.

Support within the town for Dundalk FC is everywhere. I've written about the negative side to that and it is unfortunate that, sometimes, the fans you hear the most are the critical ones. Going from being up there just for games to actually living in the town has been an adjustment. Most of our neighbours are fans too, so it's hard to escape from football.

When the going is good, that's fine. But sometimes when I have the kids with me, I just want to switch off completely.

I couldn't do that once the shit hit the fan. A load of us had been living in Dundalk, but not anymore. Dundalk was no longer the centre of everyone's life… the chairman was living in Florida, our Sporting Director in Belfast.

So I felt like I was getting all the questions.

What's going on? How did we go from that… to this?

People were frustrated. It's their town, their club. I understood that. But my reaction would depend on the type of day I was having.

I like chatting, but there are times when I'm in a rush to get somewhere. If I'm caught in that situation, I can appear to be uncaring. But I'm genuinely just trying to get to where I need to be. Then other times, I'm just in a bad mood and I might ignore someone, especially if they say the wrong thing.

Bronagh would say to me, 'You can't say that!'

'But they can't say that to me!' I reply.

At times it's not easy living in the town, but most of the time it's brilliant.

Going for a pint? I usually skip it. You can't have a quiet drink without someone coming up to talk football. They mean no harm, I know. But my brother-in-law and I went for a pint recently. Things got so bad that I got up and said I was going to the toilet.

I didn't return.

ON THE OTHER hand, when we are winning there is no better place to be. The Europa League in 2020 didn't mean half as much to us, because we were playing in empty stadiums. We couldn't see the joy on the faces of our fans.

Dundalk, like most towns outside Dublin, has felt neglected for decades. Our success has put the town on the map.

When I first arrived, the recession was coming to an end in Dublin. Money started to flow around the capital once again. But it didn't filter out. Dundalk in 2013, '14 and '15 was a different place to Dublin, just an hour up the road.

Football was an escape for the locals. I saw grown men in their eighties in tears because of what we were doing on the pitch. I know the lengths the fans went to in order to save the club before I arrived.

Andy Connolly and Paul Brown didn't take over the club to make money.

They got their reward after our European run in 2016. But it was never about the bottom line for them; they did it for the town and the club, because they were both massive fans.

Whenever we won the league or FAI Cup, the streets would be lined with fans.

Thousands would gather in the square. A stage would be set up for a triumphant homecoming. You could see the pride in everyone's face. It was some feeling for us as players. I'm grateful to have been a part of it.

But it's also the reason why I was so annoyed with where the club ended up.

COVID DIDN'T HELP, I know, but the disconnect between the club and community shocked and upset me. So too did the disconnect between the club and the players. The club didn't seem to want to hear about the past anymore.

Fine, but it wasn't going to go away unless we emulated what was achieved in the Stephen Kenny era. That's just a fact of life. Our success was so recent that people remembered vividly the glory days... and they wanted to know why things had changed so drastically.

In my view, the basics were neglected both on and off the pitch. Trying to move on without locals in the club exacerbated the disconnect with the community. And so many people who worked in the background went too.

This is a small town, everyone knows everyone.

On the pitch, Vinny wanted to move the team on in 2020.

In his first year in charge, when we won the league, we played a six, an eight and a 10, with two high-and-wide wingers. At times we played a right winger who would come inside, but he'd also play high-and-wide and Sean Gannon would still have space to go around him. We retained the fundamentals of the glory days under Stephen.

But at the start of 2020, we played a six and two eights. The talk was about being more like Liverpool. We played an inside-right instead of a high-and-wide.

Grand, a new manager has new ideas. But you will always be open to criticism if things don't work out, because you changed a winning formula. Why fix something that hasn't been broken?

We returned to a decent bit of form when Vinny returned in 2021, and I think it helped that we went back to a six, eight and ten, with two high-and-wides.

It's simple. Do what you are good at and then develop it from there.

The players – the foreign signings in particular – came in for a lot of criticism. I firmly believe the foreign lads were treated differently to any of the Irish players who also underperformed.

People say, 'Ah, they are on big wages!'

Some were, fair enough. But some weren't. Yet people still peddled that one.

So I'd say, 'Okay, tell me what they are on?'

'I don't know… eh, but they are getting too much money,' was the typical reply.

Sure, one or two might have been on a decent wage. But they were in the minority. And it wasn't their fault they were recruited by the club. If you have something to say about the playing personnel, have a go at the recruitment strategy, not the lads who were brought in.

DURING THE 2021 season, one of the foreign arrivals picked up a serious injury. I'm not going to name names, but it won't take a genius to work out who I'm talking about.

He lay on the pitch while the game was going on and he could hear fellas in the stand criticising him. It was probably only a few fans, but it had him in tears.

Then as he walked alongside our fans, there was more abuse. Again, probably from a minority. But he knew his season was over and he had to cope with that.

It's not his fault the club wanted to sign him. If someone offered you a good wage for a job, would you turn it down?

Our recruitment strategy was wrong. We let some great players go. If we'd added a couple of the recent signings to the bulk of the squad that was there, I think that, with the environment we'd created, we'd have won the league or gone very close.

But bringing in so many new players and letting so many go, changed the culture in the dressing-room completely. It changed everything.

And it happened during Covid too, so we couldn't do team bonding sessions, we couldn't socialise together. Before Covid, lads would come in and we'd look after them for the first few weeks.

Then, when they integrated into the group, we'd take a step back.

WE LET LOADS of players go and we signed some players who had no knowledge of this league. It's not an easy league to come into, no matter how good you are. It's a different environment, culture and physicality to most other leagues.

This is a great club, with great people both at the coal-face and behind the scenes. My recovery from the ACL injury wouldn't be where it is today without the brilliant work by club doctor Dualtach Mac Colgáin, and physios Danny Miller and David Murphy. They continued to help me out even after they left the club. Danny was appointed by Stephen Kenny as the physio to the senior Ireland team, but he still looked after me whenever he could, despite the fact that he still had a full-time clinic to manage.

No one wanted to be injured when Danny was around. He does triathlons – so he'd have you on bikes going up and down mountains, or going for 40- to 100-length swim sessions in the morning.

After Danny and David left, I didn't have anyone checking on me every day. I was setting up cones myself for my runs. Our fitness coach Graham Norton was brilliant too, but he left around the same time as Danny.

I didn't really know how much or how little I should be doing.

The boys would go out training and I'd be inside drinking tea and eating scones with Noel Walsh, our kitman. Chatting to him was great. But the environment within the club was shite – and I let my own standards drop because of that.

I went back to Santry four months after the injury to do strength tests. The targeted imbalance between the two legs was twenty-five percent, but I was at twenty-eight percent. I was pissed off with myself, because I have always expected to be ahead of whatever target I was chasing.

The next test would be three months later.

Halfway through, the doc, Dualtach and Danny tested me, just to see where I was at. I was still at twenty-eight percent.

My head was all over the place. It was around this time that my son Bobbie suffered a febrile seizure. At one stage it was so bad that he stopped breathing. I had to give him mouth-to-mouth in the passenger seat as we rushed to the hospital.

For weeks, I couldn't shake that image of Bobbie from my head. It was terrifying. Working on my own fitness suddenly didn't seem so important.

Meanwhile, I wasn't being held to account in terms of the work I was putting into my recovery.

Some days I just didn't turn up. No one was asking where I was. I spent a bit of time at Felda Gym, one of our sponsors, doing leg weights. But when they closed down over Covid, that threw another spanner in the works.

If it wasn't for the test with Dualtach and Danny, I'm not sure I would have snapped out of it. For the next six weeks I trained harder than ever before.

In that time, I went from twenty-eight percent to an eleven percent imbalance. I achieved in six weeks something that should have taken three months.

I remember one session with Danny. The weather was awful. We trained next to a local pitch, because we didn't want to damage it by running on it. The grass was long and the ground was like mush. Danny had me doing drills and I was bollixed.

As the sun went down, we moved closer to the streetlights so we wouldn't be working in darkness. At one stage I turned around to Danny and laughed.

He asked, 'What are you laughing at?'

I replied, 'One of my last games was against Arsenal and you're just back from being on the sideline against Portugal, and now look at us – grass up over our ankles, slogging away and using street-lamps for a bit of light!'

Danny saw the funny side.

Back at the club, Vinny Perth had returned to the dugout. I had my issues with Vinny, because of the way I felt I was treated during his first spell in charge. But in fairness to him, results picked up when he returned.

He had to work with the same shit going on in the background that hampered Filippo and the players.

We got on grand when he came back in and I tried to help out as much as possible.

Club first!!

That's how it has always been for me. His goals were the same as mine – keep the team in the Premier Division.

▪ CHAPTER 26 ▪

STRIKE!

That was the threat from the dressing-room ahead of our first-leg against Vitesse Arnhem in August, 2021.

We were due to face the Dutch side in the Europa Conference League and, for the third year running, the issue of bonuses was causing huge friction between the players and owners.

This time the lads were ready to press the nuclear button.

I had stepped away from bonus negotiations because I found Bill a nightmare to deal with. But as I was still recovering from injury, and so the rest of the lads could concentrate on preparing for the game, I said I'd help out.

The issue this time was that the club wanted to make the bonuses a percentage of net income – and they wanted to include every last expense in their calculations.

On the list were hotels, buses, plans, meals… literally anything that had them dipping into their pocket.

On top of that, they wanted to reduce the percentage again. It meant the lads were in line to collect a fraction of past European bonuses.

The Vitesse game was on the horizon and talks were going nowhere. So the lads decided that the only way to get people to listen was to threaten a strike.

I put in a call to Bill.

It was two days before the game. I was on my way to hospital to collect

Bronagh and our new baby, Jesse. It was a 30-minute drive. I chose this time because Bill was always a hard man to get off the phone. But with my drive-time deadline, I was focused, aggressive and to the point.

I said I was trying to help him, that the whole thing had become a shitshow.

Bill wouldn't budge. He told me he was waiting on information from the club. I told him that wouldn't sit well with the players, that they needed assurances on a better deal… ASAP.

Forget the half-hour drive, I spent a full hour on the phone with Bill, including half-an-hour in the hospital car park, while Bronagh was waiting inside with Jesse, all packed and eager to get home. Bronagh never found out that I was outside for so long. I hope she's not reading!

I kept the pressure on Bill. I said the lads needed information first thing the next morning – the eve of the game.

Still nothing. I texted Bill that afternoon. The players were going mad. We were so close to calling the PFAI. The plan was to ask them to draft a letter, which we would then show to the club.

I have been on the PFAI Committee and I've done a lot of work with them – I was chair of the Collective Bargaining Agreement, when we hoped to get initial rules signed off, like a minimum wage and other things to offer a basic standard of living for our members. The PFAI has done great work over the last few years for players. I took part in the first ever 'Out of Contract' players' camps in 2010, and I have sat at meetings with government over matters too.

I said to Bill in the text that it was now or never, that the players felt they had no other choice at this point but to down tools. They knew the fans might turn on them, but it was the only leverage they had. It wasn't something they took lightly, because they felt they could beat Vitesse. Simply put, the players had enough shit from the club at this stage! Luckily, Bill got back to me. The bonuses would still be calculated on net income, but what the club could count as expenses would be capped. And the percentage was upped too.

When the lads came off the training pitch that evening I told them it was sorted, that they could focus on the game.

We came close to beating Vitesse. They won 2-1 in Tallaght, but we were brilliant over there. Patrick McEleney scored twice, including a wonder-goal, and we were two minutes away from bringing the tie to extra-time.

ANOTHER BIZARRE THING emerged from that series of phone calls with Bill. He asked me if I'd run the club? I laughed, because I thought he was joking. But he said it to me again a few weeks later.

I told him I wouldn't, because firstly I was a player, and secondly I didn't have the qualifications or experience to run a club.

I had agreed a few years earlier to get involved in the business side of things and do a few hours every week, getting an insight into the running of the club, getting in sponsorship etcetera.

But I wasn't ready for what Bill was proposing. It summed up the madness of the club. I did, however, give him some advice.

I said, 'I'll tell you one thing Bill, if I had to run the club tomorrow, I'd get the best person in for each job and they would all report to me. They would all be diligent and good at their jobs'.

He asked what I meant by that.

The stadium manager was a guy called Aaron Lawless. He's a great guy and he has a really sharp mind. So much so that he's now working for me.

But Aaron came out of college with a social media marketing degree, went into Dundalk and was told, 'You're the stadium manager'.

It was the same in other departments. Square pegs in round holes.

THAT WAS DUNDALK in a nutshell under Bill and its American owners. The club was pissing money away – on and off the pitch.

The bill for accommodation must have been €15,000-a-month.

I was called in for a chat with Jim Magilton at one stage and was told that they were thinking of taking pre-match meals out of away trips.

'What?!'

Jim had been in as interim coach for a few weeks and all he was on about was standards – and I agreed with him, because standards had dropped. People were getting away with murder.

Lads were coming in from America and they weren't good enough, so the standard of training dropped.

I know of one lad who got accommodation and food include in his package. His full package wasn't far off my wages.

And they were talking about getting rid of pre-match meals?

In the end, the pre-match meal was taken away for one trip. But the team went ahead with it anyway and Vinny paid for it out of his own pocket, while the fitness coach bought carbohydrate bars and snacks.

At one stage we didn't have any tractors, so the pitch wasn't brushed for months. It's not great at the best of times, but it was awful to play on while it wasn't being looked after. Funnily enough, within a couple of weeks of Filippo's departure, the club splashed out on a new tractor and there was a marked improvement when it came to maintaining the pitch.

Jim Magilton then stepped in as caretaker manager. The contrast between Jim and Filippo was stark. Jim was more from the Dermot Keely school of f**king lads out of it.

Players were complaining that training loads were heavy, that advice on load-management wasn't being followed. And the atmosphere in the dressing-room was even worse than before. The foreign players, in particular, couldn't get their heads around the new regime.

There was no rush to bring in a new manager. It was as if the club was trying to save money by keeping Jim in the role; when Jim was saying all the time that he didn't want the job.

To me, everything was pointing towards the owners selling up.

Tighten the budget, offer one-year contracts so there is no commitment to anyone… and it's much easier to get rid of the club.

Thankfully, they did.

And thankfully, the right people came in after them.

EPILOGUE

I am a lucky man to have three amazing and beautiful girls in my life. Here I am with my mother Carmel (above) on her 60th birthday celebration and also happy times with my wife Bronagh after a league and cup double. I'm not forgetting my son Bobbie (top left, joining us at three-weeks old in Oriel Park after Dundalk clinched the title against St Pat's).

Happy families... Myself and Bronagh, and Bobbie and our daughter Jesse; Neil and his wife Hannah and their daughters Lola and Bronte... and my loving mum Carmel.

Lola and Bronte allowed me the honour of having them as team mascots on one of many memorable days as Dundalk captain.

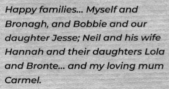

I'M LYING IN a hospital bed, praying I'll see tomorrow morning.

This bed will be my prison for the next two and a half weeks. No visitors. Damn Covid restrictions. At times, it's just me and my thoughts.

They're dark. Life and death stuff.

A young boy at home and a second baby on the way... *Would I ever see him again, would I ever see her?*

I'd been in Santry Sports Clinic a few days earlier for surgery on an ACL tear.

I was discharged, went home... and I started coughing up blood that evening. I spent four nights in hospital... blood clots in my lungs.

I was discharged again. One day later, things went rapidly downhill. I was short of breath and felt crushing pressure on my chest. Straight back to A&E. That night was the worst of my life. I genuinely thought I was going to die.

THE INJURY HAPPENED on Good Friday, so I had to wait until after the Easter Bank Holiday weekend for a scan. But I knew. By Saturday morning I had downloaded the Santry Sports Clinic ACL recovery programme, which mapped out targets week-by-week and the different exercises you should do at each stage.

Approach it with a positive attitude, I said.

In my 17 years in football, the longest I'd been off my feet was a few weeks.

Most players aren't so lucky. I was going to use this as an opportunity to come back stronger than ever.

Football happens in a blur. During the season, it's about preparing for the next game, making sure you are in top condition every Friday night.

No time to knuckle down and work on specific issues or deficiencies. Mine was acceleration. I was one of the fastest at the club over a longer distance, but those first five yards... I could be quicker.

I said to myself... *This is my chance to work on myself. No distractions, no fear of overloading.*

I had a whiteboard in my office at home. Before I met with the orthopaedic surgeon in Santry, I had already written out the various milestones I wanted to hit during recovery.

I was ready to go. Put me under.

Cut me open. Let's get this done.

'WE'LL DO THE surgery on April 30,' he said.

'What?' That was four whole weeks after the injury. Why the wait? I wanted it done as soon as possible.

He explained what he wanted me to do between now and the operation.

Build up the knee, strengthen the muscles around it. It will speed up the recovery process, he assured me.

The swelling went down around 10 days after the injury, so I kicked off three weeks of flat-out rehab. The lads at Dundalk couldn't believe it.

'I thought you did your ACL,' was a common remark.

I was in the gym doing one-legged squats, dead-lifts, step-ups… everything I could to strengthen the muscles around my injured knee.

I used a thing called 'blood-flow restriction' – a strap around the thigh that did exactly what it said on the tin – restricted blood-flow into the muscle. It's a technique used by a lot of Premier League clubs when players are recovering from injury. It helps build strength and size in the muscle.

In my last session, two days before the operation, I did some cardio. Five rounds of 300 metres on the rower, followed by 10x12kg ball slams. I came in at under nine minutes for the lot, which was good going.

I WENT INTO the clinic on Friday for the operation. When I woke up on Saturday morning, it was agony from the knee down. I have a high pain threshold, but this was excruciating. I got up to go to the bathroom and as I got back I let out a huge roar… loud enough that the doctors raced in with morphine.

I was assured that the operation was routine, it went without a hitch. I asked if the amount of pain was normal and was told it wasn't, but that everyone reacted differently to the surgery. So I was discharged and headed home. But even trying to get my leg into the car was unbelievably painful.

As soon as I got home, I worked on getting the swelling down. I had everything planned in terms of rehab. I was even looking forward to the challenge. *Things could always be worse*, I thought. *Seventeen years playing without a serious injury to this point wasn't bad. Just get on with it, rehab, work on your weaknesses, and come back quicker, fitter and stronger.* Like I learned during lockdown… crisis presents opportunity!

I lay back on the couch and elevated my foot, and used a Game Ready cold compression device to help with the swelling. But the pain wouldn't go away.

Bronagh went out with her mother for the afternoon. I was freezing, so I put the heat on. The pain got worse. It took every ounce of energy to drag myself to the bathroom for a pee. I hobbled back to the couch.

Colder again. And I was wrecked after making the short trip to the toilet.

I checked to see if the heating was on. It was. It was May 1... not a cold day.

Back on the couch I coughed up what I thought was phlegm. No one was around and I was too sore to fetch a tissue, so I swallowed it down.

When Bronagh got home she gave me paracetamol. It got rid of the shivers.

A few hours later, I coughed up some more phlegm. 'Throw me a tissue,' I said to Bronagh. I spat into it, looked into the tissue and saw it was bright red.

'F**k, it could be a clot,' I said.

I RANG MY doctor. He told me to ring Santry.

It was late at night. I was told to go to A&E.

Bronagh's mother came over to babysit Bobbie so that Bronagh, who was six months pregnant at the time, could come with me to Our Lady Of Lourdes in Drogheda. The waiting room was packed.

All I could think of was Covid. Bronagh was pregnant... she wasn't vaccinated.

I stood in agony, waiting to see a triage nurse.

Eventually I was called in. I explained that I had surgery the day before, that I coughed up blood. 'I might have a clot,' I said.

I was sure I'd be brought through quickly enough.

'There are 11 people ahead of you,' I was told. 'It'll probably take eight to 10 hours.'

'What the f**k?'

I was there with my crutches, leaning against a wall, struggling to catch my breath. I then turned to Bronagh and asked, 'Will we leave?'

Bronagh is usually the more laid-back one in our relationship. Back at the house, when I said it could be a clot, she wasn't convinced.

'They probably put a tube down your airways during the operation,' she said.

If I left it to her, I'd have been a goner!

Once we were in hospital, the roles were reversed. There is no way we are going home, she said. And we aren't going to wait for up to 10 hours either.

We decided we'd drive to St Vincent's in Dublin. We said very little to each other on the drive. It was mostly worried silence as we drove through the Port Tunnel and across the Liffey. They had a separate waiting area for people admitted with any symptoms of Covid. I had a bit of a temperature and I coughed up blood, so I was put into an isolation cubicle. I had a bed. I could lie down.

This was much better than a seat in a crowded waiting room.

AS SOON AS I saw a doctor, he booked me in for a CT scan first thing in the morning. I was hooked up to all sorts of monitors, checking my heart and oxygen levels. They even gave me a blood thinning injection.

I was swabbed for Covid and when it came back negative I was moved into the regular A&E, where I was seen by a doctor called James Foley. He often does match-nights at Tallaght Stadium.

Later that evening I was moved into a ward down the hall. The CT scan results came back and confirmed there were small clots in my lungs.

IN THE BED next to mine was Jody Lynch's dad. I played with Jody at Bray Wanderers. We spent hours talking about football.

I got a text that night. Alan Keely had passed away. We were teammates at Shelbourne for a few months. He lived in Dundalk and worked as a postman, so I'd have seen him about. I couldn't believe it. After four nights at St Vincent's I was discharged. For all the tests that were carried out, they didn't do an ultrasound on my legs and pelvis, to see if there were clots there. The CT showed low-grade clots in my lungs, but the ultrasound would have picked up on a bigger clot.

Now, I have to say the doctors were brilliant. One was a friend of our club doc and he chatted to me for a while. The bit of company was appreciated. He looked into my case. He didn't have to. But he made sure they checked my heart and gave my lungs a thorough examination. Everything seemed fine, so off I went.

I HAD THIS feeling that something wasn't right.

I said to Bronagh that night, 'I'm afraid to go to sleep'. I was afraid I wouldn't wake up the next morning. Eventually I drifted off.

The next morning I went into the club and saw our physio Danny Miller. He assessed my leg, then I went to see the lads and headed home.

Back to the couch, leg up… Game Ready on. I rang Stevie O'Donnell for a chat. Suddenly, I found myself struggling for breath. I could feel a heaviness on my chest. I hung up, rang Bronagh, who was down with her mam, and said, 'You have to take me back to Vincent's'.

WE WENT BACK into the Covid side and, as the triage came to see me, Dr Foley walked by. 'You're back already?' he asked.

'Don't talk to me!' I replied, messing.

He went in and pulled my chart straightaway, and suddenly tests for this, that and everything were organised. He obviously knew it was something serious.

I have to give credit to the staff in our Health Service. The HSE comes in for criticism, but when it comes to the frontline staff, I'm in awe. Dr Foley arranged for a CT scan straightaway and I was put into an isolation cubicle. But that night was the worst of my life up to that point.

I honestly feared I wouldn't survive that night.

I'd been in hospital and we thought I was sorted, but suddenly I was back. And feeling a lot worse. As I tried to sleep, I experienced a hot flush. It started at my toes and I could feel it creeping up my body. Suddenly, I started shaking. Violently. I managed to ring the bell. The nurse came in, checked my stats and vitals. They were fine. The shaking eased.

I tried to nod off again. The shaking. Again. I turned to the monitor by my bedside and could see my oxygen levels had dropped. Once the shaking stopped, they returned to normal.

I was really afraid to sleep now. I was terrified that I wouldn't wake up.

I sat there exhausted, but started to doze off. I was jolted out of my sleep again by the shaking. It happened five or six times that night.

I was freaking out. Here I was, one of the fittest at the club. I looked after myself, lived life the right way, didn't drink much, didn't smoke, could do 5k in 18 minutes… *How could this be happening?* Up to this point, I thought I was indestructible.

EXHAUSTION WON OUT in the end. I slept a bit, woke up and felt a great relief wash over me. But then the CT result came back. It showed a big clot. I was moved onto a ward. In the bed next to me was a man called Shay.

He was 92 years old and said he played for Bray Wanderers in his twenties. I couldn't believe he was in his nineties. Shay was a good looking man with a big head of white hair, and he was as sharp as a razor.

In the bed next to the window was a man called Michael. He was sound, witty. We had some good chats. There was no TV in the room, no music. I had my 'tablet' to keep me entertained. I asked Michael for his favourite singers. Dean Martin and Frank Sinatra, he replied.

It was a Saturday afternoon and the three of us sat up, looked out the window onto the golf course next door and listened to the music.

'You know you're alive when Sinatra is singing,' Michael said.

I'll remember that day for the rest of my life.

The next day, Michael had changed. He sunk into depression. He had been there for a long time and just wanted to get home. The doctors were telling him he was on the mend, but something inside him said otherwise.

Shay was discharged first, then it was my turn. But not before a haematologist paid me a visit. 'Are you Brian?'

She asked about my dad's cancer. She was concerned that the blood clot came so quickly after surgery.

'We are going to keep you in a bit longer, run some more tests and hopefully have you out by the weekend.'

Oh f**k, I thought.

It turned out her husband worked as a Strength and Conditioning coach for Leinster Rugby. She knew I was a pro athlete, that sport was my livelihood, so decisions would be made with that in mind. It was a massive downer and a little scary as well. *It's just a clot, what are they not telling me*, I wondered. *If they are looking for something, isn't there a good chance they'll find it?*

I got the full MOT, all the cancers… white blood cells. I was worried, but relieved at the same time that they were being so comprehensive.

I wanted to go home and see Bronagh and Bobbie. As far as Bobbie was concerned, daddy lived in the phone for a few weeks. They came down a couple of times and we met outside… sat on benches opposite each other. I wanted to give them a hug, but was worried about what I might pass on.

I was also concerned about my knee, even if it paled into insignificance when, every time I tried to sleep, I started shaking. I needed to get the swelling down so I walked around the hospital. It was nowhere near the level of activity required at that stage, but I couldn't see a physio because of Covid.

THE RESULTS CAME back. I could go home, but I would have to go on blood thinners.

Michael was due to go home soon after I left. His nephew was a porter in the hospital, so we exchanged numbers. I asked him to pass on any news on Michael.

A few weeks later, I took Bronagh and Bobbie on holiday to visit my family in Galway. It was our first time in years to see the family – and their first time to see Bobbie. I got a call from Michael's nephew. He passed away.

By August I met with a few consultants. They walked me through my reports.

I met with a junior doctor, around my age, who told me that the pressure on one of the chambers in my heart had reached a certain level.

'What does that mean?' I asked.

'Well, if you go over 30 or 35, you are…'

He was trying to find the words.

'You're f**ked?' I said.

'Yeah, something like that.' I was two-thirds of the way there.

I was told that if the clot had moved a few millimetres, I could have been done. That was tough to hear.

THOSE MONTHS SPENT recovering from an ACL tear and from the clotting gave me time to reflect on my career. I realise just how lucky I am to have experienced the success we had at Dundalk.

I ran out at some amazing stadiums, and played under those wonderfully old-school floodlights against Zenit St Petersburg. There was Alkmaar, the win against Maccabi Tel Aviv, the Legia Warsaw fans, the 2014 Premier Division decider, cup finals at the Aviva Stadium, Arsenal… endless memories.

I finally had some time to reflect on the positives – something I didn't allow myself while I was playing. It was always about the next match, the next trophy.

Most of the players in that dressing-room were never content with what we had. We wanted more. We demanded more. We enjoyed every win, but we never dwelled on them.

As I recovered from the ACL injury and from the blood clots, I had time to look back on just how lucky I was to experience these successes with some very special people… Dane Massey, Gary Rogers, John Mountney, Sean Gannon, Sean Hoare… lads who were let down by the club in the end. Robbie Benson was another one who should never have been allowed leave. His goals were massive in Europe… against BATE Borisov, Legia Warsaw and Zenit.

It's great to see some of them back in the dressing-room again – including our new gaffer… Mr O'Donnell!

But Patrick McEleney and Michael Duffy leaving… that was also heartbreaking for us as their teammates. They are two incredible players.

And also last season we lost our captain, Chris Shields. He was a massive player for us, and that was a huge blow. I was doubly pissed off with the club that they let him go while we were in the middle of a relegation battle.

Again, it smacked of the owners wanting to get as much money back as they could before selling up. They were saving on Chris' wages for the second half of the season, and getting a transfer fee too. Selfishly, I was also unhappy with Chris, because I knew that his departure would hurt our bid to stay up. But I could also understand why he left. The place was falling apart.

Now, however, it is about who we are going forward… and our identity as a Dundalk team that sees itself as winners.

Davy McMillan and Patrick Hoban are two phenomenal goal-scorers. I am lucky to count them as teammates…It's not just the players, though. It's the Dundalk fans. This is a town where there are 10 times more people walking around in Dundalk gear than in Liverpool or Manchester United jerseys. Where else would you get it in this country? It's their town, their team. And they are proud to support us. When the going is good, it's great to see the pride in their faces.

I can't put into words what it means to have local kids looking up to you, wanting to emulate you. When I was a kid, all I ever wanted to be was a professional footballer. It was never about making millions, it was all about the love of the game… of winning, of being the best I could be.

I missed those fans when we played in Europe in 2020. It didn't mean half as much to play at the Emirates without hundreds – or thousands – of Dundalk fans there. Friends and former teammates have gone on to live my ultimate dream… playing for the senior Ireland team. I can't imagine feeling any more proud if it was me walking out at the Aviva.

The stories, the craic in the dressing-room, on the training pitch, the biscuit nights, the nights out, trips all over Europe… and all the stories we CAN'T tell!

The staff at the club, the volunteers, the people who sponsor us or who help out… such as Felda gym where I did much of my rehab.

To the family and friends that I was never there for because of football, but who never held it against me… my eternal gratitude. I never slowed down or relented.

I wanted to keep going, to win some more. And I still do.

This book and my time off the pitch has allowed me to pause and reflect, and really appreciate what I have achieved.

It's been a privilege – and thankfully, it's not over yet.

Until early in the new year, 2022, I couldn't have said that with full certainty.

I still had to wait for the all-clear from the doctors. Would there be permanent damage to my lungs? Could I get off the blood thinners?

I honestly didn't know whether I would play again until mid-January.

I was on blood thinners for eight months and didn't come off them until December 31. Two weeks later, on January 14, I sat down with the haematologist.

She did her research and told me she was confident that I could return.

But there were a few scares along the way.

I was told to be really alert for signs or symptoms of clotting – and one episode saw me back in A&E on St Stephen's Day.

Because I was on thinners, I was liable to bleed a lot easier.

One morning I noticed a little bit of blood in my mouth. It was a false alarm.

Once, I was off the Warfarin in the new year I became paranoid, thinking every little feeling or sensation was a potential clot. I ended up in hospital again in early January because I felt a little bit of pressure. The doctors put it down to stress.

Once again, Danny Miller was brilliant. He reassured me at every stage. He told me it was worth going into A&E 100 times to catch it once, that I couldn't take any chances. I'd already signed my new contract with Dundalk, but if the haematologist's advice had been to retire, I would have ripped up the deal and told the gaffer to use the money on another player.

I was convinced I'd get the green light. I was desperate for another year.

STEVIE WAS taking over and I really wanted to be a part of it. I was delighted when he said he wanted to sign me back. I knew at the age of 35, having done my

ACL and missed a year, that it was a gamble for him, especially with a reduced playing budget.

I had offers elsewhere, part-time, but similar money to Dundalk, which would have suited business life outside of football. But I wanted to stay at Dundalk.

The club has taken a few steps back after years of glory, there's no doubt about that. The budget is mid-table compared to some other clubs. But if we can climb the ladder once again, there will be a real sense of achievement.

I really don't think people fully grasp the magnitude of what Stephen Kenny built at Dundalk. It was a one-in-a-million shot. It won't be easy to get anywhere near that again, particularly in a league where so many other clubs are so strong. Just look at the budgets and squads at Shamrock Rovers, St Pat's, Derry, Bohs and Sligo Rovers. And Damien Duff's arrival has rejuvenated Shelbourne.

But there is a real hunger to get the club back to where it belongs.

I don't know how far we'll go while I'm still playing, but at the very least I want to be a part of starting that journey.

The environment is already so much better than in recent years.

I know the club's ambitions, the owners' ambitions and the gaffer's ambitions – and it's not going to be a quick fix. This is all about rebuilding a club, not just about targeting a league win this year. Building something that will endure, and that the town will be proud of again!

I know as I get older, I will enjoy every moment of it.

I love football and Dundalk FC is a part of my life now and forever.

I didn't want to jump ship and say, I was there when we won this and that, and competed in Europe. I didn't want to be there for the best bits and then leave when the hard work started.

I signed back on a big wage cut from my last contract because Oriel Park is a nice place to be once again. People are walking into the dressing-room once again with smiles on their faces. Lads are sitting down again playing board games after training or having food together.

They aren't rushing to get home as soon as the session is finished.

Up to mid-January, I wasn't sure whether I'd play again.

But I was certain about one thing…

I wanted to give it one last shot.